THE CONSTRUCTION OF BELIEF

The Construction of Belief

Reflections on the Thought of Mohammed Arkoun

Edited by

Abdou Filali-Ansary and Aziz Esmail

SAQI

THE AGA KHAN UNIVERSITY
Institute for the Study of Muslim Civilisations

First published 2012 by Saqi Books
In association with the Aga Khan University Institute
for the Study of Muslim Civilisations

Copyright © Abdou Filali-Ansary and Aziz Esmail 2012
Copyright for individual texts rests with the authors

ISBN 978-0-86356-424-6

A full CIP record for this book is available from the British Library.
A full CIP record for this book is available from the Library of Congress.

Printed and bound by Bookwell (Finland)

SAQI
26 Westbourne Grove, London W2 5RH
www.saqibooks.com

Contents

Professor Mohammed Arkoun
(1928–2010)

Professor Mohammed Arkoun was a prominent and influential figure in Islamic Studies. In a career of more than thirty years, he was an outstanding research scholar, a searching critic of the theoretical tensions embedded in the field of Islamic Studies, and a courageous public intellectual who carried the banner of an often embattled Islamic modernism and humanism.

Arkoun was born into a traditional extended family in Taourirt-Mimoun, a small town in the Great Kabylia, in February 1928. As a Berber in colonial Algeria, he initially spoke neither the language of the colonial rulers nor that of the Qur'an, and as a result he found himself marginalised from an early age. He attended a college run by the White Fathers and completed his schooling in Oran, and in Algiers. He began degrees in Arabic literature, law, philosophy and geography. He established his scholarly reputation with his early studies (1969, 1970) of the Persian historian and philosopher Miskawayh. As he began to consider how one might rethink Islam in the contemporary world, his sophisticated questioning provided a welcome counterpoint to the highly ideological interpretations that had dominated debate in both the Muslim world and the non-Muslim West.

As Professor of the History of Arab Thought at Vincennes University, Arkoun accepted a chair at the Sorbonne Nouvelle in 1980. There, he was the director of the department of the history of Arab and Islamic thought and editor of the magazine Arabica. He not only maintained Arabica's very high standard of scholarship; he considerably broadened its scope and urged it to play a significant role in shaping Western-language scholarship on Islam.

Arkoun is the author of numerous books in French, English and Arabic, including *Rethinking Islam* (Westview Press, 1994), *L'immigration, défis et richesses* (Centurion, 1998) and *The Unthought in Contemporary Islamic Thought* (Saqi Books, 2002). His shorter studies appeared in many academic journals and his works have been translated into several languages. In 2001, Arkoun was asked to deliver the Gifford Lectures, which enable a notable scholar to contribute to the advancement of theological and philosophical thought; there he was announced as the recipient of the Seventeenth Georgio Levi Della Vida Award for his lifelong contribution to the field of Islamic Studies. As a visiting Professor, he taught at the University of California, Princeton University, Temple University, the University of Louvain-la-Neuve, the Pontifical Institute of Arabic Studies in Rome and the University of Amsterdam. He also served as a jury member for the Aga Khan Award for Architecture. At his passing, he was Emeritus Professor at La Sorbonne as well as Senior Research Fellow and member of the Board of Governors of The Institute of Ismaili Studies (IIS) in London. In October 2009, the IIS organised a symposium in honour of Arkoun's efforts to renew the study of Islam.

Professor Arkoun died in September, 2010.

In an obituary, one of the contributors to this volume, Ursula Günther, wrote of Arkoun's humanism and his approach to teaching. "Mohammed Arkoun was not only a sharp-witted intellectual and humanist from the depth of his heart, with a subtle sense of humour," she observed. "He was also a passionate, charismatic speaker and a dedicated teacher. He felt a part of all that is capable of opening up new links to intelligence, as he put it, and saw himself as 'an intellectual in revolt'. May his idea that thoughts develop a life of their own prove right, continuing to take effect beyond the walls of cognitive demarcations and dominant ideologies."[1]

Notes

1.   Ursula Günther, "Obituary for Mohammed Arkoun: A Pioneer of Modern Critical Islam Studies", Quantara.de, 21 September 2010, Web 7 March 2011 <http://www. qantara.de/webcom/show_article.php/_c-478/_nr-1104/i.html>

Preface: Situating Arkoun

Abdou Filali-Ansary

In an article that was a tribute to Claude Cahen, Mohammed Arkoun begins by quoting a sentence from the late Professor, written when he in turn was paying tribute to another distinguished colleague. The sentence reads as follows:

> Respect for the memory of a deceased man implies, in the first place, respect for science and for the readers he (Maurice Lombard) had. It is thus that I would like to be treated if the same thing happened to me.[1]

This volume was conceived, planned and realised as a tribute, and, as befalls a festschrift volume, with the blessings and active participation of the late Professor Arkoun. The idea of respecting science first and foremost was in fact the only possible option in an endeavour that seeks to pay tribute to Mohammed Arkoun, regardless of the feelings and attitudes of those present. The main "struggle" (the French word "combat" was prominent in titles chosen by Arkoun for his interventions) was to make science prevail over myth and belief. The chosen topic *The Construction of Belief*, for which credit must be rendered to my friend and colleague Dr Aziz Esmail, alludes to the "Copernican Revolution" that has engulfed the humanities and social sciences in recent decades, through which belief is not seen as a given that overwhelms individuals and communities, thereby defining their symbolic world – but rather, as a complex set of views and attitudes that emerge through historical and social processes liable to observation, analysis and scrutiny. The chapters of this volume all illustrate ways in which the

Copernican Revolution has prevailed in academia, as the only objective way to approach the discussion of belief, now seen as a human artefact – regardless of the claims implied by that belief. Such an objective approach to the study of faith becomes particularly significant in the case of Mohammed Arkoun, given his impassioned stance on and contribution to prevailing scholarly approaches to "Islam" and all things "Islamic".

In a way, every scholar and every thinker is unique. However, we are tempted to say that some may be more unique than others, and that Mohammed Arkoun is one of these. The obvious argument for this is his general style, which combines, in his writing and his lectures, (which he understood as interventions) a strict scholarly rigour with a great display of vehemence. Concern for exactitude coupled with intense emotion are not often seen together, however they are what marks the "uniqueness" of Professor Arkoun. This is witnessed in the language he chose for his speech and his writing, and by the image he had of himself and his role in the context of academia and well beyond. There are however other reasons, which make it important and at the same time difficult, to situate him in the contemporary landscape of discourse about things "Islamic".

If we look at the intellectual ferment in Muslim contexts during the twentieth century, we can identify with relative ease a number of salient currents, although categorisations and classifications are abundant and differ sometimes quite substantially. One of the main trends to emerge during the twentieth century was the legacy of nineteenth-century reformism. This influenced above all the "modernists", who believed that Muslims had a unique cultural offering – a vision laid down in the sources of their faith – and who felt that this vision and the dynamic it entails had been obscured by literalist traditions. Once polished and brought back to its original purity, this vision would provide the impetus for a collective return to rationality, discipline, morality and strength. This conciliatory and self-assuring message, while still resisted by staunch traditionalists early in the twentieth century, was challenged by a turn that proved to be deeply disruptive.

Following the quick collapse of traditional institutions in the Muslim world, including the disintegration of political centres of power, new questions were raised from within the ranks of future reformists. Ali Abder Razek was to fire the first shot by raising bold questions about what had been considered to be core or essential beliefs, such as the political message of religion. The questions were most disturbing as they came from a religious scholar and cleric, formally trained in the strictest traditions and, more importantly, not exposed to ideas or views from modern philosophy or political thought. A new seed of dissent was sown, reviving an atmosphere of heated controversy that had been forgotten for centuries.

We now know that other Muslim thinkers had raised elsewhere, more or less at the same time, similar questions that had been set aside or repressed by a heavy-handed tradition. The book by Ma'ruf al-Rusafi was written in 1934 but could not be published until 2002. There were other intellectuals with a comparable profile to al-Rusafi and Abder Razek, who felt strongly about the limitations imposed by a frozen tradition and expressed their need to break free by daring to pose bold questions, but without reference to or use of the methods and concepts derived from modern thought and scholarship. These include Mahmud Mohamed Taha and Ahmad Kasravi.

At a later stage came a generation of thinkers who had been exposed to modern ideas about religion, politics and their conflicting relationships in European contexts, especially since the Enlightenment. They were also exposed to modern approaches to questions of religious and cultural heritage, especially historical-critical scholarship, and came to discover endeavours that aimed to apply these methods to the heritage of Muslims. Mohammed Arkoun is definitely of this later generation. He emerges as someone who has assimilated and mastered concepts and theories of contemporary social science and philosophy, particularly in the forms and terminology that were worked out within French-speaking academia. However, he does not seek to advocate some kind of religious reform by redress or to correct traditional views through a scholarly re-examination, as was attempted by a number of Muslim scholars of his generation, for example, Fazlur Rahman, Abdelmajid Charfi, Abdolkarim Sorouch. Rather, he stresses that we need to subvert, not to reform. He fully adopts the scholarly agenda, but with a substantial reservation. In short, his principal aim was to broaden the impact of the "Copernican revolution" accomplished by historical-critical approaches, to question one specific type of categorisation still in use not only in public debate and discussion but also within an academia that had embraced historical-critical methodologies. Indeed, it was the categorisation that singles out Islam and Muslims as one, broad, enduring and efficient reality in the past as well as in the present, that Arkoun spent his lifetime passionately questioning.

Arkoun's aim was to scrutinise and dissolve notions which were derived from ideologies and that had shaped the perceptions of realities in the past and still remained in use today. The "Copernican revolution" was not, in his view, complete and effective until it dissolved the remnants of ideologies that had prevailed in various historical contexts, including those inherited from the "rational" Enlightenment. Many have consequently situated Arkoun within the wave of postmodernism, but there is a need for caution here. He does not reject the ideal of truth, or the ambition to reach some degree of reliable, well-supported forms of representation. All discourses are definitely not equal in their claims to truth and it is important to dispel the illusions and distortions that have accumulated through, and can be fully explained by, various historical processes. In a few paragraphs in a paper bearing a title which could be considered to be his "manifesto", "Transgresser, déplacer, dépasser" (Transgress, displace, overcome), Arkoun formulates his most formal statement about history:

> The philosophical substance of modern historical thought can be made explicit in the following epistemic and epistemological propositions:
> • All human social units, whatever may be their size, are subject to mechanisms of transformation, change, evolution either in the direction of integration, complexification, heading towards hegemony, or, to the contrary, in the direction of disintegration and weakening that may lead the unit to effacement, dissolution, demise;
> • All that happens in the life of social units is the consequence of the continuous play of external and internal forces which determine the wills, initiatives and perceptions of social actors, thus labelled precisely in order to highlight the theatrical setup of power behaviour in particular;
> • Spheres of the supernatural, of divine or metaphysical transcendence, of active and omnipresent gods or of one, living but distant god, of magical, popular, legendary, religious beliefs, all linked to the imaginary, are equally products of social actors. As such, they must be submitted to the same analytical and critical investigation as conducted by social sciences in order to assess their pertinence and their effect in the historical shaping of societies;
> • The historical argumentation which underlies all modern historical writing aims at progressively absorbing the sociological reasoning as defined by Jean-Claude Passeron,[2] with the clearly stated ambition to objectify the actors' subjectivities.[3]

The frustration, short temper and lack of patience Arkoun showed are clearly due to the fact that his campaigning did not yield the desired effect. He felt that he was completely misunderstood, as he was often faced by a polite but coldly dismissive silence. There was, no doubt, something that created embarrassment among his audiences. An assessment made by Ira Lapidus of one of Arkoun's works is perhaps not untypical:

> In a series of recent works he [Arkoun] has become the leading French-language spokesman calling for a rethinking of Islam in a modern mode. Unfortunately, his book is full of French academic jargon, scholarly polemics and allusions to subjects that will not be familiar to ordinary readers. [...] it is also a frustrating work to read because Mr. Arkoun raises important questions, announces that further research is necessary and leaves them unresolved.[4]

Arkoun was perceptive in calling for an outright adoption of historical-critical approaches. It is the case that in most Muslim contexts education in religious matters, and the prevailing perceptions in general, are overwhelmingly dogmatic and built upon assumptions that are often unacceptable to the modern mind. Religious instruction is given in ways which were widespread during pre-modern times, shaping the minds of people for a lifetime. At the same time, in order to achieve consistency, Arkoun was also right in insisting that the historical-critical attitude be taken seriously, and therefore be applied to the concepts and terminology used to represent history and culture where they come to define collective identities and common aspirations.

Pushing the "Copernican revolution" achieved by modern social sciences to its ultimate consequences, ensuring that it is comprehensive and consistent in Muslim as well as in "Western" contexts, seems well overdue; particularly, if we take into consideration the pernicious effects of the uses and misuse of categories such as "civilisation", "culture" and "religion". The vast accumulation of literature intended to dispel the idea of a clash of civilisations gives us a very good reason for a systematic reconsideration of categories that we take to be elementary building blocks for public discussion. Without a thorough comprehensiveness and consistency, without a methodical critique of such categories or concepts, it becomes impossible to destroy the false idols that populate our imaginations. Misunderstandings created by the uncritical use of these categories weigh heavily on perceptions in the public opinion, and create deep gaps between the understanding brought about by scholarship and by perceptions that are firmly rooted in societies. All this, Arkoun was well placed to perceive, understand and feel the need to fight. Having found himself on the margins of two societies with different historical heritages and a history of intense confrontation, he was able to perceive acutely the devastating effects of categories, concepts and terms that are understood to be markers of elementary realities.

There remains a gap between the ideal Arkoun called for and the social and anthropological realities on the ground. It is striking to call for subversion against, rather than reform of, deeply entrenched but grossly inappropriate views. Attempting reforms that may amount to simple face-lifting, while leaving fundamental attitudes unaffected, will not bring about the change that Arkoun (and many contemporary scholars of Muslim background) felt to be overdue. But this does not take into consideration the religious needs ('spiritual aspirations', if we wish to follow the established terminology) in societies at large. In this way Arkoun was a utopian intellectual, not in terms of what he insistently requested from fellow scholars, but rather in regard to what he hoped to achieve in the public sphere. He simply seemed to be insensitive to the fact that societies do need myths and allegories, that no established religion can be subverted through rational argument (otherwise, which popular religion would have survived?), that religious attitudes evolve not because people are convinced to adopt change, but rather when they are 'seduced' by rival alternatives. Preaching a form of enlightenment that is not accessible to the multitude, he seemed to be insensitive to the Rushdian (or Averroist) principle, following which the social order needs to be built on foundations derived from supernatural perceptions, at least until secular worldviews can and do prevail. At moments, his thought seemed to be frozen in sophisticated phrases that he derived from scholarly works little known to those whom he addressed. He also became increasingly reluctant to listen to the world around him, to interact with other thinkers who were voicing concerns similar to his own, which may explain the little influence his thought has had in predominantly Muslim contexts.

Ultimately, Arkounian views, utopian as they may be, may not have caught the interest or understanding of the multitude during his lifetime, but they do call upon ideals that are universal and of all times. They may inspire and motivate scholars in the future, as there should be individuals who are prepared to brave the hurdles of his terminology and make their way to the numerous gems that his message contains. He may, with time, find his place next to great and fecund utopians like Rousseau or Proudhon who, long after their demise, continue to inspire, at least within circles of committed devotees.

Notes

1. Mohammed Arkoun. *"Transgresser, déplacer, dépasser"*, in Arabica; T. 43, Fasc. 1, *L'œuvre de Claude Cahen : Lectures Critiques*, pp. 28–70.
2. *Le raisonnement sociologique: un espace non poppérien de l'argumentation* (éditions refondue et augmentée), (Paris : Albin Michel, 2005).
3. "Transgresser, déplacer, dépasser", pp. 57–8 (my translation).
4. "Islam without Militance", in *The New York Times*, 21 August 1994.

Mohammed Arkoun:
A Personal Tribute and an Intellectual Assessment

Aziz Esmail

I (i)

I first met Mohammed Arkoun in the late 1980s in the United States. The occasion was formal. It was a small seminar on an Islamic issue (a "workshop" – a word academics do not mind using nowadays, borrowing factory idiom). Arkoun spoke with the force, the vehemence which – as I was to discover – was characteristic of him. He made a strong, immediate impression on me. The vehemence was striking, if only because it is unusual in learned seminars, at least in the Anglo-Saxon world. But this impression could have faded, and his passion might as easily have been something to deplore as to admire (for passion in the absence of intellect is always deplorable, and of Arkoun's intellect I was able to take true measure only afterwards). What caught my attention were a few telling remarks of a serious kind. They left me intrigued.

The remarks impressed me less for themselves than that they came from a professor of Islamic Studies. This, in turn, made an impact because my own experience of Islamic Studies had been a great disappointment. For this reason, Arkoun's approach struck me as a rare intellectual treat.

In a piece on Arkoun I must check a temptation to digress to myself. But to convey why I found in Arkoun a person rare of a kind I must say a word about why I had found academic Islamic Studies unsatisfactory. For it was this common perception which fed the intellectual friendship that was to flourish between us.

(ii)

Graduate Islamic Studies had never been an aim of mine. It was a product of pure chance. On the other hand, religion represented a very powerful force in my life, and it was this, perhaps, more than an intellectual attraction to the field, that impelled me towards Islamic Studies.

I had been born and brought up in the Ismaili faith in its Indian subcontinental form. In culture – language, custom, food and entertainment – my world was Indian. (In cultural matters we were unconcerned to sift supposedly "Islamic" elements from supposedly others. In this respect we enjoyed the blessings of unselfconsciousness, denied to more recent generations in similar contexts.) The land – East Africa – was ruled by the British, and so our schooling was in the British mode, in modern subjects, with supreme importance given to English, a necessary means of advancement in the world.

Our religious ideas and practices belonged to a remote past. They carried a sense of the timeless and the transcendental, of pleasure and passions not of this world. Carried in our Indian vernacular, they were at once intimate and untouched by ways of modern thought. But the teaching of our faith at the time (as now) advocated a harmony of the ancient and the modern. It lauded the spiritual, but also embraced the modern world. So, someone like me, participating in at least two worlds, did so not only without conflict but with a sense of fulfilling a mandate. Yet it is hard to over-emphasise how distinct the two worlds then were. At school the teachers of all secular subjects (in my time) were of other faiths. This was never an issue. The religion was not allowed to encroach unduly on our time at school, and certainly not on what we studied. So, although one had no way of realising this, the school – or more accurately, what we learned there – was a microcosm of England, itself a microcosm of the modern West; while our religious and cultural pursuits were a microcosm of the Indo-Islamic world, in an African setting.

This simple experience (common to so many people in so many lands in so much of modern time) was for me to become in later, more self-conscious years an object of analysis and wonder and a wish for integration. At school my mind was long excited by science rather than the arts (though, happily, we did not think of them yet as alternatives). At the same time my knowledge of our sacred Indo-Islamic poetry (even this hyphenated word belies its freedom from duality) fostered an early sensitivity to language. Later, this sensitivity was carried over to my studies in English at university. The realism of English literature offered me a counterpoint to mysticism, and although I never objected to the literature as "foreign", and though it was to open to me the new world of European thought and culture, it took me back to my own setting and background in a wish to understand it anew with the discipline, largely self-taught, of thinking about literature.

In due course, seeking more than means of cultivation, seeking means of rigorous and methodical analysis, I turned to other subjects. Philosophy, which I was later to teach, became an enduring interest. So did psychoanalysis; and later, sociology and anthropology.

This was the intellectual make-up that had come to be mine. I do not call it inter-disciplinary (though that would not be altogether incorrect). Having had an "inter-disciplinary" background, I have grown to realise the folly of pursuing it as a deliberate, artificial end. The ideal form of inter-disciplinariness is where it is inherent in the way a subject is understood; when, in other words, it is organically present – unsought, unnamed – and has the properties, so to speak, of a compound rather than a mixture.

If, then, I turned to Islam as a subject of study, I was less after knowledge understood as facts than knowledge understood as perspective. I hoped to be able to use the ideas in the various disciplines I was interested in to this end. Ultimately, I suspect, I was also concerned to bridge the two worlds I had mentally lived in. It is very likely that every motivated student of humanistic topics is at bottom a seeker. What he or she seeks is inevitably personal. This becomes a liability if the search becomes romantic or self-indulgent instead of self-transcending. It is not the business of universities to serve personal odysseys. But if a subject like philosophy or religion or art or literature is conceived in a way which a student cannot use for personal as much as for professional development, it is safe to say that it must be badly conceived.

I have allowed myself these personal observations to qualify rather than inflate my claims about the field. I do not present these claims as objective. But neither are they capriciously personal. The personal factor in one's estimation of things can be a means to more general, impersonal truth. Whether this is so or not in the present case is, of course, a matter for debate and discussion.

(iii)

Let me highlight, then, some of what I see as serious drawbacks of Islamic Studies in Western universities, especially at graduate level. To anyone sensitised to them they were too obvious to be missed. I have the past decades in mind, but I suspect the deficiencies have not entirely disappeared.

To begin with, the subject itself is anomalous. By definition Islamic Studies is the study of Islam. But what is Islam? The obvious answer is: the religion of that name. But, as it happens, Islamic Studies turns out to be a historical study of *societies* called "Islamic". The field spans politics, economics, cultures, jurisprudence, intellectual and literary traditions, and of course, religious ideas and practices. To do justice to these would require the skills of what at present are the separate disciplines of philosophy, literary criticism and the social sciences, together with knowledge of sources and texts in primary languages.

The point is not that this is too tall an order for anyone (though this is so). It is, rather, that the field, has rarely, if ever, appreciated it as a tall order. It has failed to perceive, for example, that "Islamic" philosophy cannot be properly understood without a training in the history and methods of philosophy; that "Islamic" political and social institutions cannot be grasped, beyond superficial judgements, without appropriate conceptions of social and political order; that cultures, like languages, are systems rather than elements, and require, for their understanding, tools equivalent to (if not indeed overlapping with) those of linguistics; that, in short, none of these yield full or systematic meaning through history understood solely as narration.

Islamic Studies makes sense only as a field built jointly out of contributions of perspectives such as those of history, sociology, psychology, linguistics and philosophy. This is precisely what in its traditional form it has never been.

To reiterate, however, the problem is of a different order than one that can be corrected by an injection, from outside as it were, of an inter-disciplinary cocktail.

The two principal disciplines in the tradition of Islamic Studies are philology and history. Philology is a demanding and rigorous discipline dedicated to the study of texts. But texts are only part of a society's expression, and in pre-modern times this part was but a tiny sliver. This was an obvious consequence of the highly limited literacy (by the standards of even a century ago, let alone today) as well as the absence of print.

Consequently, although the classical Islamic world abounded in texts, many of them bearing witness to great learning and sophistication of mind in their authors, it is easy to forget that their content does not represent the mental outlook (itself pluriform), the beliefs and practices we call "Islam", of people at large. This is true even of a non-scholarly text like the Qur'an, whose study and exegesis in colleges (madrasas) was a pursuit of legists and theologians, while in society at large its presence was liturgical and ceremonial, with little (if any) role for intellectual or analytic endeavour.

History, the other discipline which has shaped traditional Islamic history, is obviously an important subject of relevance to this field. At its best it too is a solid and demanding enterprise. But, being mostly an art rather than a science, it is apt to vary greatly in how it understands its subject matter. The superficiality or otherwise of its understanding will directly reflect the superficiality or otherwise of the author's mind and life-experience, or of the tradition in which that mind has been schooled. A tradition of due complexity is carried forward by good minds in its service. But it will withstand, at least for some time, the absence of good minds to carry it forward. On the other hand, a tradition of study which is devoid of a rich vision of life will not benefit from the availability of good minds. These are likely to be infected with the mediocrity of the tradition, and so forfeit their potential. Or they will turn to other pastures of intellectual sustenance.

In this respect history is at one with the other arts. A novel or a play, a work of paint or music, will be only as shallow or profound as the vision of life of its author. And we can all, in our different ways and with our different tastes, tell the difference between a glib and a rich specimen in any of these fields though we may differ in our choices and the criteria for our choices.

There have been good minds at work in modern historical studies of Islam, just as there are bound to be good (and bad) minds at work in any field of knowledge. But the tradition of knowledge-gathering in which a good mind is schooled may do either justice or injustice to that mind. It may give it a wide scope to exercise and grow its talents. Or it may direct it into a tunnel. And by doing so it may shrink the possibilities of what may be an originally fine intellect and imagination. It would do so by failing to afford the scope a good mind needs in order to flower. At bottom this is the fault of the tradition of scholarship in question. But in the end it is both the scholar and the scholarship which, depending on the degree of their identification with the tradition, come to suffer from its faults.

Islamic Studies has long been hamstrung, in its domain of historical research (so I would argue), by a remarkably restricted understanding of what history can and should be. It looks upon history as a narration of events, people and dynasties, along with their ("Islamic") principles and practices. But the history of a people must take account of the broadest complexities of human nature, both as they are reflected in people, and when people become "a people". In short, the best insights of the better part of psychology and anthropology, of history analysis, and even of philosophy in so far as it alone raises questions about the relation of mind to world, are essential at the core, and not merely at the margins of history. But such humane breadth – essential to the idea of humanities – is seldom to be encountered in works of Islamic history.

In Europe, history went through a process of self-consciousness, thanks to a long tradition of thinkers – Vico, Hegel, Benedetto Croce, R. G. Collingwood, E. H. Carr, Fernand Braudel (the list can be long). However, very little of this reflexivity ever percolated into Islamic Studies. Its boundaries, it would seem, have long been the boundaries of a ghetto.

The first question any historian must ask is what one is to take as the unit of their study. For their "subject" is not quite out there waiting to be studied. But this question has rarely been asked of "Islam". Marshall Hodgson was an exception.[1] He took an informed decision to pick not "Islam" as his unit of study but rather the civilisation associated with Islam. This begged the question as to what kind of an entity a "civilisation" was; what justification there might be in treating the "Islamic" (or, in Hodgson's proposed terminology, "Islamicate") civilisation as an entity in its own right; and what role Islam may be seen to have had in the life of this entity, seen as a civilisation.

It will be apparent from this that Hodgson was, in a word, a "reflexive" historian, consciously defining and postulating the object of his study rather than taking it for granted. One may disagree with his postulates; but one cannot criticise him for unawareness of their necessity.

The need to define adjectival uses of the term "Islamic", whether to define the societies concerned, or sections of it, is a need that may be shirked only at the price of intellectual confusion. It was one of the merits of Oleg Grabar's work on Islamic art, quite apart from whatever may be judged by a specialist to be the merits of his scholarship that he asked, and attempted uncively to define, in what sense one might possibly think of Islamic art as Islamic.[2] One can only wonder whether his readiness to probe this question owed itself to his background not in Islamic Studies but in the history of art, and of Islamic art as an area within it. It is reasonable to believe that it was this better chartered territory and a better defined discipline which accounts for this conceptual self-awareness in his work.

In general, we find an important difference in the work of those scholars in Islamic Studies who bother and try to illuminate their object of study through resort to theoretical concepts and of those who do not do so. The career of Prophet Muhammad acquires a more than factual interest in Montgomery Watt's hands because of his attempt to understand it as a composite of socio-economic circumstances as well as religious vision.[3] Similarly, his treatment of early Islam has the potential to interest students of history more generally because of the concepts he borrows from Durkheim and Weber. Again, his attempt to understand religion as such in theoretical terms, however rudimentary, gives the subject an interest beyond that of a believer. Watt's scholarship may look inadequate in the light of up-to-date knowledge. (Not being a specialist, I cannot comment.) His forays into sociology and psychology certainly have something of a fragmentary, even amateurish flavour. But none of this detracts from the pioneering quality of his endeavour in its time, and hence, its historically exemplary character.

Examples such as these show that Islamic Studies cannot be written off wholesale. They show that there have been exceptions to the rule under criticism here. But what this says, and what I hold, is that they are indeed exceptions to the rule.

Let us address a category of intrinsic importance to the study of Islam: the category, namely, of religion. Few scholars in not only Islamic Studies but so-called religious studies appear to realise or admit that "religion" is indeed a category; that as such, it is posited or constructed rather than found; and that it therefore requires assessment, at any given moment, of its usefulness or suitability in the light of our knowledge and outlook.

This does not mean that it is an empty category, or that to question it intellectually is to deny the role of faith or spiritual insight in the dimension of life associated with it. In any case, I see no necessary conflict between spiritual sensitivity and intellectual scepticism, and would even assert that the former is deep and honest only when in companionship with the latter. At any rate, in scholarly study, category analysis is indispensable.

When it is lacking, the least of the results is the lack of a typology – that is, a failure to distinguish between types of religious thought and experience. How, for instance, might we distinguish the kind of experience present in the Qur'an from the kind of speculation characteristic of theology (*kalām*)?

What, again, is meant by "mysticism" or "esotericism"?

There is a tradition of scholarship in modern Islamic Studies devoted to

Sufism, "esoteric philosophy", "theosophy" and the like. The subject-matter covered by these (to my mind vague) labels is, as it happens, remarkably rich. But the manner in which it is treated in this tradition is not by way of inquiry but with a view to celebration and exaltation. One would look in vain, in this tradition, for philosophical critique or argumentation, psychological analysis, or attempts to locate the phenomena concerned in a more general anthropology. The scholars who write in this vein are apt to look upon such options with indifference if not disdain.

I regularly encountered indifference to the idea of such inquiry in personal conversations with Annemarie Schimmel, who loved Sufism, knew enormous swathes of its poetic texts by heart, and had less than zero interest in what she would summarily dismiss as "philosophical" or "intellectual" intrusions into a domain to which "love", and "love" alone, held the key. This reflects a very different kind of investment in the subject from (say) that of Reynold Nicholson – whose attitude to mysticism is better described as an intellectual (literary) interest rather than investment in it.

In this outlook there is no room for sceptical evaluation or even critical appreciation where the term "critical" is taken seriously. There is no means, therefore, for suspending judgement about metaphysical claims and abstaining without *a priori* acceptance or rejection, from taking the claims of ancient masters at their face value. There is room aplenty for questions, but scarcely for questioning the texts. What is thus possible is not inquiry but learning – learning of a certain sort, designed to foster appreciation and nurture allegiance. As a result the preferred student is the one inclined towards discipleship rather than independent judgement; one who is engaged on a quest rather than cultivation of the mind.

I should add that I have little tolerance for the opposite kind of mind to that of an acolyte – a mind bent on scepticism as a sport, taking delight in debunking. Critical inquiry belongs to a very different kind of outlook from that associated with the kind of criticism which takes pride in its aggressiveness. Criticism in this sense (the word is ambiguous) is a sign not of intellectual cultivation but of intellectual vandalism. The two are as apart as chalk and cheese. Moreover, I believe that love for a subject, a wish to be inspired by it, and to pursue learning with passion, are qualities not only valuable but essential to true intellectual accomplishment. One is a dubious student of music who is deaf to its pleasures. Likewise, I doubt whether the study of religion, not only by a student whose mind is closed to seeing anything good in it but also by one who is religiously unmusical (to use an expression from Max Weber) is likely to eventuate in a contribution to human knowledge in this field.

It does not take much of an argument, however, to apply the same idea to the mind closed in an opposite direction. But there is more to it than that, of a specific sort, in the area we are considering here.

There are three activities of the mind here which it is useful to distinguish. There is first of all the doctrine and symbolism, for example, running from Yahya al-Suhrawardi, through Ibn-al-Arabi, to Mulla Sadra. To link these names like this is to see at once both what united them and what distinguished them, so that if we speak of them as constituting a "tradition" we must do so by understanding "tradition" in a looser and more historically contextualising sense than those scholars nowadays who think of it as a harmonious whole given for all from times immemorial.

The point I wish to make here is that such a tradition can only legitimately continue as it is, without the injection of meta-level philosophical or theoretical considerations I have mentioned above, as long as the cultural or intellectual ethos in which it is excluded remains essentially unaltered.

The fact is, however, that with the altered paradigm of the modern sciences, both natural and human – a reflection, in turn of a profoundly changed world – the old paradigm, with its assumptions about being and knowledge, cannot be maintained, except at the price of intellectual ghettoisation, without a fresh inquiry, at a meta-level, by means of categories from the combined domains of modern philosophy, psychology and anthropology. It may well be that we might find some of these categories inadequate when confronted with this subject-matter. If so, it would be a stroke of good luck, contributing as it might to new horizons both in the tradition and within the sphere of modern knowledge.

The approach to mysticism or esotericism by scholars in modern universities which I have outlined above differs from both these phenomena. It eschews modern categories. But it is also at a great remove from the very subject-matter it eulogises. It is far more inspiring as well as instructive to read from Jalal-al-din Rumi's *mathnawi*, even in translation, than to read Schimmel on Rumi's "symbolism". Modern studies of mysticism in the style I have characterised above are hybrid phenomena. It is not intellectual enough, yet it is informed by genuine scholarship. It is not of a piece – being situated in a very different time and place – with the mystical or gnostic doctrine and practice of historical times, yet pays allegiance to it. It is a kind of academic neo-mysticism.

How might such a curious hybrid, coy of intellectual challenge, yet learned, come about in religious studies? Part of the answer is unintentionally apparent in the name "religious studies". Designed to study religion, it has a tendency to be religious. Both aspects fall short of their ideal prototypes. Genuine religious participation is unaware, or only notionally aware of itself as religious. And religious enthusiasm, whatever form or name it takes, acts as a brake on objective inquiry.

The half-way house that religious studies tends to be in cases such as the one we have just considered is reflected, among other things, in the lack of theoretical self-awareness in the field. The only major "theory" it has adopted is phenomenology. In the pioneering work of Micae Eliade, phenomenology takes the form of the so-called "history of religions". One of the criteria for a successful history of a subject is that the subject must be a sufficiently coherent and comprehensive unit. Religion is an inseparable facet of social existence. To abstract it from social and psychological realities is to substitute something unreal for these realities. That is precisely what we find in the accounts of religious phenomena in Eliade or his associates, like Henri Corbin. Louis Massignon was different. He was a religious visionary with feet planted firmly in history. His subject, appropriately, was a single life (Mansûr al-Hallâj). In Massignon's pages Hallâj lives as a real historical figure. His demographic and sociological milieu is painstakingly recorded. Unlike Corbin's figures, he is a flesh and blood character. His spirituality is nowhere compromised or underplayed. Quite the contrary: it breathes through the entire work. Massignon's study, then, is a work of genuine scholarship. Its animating spirit is that of a spiritual humanism. Once again, the exception draws our attention to the rule.

Phenomenology, founded by Husserl, is a philosophy, hence subject to philosophical critique and assessment. In religious studies its philosophical status is hardly ever inspected – for graduates in religious studies are not required to have philosophical training, and professional philosophers like to keep to themselves. (Matters are different in theology.) In practice, phenomenology in religious studies serves as a code name for something like non-judgemental descriptivism. But what is the point of describing? A re-statement of religious phenomena in (say) Marxist or Freudian terms, whether valid or not, has a self-evident significance. But if the idea is to avoid such trans-location, deplored as a way of explaining away the object while professing to explain it, why re-state at all? Why not simply stop at editing and publishing the texts concerned?

These are methodological and epistemological questions which remain, in this field, infrequently and insufficiently explored.

If, then, we were to jettison religious studies and re-allocate its subject matter – epistemologically and methodologically – by linking it to the conceptual frameworks, we may well serve to re-invent it into a more comprehensive human narrative. The effort is worth making.

For lack of this, our Judaeo-Christian-Islamic heritage remains effectively dissociated from the Greco-Roman as well as modern scientific heritages. The world of secular scholarship today has yet to take due measure of the phenomenon of prophecy in Hebraic and Arabic history. The insufficient attention hitherto given to this major influence in the history of culture is due to the twofold dissociation in modern culture, hence also academic culture, of the religious from the humanistic, and of Islamic Studies from Judaeo-Christian Studies.

One cannot do justice to prophecy in Islam without reference to Hebrew prophecy, Christian messianism and other related phenomena as parts of a single phenomenon. This underlines another major problem in Islamic Studies as a field: the artificial isolation of its field from other Mediterranean and Near Eastern cultures and faiths. It can be said that Islamic Studies is at once too disparate and too narrow a field, in terms of both time and space.

Take, for instance, philosophy. It goes without saying that knowledge of an Avicenna or Averroes is deficient without due knowledge of Aristotle and late Hellenistic philosophies. But it is less often realised that our perspectives on these great Muslim thinkers are also the poorer without knowledge of Kant and those who came after him, down to Nietzsche, Heidegger and their successors. After Kant's repudiation of metaphysics, and subsequent elaborations on this "Copernican revolution", metaphysics, once the "queen of the sciences", ceases to be business as usual. One may choose to discard it or to re-assess it (and perhaps, more valiantly, attempt to re-instate it). But what one may not do, if one cares for intellectual integrity, is to resume today from the day before yesterday as though there had never been a yesterday. An ancient world-view cannot be resumed in a later age as though there had not been an intervening age, an age which did not simply follow the earlier era, but owed its being to its confrontation with the latter.

Yet we have scholars of gnostic Islam who proceed as if metaphysics were as epistemologically secure today as it was before the advent of intellectual modernity. Or, similarly, to ignore its extra-philosophical roots. It is, in fact, hard to imagine an Avicenna or Averroes returning to the world of today and not taking the keenest interest in modern physics, biology, philosophy and the human sciences. Knowing what we do about them, the comprehensiveness of their interest in all things human, and their credo, expressed by their intellectual forebear al-Kindi, that knowledge should be welcome no matter from where it comes, it is hard to think of them as discounting these modern sciences in their understanding of being.

Arabic or Persian philosophers stand a better chance, then, of being understood by historians of philosophy than by historians of Islam. The history of Islam may be better understood if the history of mentalities is joined to the history of events and ideas in Islamic contexts. The origins of Islam are still insufficiently understood. It is safe to say that whatever further research may be needed for this purpose, research alone will not suffice; that prophecy, revelation or book, crucial to belief as well as in history, demand attention. Moreover, these are best addressed in a comparative (Judaeo-Christian-Islamic) light.

What is true of the classical age of Islam is also true of its modern age. The only adequate basis for understanding modernity is a comparative one. Just as the problems of the developing world may be properly understood only in a global perspective, so too do the nature of modernity, its effects on conditions of life and the shape of the human mind, its impact on old traditions and religious views of the world, call for a comparative perspective in which alone the specificities of the Muslim world may be understood without artificial isolation from world history.

These perceptions and a growing sense of intellectual isolation drove me away from Islamic Studies and to other fields of the humanities and sciences in the decades which followed my higher education.

Towards the end of the 1980s I took up a position as the Dean of the Institute of Ismaili Studies in London. With this position came a privileged opportunity to relate my intellectual background to the practical imperatives of cultural and educational development in a community with a strong attachment to its faith balanced by a philosophy of productive adaptation to the modern world. With this position my questions about the nature of Islamic Studies took on a more practical, urgent and outwardly responsible aspect.

Intellectual life, however, requires the tonic of shared ideas and conversation. To Mohammed Arkoun, who lamented the state of Islamic Studies as much as I did, and for overlapping reasons, I owe the conversations which nourished my renewed interest and endeavour. And although my intellectual formation and temperament were different from his, and although my personal background, unlike his, was shaped by strong spiritual commitments, on the intellectual front he remained a constant interlocutor.

This was especially so when we became colleagues on the Board of Governors of this organisation.

In the following section I offer a summary sketch of Arkoun's thought as I understand it. I do so neutrally, without interjecting my own opinions or reactions. In the last section I offer the rudiments of an evaluation.

II (i)

In our day it is no longer possible to speak of Islam except by enclosing it in quotation marks. This remark of Arkoun's can be taken as an indication of his entire approach to Islam.[4] It signals what he himself was often to call a need for *problematisation*. Where most people who speak of Islam assume that "Islam" represents something definite – for example, a set of *usul* (principles) and *arkân* (rites); or "submission to the will of God" – Arkoun, relying on the ear rather than on definition, had it trained on *usage*. Individuals and groups employ the word "Islam" variably, depending on their interests and their passions. The connection is, by nature, un-conscious. (I hyphenate this word both to imply active barricading of consciousness and to distinguish it from the Freudian unconscious.) Arkoun thought it the duty of a scholar of Islam, confronted by a specific instance of "Islam", whether in a political or religious connection, to probe the subsoil of interests, passions or longings which fuel its appeal. Needless to say, the same rule would apply to any other terminology functioning as social rhetoric.

(ii)

Arkoun's approach thus involves a rejection of taking Muslim rhetoric about Islam at face value. To this extent his approach belongs to what the philosopher Paul Ricoeur calls the "hermeneutics of suspicion". But so do Marxist and Freudian styles of interpretation. Arkoun's approach differs from these. For this reason, this broad category defined by Ricoeur must be narrowed to enable his method to be characterised more specifically.

In a nutshell, Arkoun's approach is that of critical deconstruction. The cradle for this idea is postmodernism. Key terminology from postmodern jargon pervades Arkoun's writing. Examples include *l'imaginaire* (translated unattractively in English as "imaginary", as a noun); "deconstruction"; "logocentrism"; "archaeology" of knowledge; and "mimetic rivalry".

A principal/formative influence on postmodern thought is Nietzsche. Nietzsche's repudiation of metaphysics was more total than Kant's.

While Kant retains notions of reality and truth, though with significant philosophical caveats, Nietzsche actively eschews them. It is only after Nietzsche that it becomes possible to speak of knowledge as "produced" rather than obtained. Though it would be simplistic to equate Nietzsche's position with those of postmodernism, its focus on the uses rather than references of discourse can easily be traced to him. Famously, or infamously, to Nietzsche we owe the idea of a claim to truth as a bid for power. In the Nietzschean way of thinking, knowledge, truth and the other constants of traditional metaphysics are seen as, ultimately, tools or masquerades of power.

This whole picture of the world – too tendentious to be called a theory, and too unsystematic to be called a philosophy – informs Arkoun's work. His theoretical framework was not original. Where he stood out was in his application of it to the study of Islam, in which there was (and remains) a dearth of theoretical perspectives.

The two pillars of Arkoun's analysis are history and anthropology. History is all-determining. This follows naturally from the rejection of metaphysics, which also opens the door to anthropology. The two methods should ideally coalesce into an anthropological history, or historical anthropology. Such a project would differ profoundly from "positivist" scholarship of traditional Orientalists. I believe it is an accurate statement of Arkoun's view of the prevailing tradition of Islamic history to say that it subscribes to the cult of facts. Obsessed by chronology, fastidiously philological, it offers no light on the forces at work in the contemporary Muslim world because, halting at the surface of the texts, it fails to penetrate to the historical forces contemporary to the texts. The result is what Arkoun frequently called "dead" history.

It would be wrong to conclude that Arkoun thought little of Orientalist scholarship. On the contrary he considered its achievements both impressive and indispensable. He was never unsure of his identity as a scholar of Islam. He thought and wrote as a scholar. His historical ideas were, just like Orientalist scholarship, textually based. But to this he joined a keen curiosity and natural flair for anthropology, in whose theories he was deeply interested.

Historians and anthropologists are traditionally dispassionate, maintaining a principled adherence to detailed observation and inquiry. But Arkoun thought and wrote with passion, a passion which frequently boiled over in vehemence. His was the passion of a campaigner, albeit an intellectual campaigner who disdained conventional politics as much as he disdained the edifice of the modern state.

In this, his campaigning zeal, he stood in the old tradition of the "committed" intellectual who is concerned to expose the mask of reason which legitimises vested interests. Although he detested Marxism, he was at home with the concept of ideology first promulgated, in its modern form, in Hegelian and Marxian thought, and elaborated in the sociology of knowledge.

In the postmodern climate of thought the old notion of ideology took a new turn under the influence of men like Nietzsche and Heidegger. Arkoun was not concerned with defining or evaluating the notion. This was probably for the best, as his strength lay not in philosophical revision or analysis, but in applying this and other such concepts to the hitherto untouched field of Islamic history. Doing so brought additional issues to light, necessitating other theoretical concepts, to some of which Arkoun was to give his own twist or spin so as to help illuminate the history of Islam. In the process he touched on important issues still deserving continued attention.

The critique of ideology is an unmasking enterprise. It attacks mystification. An especially interesting analysis in Arkoun's work is to be found in the argument that religion theologises mundane events. In the process it turns social actors into theological categories. Thus, Arkoun was known to speak of Muhammad bin Abdullah in distinction from Muhammad the Prophet – not in any way to belittle the latter, but to emphasise that prophecy was an interpretation, drawn from the universe of symbols already present in the Hebrew bible and more generally in the Near-Eastern milieu, of the strivings and ideals of a social actor. Similarly, the men around the Prophet, whose interests led them to support or opposition, or into hedging their bets, are to be encountered in a theologised form in the discourse of the Qur'an, as *mû'minûn* (the faithful), *mûshriqûn* (polytheists) and *mûnâfiqûn* (hypocrites, with guile in their hearts).

This is one of the most interesting and original ideas to emerge from Arkoun's theoretical interest, applied to the materials of Islam. Just as Marx is said to have stood Hegel on his head, so Arkoun makes theology stand on its head. When theology, which takes itself to be foundational, is made to stand on its head, it shows up its real foundation which, in Arkoun's view, is society: the sphere where men organise themselves to pursue their interests and ideals, and in the process form alliances, wage warfare, and not least, manufacture and uphold ideologies.

There is, in fact, a double movement involved. In the first instance, social realities are transmuted into theological *imaginaire*. Deconstructive analysis seeks to return theology's celestial escapades to its earthly roots. It is, in other words, the re-tracing of a process from its end-point to its origin. It is, we might say, like the return of evaporated water, condensing as rain, to the earth where it rose.

Whatever we might say in defence or criticism of this scheme, it is quite evident, when one thinks about it, that religious discourse frequently mystifies the facts of history. Its claim to unveil a higher reality appears all too often to go hand in hand with an apparent determination to veil naked human interests, whether for power, status or possession. If one were to look for a core in deconstructive analysis which would remain persuasive when the rest of its principles were rejected, whether as being reductive or on some other such grounds, it would be an appeal to the humanity of the figures and motivations which are reflected (and disguised) in religious ideologies.

It is in this sense that the prophet of Islam (like other prophets, messiahs, saints or whatever) is to be regarded primarily as a social actor, and only secondarily (though not, as we shall see, reductively) in the light of a religious interpretation, as a prophet.

(iii)

The above, I believe, is an accurate distillation of Arkoun's position in this regard. To distil it in these terms pushes to the fore a question which may otherwise be lost from view. Put simply, it is: can a believer, wishing to continue to believe, accept Arkoun's approach? Put differently: are belief and deconstruction compatible? We may join this to a further question: can a believer make use of – that is to say, profit from – Arkoun's ideas? However, since this second question presupposes an affirmative answer to the first, we may coalesce the two and deal with them as one.

Broadly, a reflective believer has two options in the face of what Paul Ricoeur calls "hermeneutics of suspicion". He may hold that faith can well survive and even gain from such a confrontation. Or he may assert that it has value for an intellectual, but that it is imperative that ordinary men and women be shielded from it.

Both these expedients have in fact been proposed. The first has been argued, in another context, by Paul Ricoeur.[5] The second was the characteristic position of classical philosophers, living in Muslim communities, Jewish communities or Christian communities – men like Ibn Rushd (Averroes) and Ibn Maimûn (Maimonides).

I include classical philosophers like al-Fârâbî or Ibn Rushd even though, quite clearly, they have nothing to do with modern critics of ideology, because their position on matters such as God's knowledge or the eternity of the world was at strong variance with that of religious orthodoxy.

Their position, however, which was essentially that of Platonic political philosophy, was founded on an emphatic distinction between knowledge due to an elite (*al-khâṣṣ*) and to the rank and file (*al-'amm*). Neither could be practical or acceptable today. In parenthesis, it is also worth noting that Arkoun, with his strong distaste for the notion of an elite, was nothing if not hostile to Platonic political philosophy or the metaphysics allegedly connected to it.

As for the first of the options stated above, it is doubtful whether it can be upheld, beyond the private conscience of a solitary philosopher in a community of faith, by the community at large.

One may, of course, reject all deconstructive analysis altogether. But a theologian who does so would need to reckon with the *prima facie* credibility of the insights from historical sociology. He would also need to show why an alternative view, appealing, say, to a "beyond" (however this is understood), is rationally more satisfactory.

If it can be shown that Arkoun's argument misses something essential, it would, in a word, be *reductive*. Is it so? What place, if any, does the outlook of faith have in his thinking?

The question of the reality (or otherwise) of religious belief is a question of utmost importance in human self-understanding. Modern systems of thought do not always seem to grant this importance. Arkoun is among those who do. The following remarks make this clear:

> It is necessary to accept as objects of history, psychological analysis and historical anthropology what the 'believing' reading calls God, prophetic function, the revealed and revealing Word, the sacred, retribution, prayer, trust in God and so on. Historians have already used all this religious vocabulary; but they have presented it in a scientific culture based on a prejudice in favour of rationality which has long been that of Aristotelian categorization continued [in] the Enlightenment whose strategies, argumentation and themes aimed precisely at the substitution of its 'scientific' sovereignty to that of religious reason ...[6]

The criticism of the Enlightenment here is not incidental. It was a cornerstone of Arkoun's thought. Like many postmodern authors, he saw the philosophy of the Enlightenment as an ideology. To his mind it deserves the same deconstructive treatment as religious ideologies. In common with other postmodern authors, Arkoun did not accept the existence of any such thing as objective reason. There were only "reasons": discourses of one kind or another.

Adjectival qualifications of reason, which are a commonplace today, occur in Arkoun's writing. Examples are allusion to "religious reason" or "Islamic reason". Needless to say, before postmodernism, such expressions would have been rejected as linguistic errors or barbarisms.

The title of one of his books, *Pour une critique de la raison Islamique*, illustrates this usage. The Kantian echo in the title is however ironic, for Kant, although he took reason to be humanely anchored, would have recoiled at any suggestion that it was socially constructed. But for Arkoun that is precisely what reason is. Hence, the Enlightenment's appeal to Reason as a universal ideal is, in his view, deceptive. The ideal is but an ideological extension of modern Europe's belief in its entitlement to world mastery.

The Enlightenment is not what it saw itself as: the summit of human rationality. What it saw as objective reason was in fact a particular projection of reason, which effectively flattered the self-image of an ascendant Europe. Its pretension to universal rationality was a fraud.

It would follow that a rejection of religion in the name of reason is a suspect position. This was one of Arkoun's emphatic themes. Teaching and writing in the French context, he was aware of the militant face that modern secularism can take. To Arkoun militant secularism is a mirror image of religious militancy. It is a war of dogma with dogma. Both the contemporary so-called revival of religion and the attack on it by secular reason are, in his view, positions fit only to be combated and overcome.

The task of scholarship cannot stop here, however, for, the even-handedness implied in this position requires acknowledgement of the believer's outlook and sensibilities. But if such an acknowledgement were to be combined with a critique of religion as ideology, what is needed is a conception of religious faith as somehow distinct from the ideological use of religious symbols.

Since Arkoun's theoretical positions are a part of his reflections on Islam, it is best to look at these for clues to his perspective on faith. The most convenient for this purpose are his reflections on the Qur'an.

(iv)

The Qur'an is a book. Its being – or rather, having become – a book is for Arkoun the first epistemological obstacle to a true appreciation of the phenomenon called "revelation". For the book, or rather the corpus (*mushaf*) is a kind of packaging, a fixation, of an oral discourse which by its nature was open-ended and spontaneous. The passage from the primary to the secondary, from the spoken to the written, was for Arkoun a problematic development. Speech is open-ended. A corpus is bounded. The Qur'an as speech or recitation is one thing; as a *mushaf* it became, in Arkoun's telling words, an "official closed corpus".

The collection authorised by the Caliph Uthman bin Affan (644–656) had far-reaching effects. It led, in succeeding decades and centuries, to the rise of a "functional solidarity" between state, jurist-theologians, state bureaucracy and the written word.[7] Even so, the Qur'an was not one-dimensional. Its content became a prolific source for exegesis and commentary, theological doctrine and, not least, religious jurisprudence and law (*fiqh* and *shari'a*).

At the same time the "mythical" idea of the Qur'an, present in the original discourse, remained the living source of a rich *imaginaire*. The mythical aspect visualised a descent of the divine word from a heavenly archetype, the *umm-al-kitâb* ("Mother of the Book"), relayed to humanity through an inspired messenger. But this *imaginaire* was exploited to legitimise true belief (literally, orthodoxy). Given the numerous groups competing for material and spiritual supremacy, the *imaginaire* crystallised into competing orthodoxies, such as Sunni, Shi'i or Khariji, each subdivided into groups with competing and exclusive claims to truth. By their very nature, these standardised orthodoxies could not accommodate the practically infinite diversity, unavoidable in a complex civilisation, of temperaments, intellectual styles, literary traditions and lifestyles. There was thus a standing employment open to "managers of the sacred" whose task was to define true belief and hunt down heresies.

It is obvious that this description also applies (with suitable adaptations) to the other "Societies of the Book" (Jews and Christians). Each group (or sub-group) defined itself through "mimetic rivalry" with the other. One of the implications of this view is the need for a common approach to the socio-religious milieu of the Mediterranean world in which the "Societies of the Book" were shaped. Their impact on the modern world and the consequences of the impact on them by the conditions of the modern world likewise deserve a common approach.

In this scheme, the history of Islam might be viewed as a passage from the "Qur'anic Fact" to the "Islamic Fact".[8] This implies a departure from a discourse which nourishes faith to a discourse which feeds ideology. The former is to be found in the rich reservoir of myth, metaphor and symbol in Qur'anic and Biblical texts. These literary modes, namely symbolic evocations of God, the heavens, the heavenly book, angels, the Last Day, and so on, ensure an open space of meaning, potentially internalised by the believer. Transcendence understood in these terms is to be contrasted with transcendentalisation, or sacralisation, of ideas and institutions meant to immunise them from questioning or challenge. Whereas the "Qur'anic fact", like all mytho-poetic discourse, opens a space for thought and imagination, its codification into the "Islamic fact" tends to abolish this openness.

The distinction between the phenomenon of the Qur'an and the phenomenon of Islam is part of Arkoun's general view of the revelation. It calls to mind the approach of modern Muslim reformers (like Fazlur Rahman and Mohammad Iqbal) who were inclined to see Islamic history in many ways as a falling away from the Qur'an – a loss, over the centuries, of the dynamism of the original revelation. But Arkoun thought little of reformists. In any case, his "Qur'an" is not the *mushaf* or book. And unlike authors who take the idea of God's word as a given, Arkoun (who was partial to epistemology rather than ontology) focussed on the *linguistic* features of the revelation, insisting that the idea of the "word of God" be problematised rather than assumed.

(v)

Over time, however, Arkoun's reading of the Qur'an became more critical – we might even say, more ambivalent. Although he retained his view of Qur'anic discourse as meaningful for a believer as opposed to an ideologue he was more inclined, in the latest phase of his scholarly work, to find in it the seeds of what would amount, in stark terms, to ideology. This development in Arkoun's thought coincided with an interest in a section of the Qur'an, namely Sura 9, which poses a great challenge to modern Muslims who are eager to dissociate Islam from the barbaric acts of violence which are carried out in its name nowadays. Sura 9 contains a call to arms against the "enemies of God" (labelled as polytheists) combined with a promise of mercy and reconciliation to those who relent.

Although it would be far-fetched to find sanction for contemporary acts of violence or terror in the so-called "verses of the sword" in this section of the Qur'an (or others like it) – all one needs to appreciate this is a sense of historical context – they can hardly be passed over in silence. However, to do otherwise takes courage in the current climate. It is to Arkoun's credit that he showed courage by tackling these issues head-on.

Arkoun's analysis went further than simply declaring that context determines meaning. If this is all that mattered, the idea of *asbâb al-nuzl*, "occasions for the revelation", standard in the writings of classical exegetes, would be sufficient for modern enlightened approaches to scripture. But, can anyone honestly hold that after the profound changes and advances in our understanding of human knowledge ushered in with the rise of the modern world and the modern mind, these few rule-of-thumb platitudes – platitudes like taking account of context; interpreting anew with the times; symbolic interpretation – are the only harvest at hand? If so, it is a pretty meagre harvest. Anyone who is acquainted with modern philosophy and the human and natural sciences – indeed, anyone acquainted with the way Christian theology has attempted, sometimes with superficial enthusiasm, at other times with more discrimination, to deepen its thinking in the light of modern knowledge – cannot but be struck by the slender intellectuality of these maxims. Islamic theology today needs to go far, far beyond these easy incantations.

It cannot be said that Arkoun went far in his anthropological investigation of these issues (theology was not his chosen field) but he did make a start.

Shunning apologetics, Arkoun defines the context of the verses in question as the decisive victory of a party (here, the prophet and his immediate supporters) over its erstwhile opponents. A decisive victory empowers the victor to demand surrender of its enemies on the victor's terms. This is the concrete context which must be seen, to begin with, in full clarity (so Arkoun argues) without letting theological sentiments mystify it into something intangible or sublime. It is the "immanent" (socio-political-historical) dimension of revelatory discourse.[9] The tone, themes and length of the sura indicate a process of "institutionalisation" of the "word of God in human concrete history" after the final re-conquest of Mecca.[10] The terms in which this is understood are inextricably religious and worldly. The theme of *tauba* ("repentance") from which Sura 9 takes its name is "religious in principle, but political in fact".[11] It is part of a "mythical-historical consciousness" guiding socio-political action while elevating it to the plane of religious meaning.

So far, Arkoun's exegesis would seem reductive, with religion being seen essentially as a mystification of down-to-earth events. But he does not stop here. What needs to be recognised is a certain "disproportionality between the initial contingency" of the socio-military-political events and the "inexhaustible dynamism of the mythical-historical consciousness that draws nourishment of it".[12] While it is hard now to be sure whether Arkoun would have agreed with our use here of Paul Ricoeur's excellent words from another context, we could say, in Ricoeur's terms, that the language of the text carries a "surplus of meaning". A certain similarity to this notion is to be seen in the kind of time Arkoun sees at work in the Qur'an. With its emphatic concern with the history of salvation, Qur'anic time is basically "existential". "Every instant is filled with the presence of God", a presence "reactivated in the 'heart' of every believer as he performs his daily religious practices, meditation, rememorisation (*dhikr*) of the History of Salvation and liturgical recitation of the revealed Word".[13]

This existential meaningfulness is precisely what is lacking in political invocations of the Qur'an by contemporary Islamists. In Arkoun's words: "Today, Qur'anic time is pulverised into a mass of social and ideological times whose common characteristic is that they empty historicity of the truth gained from experience of the divine."[14] It follows that a true restoration of the existential dimension of the revelation requires not a "re-interpretation" of verses, nor research into the "occasions of revelation" (*asbâb al-nuzûl*), but a reconstitution of the categories in which we might understand the very phenomenon of revelation. Such a reconstitution may well provide a new, humanist basis for a foundation for Muslim thought and practice today.

III

It is time now for an assessment. Given the constraints in the length of this article, I must content myself with very brief – perhaps even laconic – observations. Besides the circumstantial need for brevity, this may also be excused by the fact that like the work of some scholars but unlike many others that one could think of, Arkoun's work at his death was in process, and hence remains unfinished, preventing rounded assessment.

Still a few things can be said. His work was an intellectual campaign. It has all the merits and drawbacks of an intellectual campaign. We misjudge it if we see it in any other terms.

His campaign, moreover, was by the nature of the case essentially adversarial. It was deconstructionist, not constructionist. It should be noted that I don't say that it was not constructive, for, in the right circumstances, destruction can be constructive. Arkoun was intensely troubled by what he saw as the intellectually retrograde and mendacious potential in both religious and secular ideologies. He saw the former having a stranglehold on Muslim minds today. Of the latter he saw recurring evidence in the attitudes to the Muslim world in Western media and politics. Yet in attacking the Western attitudes he was never defensive. Stubbornly, he refused to hail the achievements of Islam in the past, because he viewed the habit of Muslim modernists – who acclaim the Islamic past as the pinnacle of human achievement, and lament the present condition of Muslims as being due to a failure to follow true Islam – as part of the same mendacity and self-delusion which were responsible for failings in Muslim society.

He did not deny the genuine achievements in learning, invention and thought in classical Muslim history. But he saw them as existing alongside failures, like the disappearance there of independent philosophy after Ibn Rushd, in contrast to its blossoming, after the scientific revolution, in Europe. He acknowledged the more mythopoetic tradition of thought commonly called "esoteric philosophy" as worthy of interest, but insisted that before anything else it should be rigorously named and defined rather than merely celebrated.

By the same token he was forthright in his praise of the achievements of Western modernity. He had no sympathy whatsoever for wholesale comparison or contrast between "Islam" and the "West", no matter which of this pair of ultimately fictitious wholes was glorified and which was vilified. And even as he paid due tribute to the attainments of the historical Muslim world, he was careful not to call them "Muslim" or "Islamic", knowing that it is a form of special pleading to attribute them to religion; that not a few of the contributions came from Jews, Christians, "heretics" and humanists (like Miskwayhi, the subject of his doctoral thesis); and that the very notion of the Muslim or Islamic world, even in history, was problematic. With this last point in mind, he often advocated a more circumspect expression, like the "Islamic context" in place of (say) "Muslim" or "Islamic" civilisation.

In all this he was properly a historian who, in the best tradition of modern scholarship, sees his role as one of adjudicating rather than taking sides. Perhaps paradoxically, he was unlike a modern liberal historian in inveighing against what he took to be false, manipulative, cynical or self-aggrandising in Islamic discourse. This made him a polemicist. It remains open to question whether his work would have had a superior quality if he had been less strident or didactic – if, that is, he had been more of the scholar he had been and less of the controversialist he increasingly became. Perhaps, in the end, a writer who takes pains not to raise his voice even when he holds very strong judgements on what he writes about is more likely to earn a hearing than one who, raising his voice, proclaims them in every statement he makes.

It hardly needs saying that Arkoun belonged to the second category of scholars. As time went on, one noticed a disproportionate time spent, in his addresses or writings, in bewailing what scholars of Islam were failing to do, than on doing himself, in content or detail, what they were leaving undone.

But then again, to take issue with his partisan fervour may be moot. Indeed, it may beg the question, for he rejected the very principle, central to the doctrine of liberal scholarship, of neutral objectivity. He defined the role of a scholar differently from that in the liberal tradition. And although one may oppose his definition, it cannot be shown to be false by simply opposing it. In any case, one need not go along wholly with Arkoun to agree that so-called "disinterested" knowledge is, even as an ideal, an imperfectly realised thing. This may not be a conclusive argument. But once the debate is raised it becomes, by liberal doctrine's own commitments, inescapable.

In any case, the criticisms of traditional Islamic Studies I have made in the first section of this paper do not presuppose acceptance of Arkoun's particular position. What the criticisms do is to put traditional Islamic Studies into question. Arkoun came to these questions in his own way. He answered them in his own terms. To a scholar unsympathetic to either Arkoun's questions or to the questions more generally, one can only say: the questions have been raised. Once they have been raised, to pass over them in silence is wrong.

Not least of Arkoun's contribution, then, is that he asked questions – big, important, urgent questions. He had his own answers to them. Whether they come to be accepted and, if so, how widely, is another matter.

Less question-begging were two other, perhaps inter-connected flaws (to my mind) in his work. I have already mentioned one of these by referring to the influence of postmodernism in his work. This influence is in fact exclusive enough to amount to affiliation to the school of thought in question. Postmodern thinking takes certain ideas so much for granted that they are effectively taken to be facts. I have in mind the idea that truth is a synonym for socially constructed claims and beliefs; that these represent the interests, in particular the will to power, of the social agents concerned; that as the will to power leads to conflicts and inequalities, truth-claims are a "site for contestation"; and that the essential task of critical scholarship is to deconstruct all this.

On these doctrines all I can say here, without offering reasons (for this would take us too far afield), is that I personally find these doctrines repugnant. I find them dogmatic; and when seen in the long perspective of Western philosophy from the Ancient Greeks to today (not to mention the philosophies of other continents), I find them parochial, in terms of both time and place.

Linked to postmodernism – perhaps, in fact, warp and woof with it – is its barbarous idiom. The postmodern mind worships theory; the domination of theory in academic humanities and social sciences today is a phenomenon deserving of analysis in its own right. It is, again, a highly parochial affair, the self-vindicating code of a coterie of scholars and commentators who talk to themselves rather than to the broad history of letters.

Even a cursory glance at Arkoun's writing shows its well-nigh impenetrable character. Yet there is genuine illumination to be found, at least at points where his theoretical concerns are in contact with the data of Islamic history. It is a paradox that Arkoun, who believed passionately in the intellectual's social mission, wrote in a manner inaccessible to all but scholars acquainted with a specific kind of scholarship. In any event, he remained a professional scholar, rarely straying (at least in his books) from his chosen specialism. He wrote for a specialist audience. His interlocutors, in print and formal exchanges, were from the specialist academic world. But he remained dissatisfied with their evident lack of understanding or appreciation (there were exceptions, though in his view, they were few and far between). While being faithful to the canons of academic scholarship, and while continuing to write in terms which spoke to a minority of scholars of Islam, those with a taste or capacity for theory, he yearned for a wider influence of his work. He was always pleased when his work struck a chord with individuals, especially in the Muslim world, some of whom became his eager admirers.

It is reasonable to hold that Arkoun's thought has a potentially far greater scope than what is visible in his writing thanks to the straitjacket of theory and idiom by which it is bound. Perhaps it is a task well worth attempting, by existing or future students of his work, to emancipate his insights from the cradle in which they were formed, and develop them in new directions.

Development is what Arkoun's work deserves. He left many ideas nascent or undefined. This was less due to lack of time or opportunity – he had a long career – than due to two other factors. He was continually building on his ideas, though the basic themes remained steady. And he was not a systematic thinker. He did not develop his ideas in a logical step-by-step way. His intelligence worked by way of flashes of insight and theoretical conceptualisations. It will take someone familiar with the actualities of Islamic history to see how and to what degree his concepts endure the test of data; and someone with philosophical or logical acumen to evaluate the logic of his theories.

One aspect of his work which requires careful thought is the one mentioned in the foregoing pages: the degree of its suitability or otherwise for an intellectually grounded understanding of the nature of faith. Although I have mentioned Arkoun's positive stand on the place of belief in human societies, it remains an embryonic idea. He did not develop it to any degree comparable to that of his other ideas. This was probably due, in part, to his not being a philosopher of religion. His partial contemporary, Paul Ricoeur, who had a philosophically developed view of religion (within the framework of hermeneutic phenomenology), is in this respect a contrasting example.

Arkoun seemed convinced that radical criticism of the kind he offered was valuable to believers as well as scholars. But it is not clear that the two mindsets are similar enough to find this approach altogether congenial. The fundamental question is an old one. It was first raised by Plato in his discussion of the respective claims of myth and philosophy: the question of lasting relevance. It is not always raised clearly or explicitly. But it has not vanished, nor been resolved.

I may illustrate the importance of this question, as far as scholarship is concerned, with the aid of a remarkable recent book by Aaron T. Hughes.[15] This is not the place to discuss his basic premises about truth and knowledge. What is clearly laudable about his work is his refusal to side with the scholarly apologetics and anodyne defences of "Islam" (the quotation marks deserve notice) which only too many scholars of Islam are nowadays prepared to champion under the banner of "expertise". Hughes' forthright insistence that there is, and ought to be, a firm dividing line between scholarship and apologetics was, if anything, overdue in this field.

What position must someone speaking from within a religious community take in this matter, however? Hughes is prepared to make an exception for "theologians". "Theologians" here may be understood to mean religious leaders or preachers who speak to or on behalf their communities. Every reflective practitioner of "theology" in this sense will appreciate the difference between scholarly pursuit of knowledge and the kind of partisanship demanded by "theology". But this is not a finally satisfactory position. The difference being drawn by Hughes raises important questions in its own right.

Does the difference mean, for instance, that commitment to a faith excuses (or even necessitates) intellectual compromises, not to mention duplicity? Are there two "truths", or two approaches to a common truth? This question is seldom examined in modern terms, let alone answered. Whatever the answers – which could conceivably involve a renewed consideration of what Aristotle called "rhetoric" or, more generally, the relation between knowledge and politics – the question, surely, is of continuing importance in an age when the religious and secular have become embattled notions.

Arkoun did not elaborate on this issue. But his thought certainly has implications for it, if only because unlike secularists, atheists and positivists, he is never condescending towards expressions of belief.

Arkoun's rejection of modern disbelief gave him an impartiality and equidistance which makes him potentially of interest to believers. Just as, in his view, rational enlightenment remains "unthought" (and perhaps epistemologically unthinkable) in terms of dogmatic religion, so belief remains poorly understood and even unthought (and perhaps unthinkable) in dogmatically secularist cultures.

To repeat, it is as much for the questions that Arkoun raised as for his conclusions that we are indebted to him. In the field of Islam and religion more generally, there are (as ever) intolerant dogmatists, liberal apologists and intolerant adversaries of religion. Arkoun stood apart from all of these. There are believers whose point of view is confined to their own communities. Others favour religious dialogue, but, all too frequently, in intellectually academic terms. Again, Arkoun was a man apart. The ground on which he stood was not that of religion or anti-religion. He might not have fully defined the alternative ground – what he called, without enlarging on it, "emergent reason" – on which he wished to stand. He was critical too of what in modern times passes as humanism. But at this point one must turn from his books to the person he was. Those who, like myself, knew him personally will remember him as a man of intellect as well as humanity; a man capable, despite first impressions (not always easily offset), of tender feelings; and a man at times movingly alive to the life histories of those he knew, to whom he was ever generous in friendship and affection.

Notes

1. M. G. S. Hodgson, *The Venture of Islam*, 3 vols. (Chicago: University of Chicago Press, 1974).

2. O. Graber, *The Formation of Islamic Art* (New Haven/London: Yale University Press, 1973)

3. W. M. Watt, *Islam and the Integration of Society* (London: Routledge and Kegan Paul, 1961)

4. "We can no longer use the word 'Islam' without quotation marks." *Expressions of Islam in Buildings:* Proceedings of an international seminar, Aga Khan Award for Architecture and the Indonesian Institute of Architects, October 1990.

5. "Religion, Atheism and Faith" in *The Conflict of Interpretations*, ed. D. Ihde (Evanston: Northwestern University Press, 1974).

6. M. Arkoun, *The Unthought in Contemporary Islamic Thought* (London: Saqi Books/ Institute of Ismaili Studies, 2002), p. 136.

7. M. Arkoun, *Rethinking Islam: Common Questions, Uncommon Answers*, trans. ed. R. E. Lee (Oxford: Westview Press, 1994), p. 36.

8. *The Unthought in Contemporary Islamic Thought,* pp. 261–267.

9. Ibid. p. 90.

10. Ibid.

11. Ibid.

12. Ibid. p. 91.

13. Ibid.

14. Ibid. pp. 91–92.

15. A. T. Hughes, *Situating Islam: The past and future of an academic discipline* (London: Equinox, 2007).

The Authenticity of Sacred Texts

R. Stephen Humphreys

The central problem in the study of the beginnings and early development of Islam is authenticity – that is, in what sense are the texts on which we rely that which they claim to be? Do they in fact embody the actual words produced during Islam's first decades? Insofar as they depart from original statements, do they nevertheless reflect on some level the ways of thinking, the social and moral ethos of Islam's beginnings? Does every text need to retain its primitive shape to claim some level of authenticity, to give meaningful testimony about the persons and events that it purports to represent? This is a problem that confronts both medieval and modern Muslim writers as well as non-Muslims, though of course each of these three groups approaches the problem within a distinct frame of reference and has a very different stake in its outcome.

In Western scholarship, this problem was first posed in a systematic way more than century ago, in Ignaz Goldziher's famous monograph on the hadith.[1] It was picked up by a number of his formidable contemporaries, in particular Julius Wellhausen,[2] Leone Caetani,[3] and (in a somewhat erratic and idiosyncratic manner) Henri Lammens.[4] Their solutions to the problem were provisional at best, as they themselves recognised, but were not developed or revised in any systematic way until Joseph Schacht's groundbreaking *Origins of Muhammadan Jurisprudence*,[5] the implications of which have yet to be exhausted or even fully understood.

A quarter of a century later, an even more radical challenge was launched by John Wansbrough, Michael Cook and Patricia Crone. They were inspired by Schacht's arguments, but they went even further, in effect declaring null and void everything that had been written about the whole period of Muhammad's prophetic career and the early Arab-Muslim conquests (in effect, the six decades from 600 to 661). On a different level, the work of Albrecht Noth and Lawrence Conrad[6] suggested that most Arabic historical writing from the late eighth and throughout the ninth century could be reduced to a body of free-floating topoi and motifs, few of which could be securely attached to any real persons or events. That is, Noth argued, the same stories were told over and over again, but with differing locales and casts of characters.

These challenges to the early Islamic textual tradition could be neither ignored nor easily assimilated, and they have provoked a burgeoning and very sophisticated set of responses. Leading names would include Lawrence Conrad, Michael Lecker, Fred M. Donner,[7] Chase F. Robinson, Robert Hoyland,[8] Harald Motzki,[9] Gregor Schoeler, Stefan Leder, Alfred de Prémare, Josef Van Ess and (quite recently) Suleiman Mourad.[10] There is as yet no consensus, and probably never will be, but it is fair to say that the way scholars (Muslim as well as Western) think about this textual tradition has changed forever. We are far more aware of the problems and possibilities of the Arabic texts than we used to be. We have also learned that it will not do to examine them in isolation from the other linguistic-cultural traditions of West Asia during the seventh to ninth centuries; Arab-Muslim writing must be situated and interpreted within a broad context: Syriac first of all, but also Greek, Coptic, Armenian, Georgian and even Latin.

However, our discussions of texts from or about early Islam have been confused and unnecessarily complicated by the fact that the term "authenticity" is very freely used but almost never adequately defined. "Authenticity" is what we seek and devoutly long for in these texts, but we mean many different and perhaps contradictory things by it. Within the discourse on early Islam, whether scholarly or apologetic, authenticity is more an ad hoc notion than a rigorously articulated concept. We think we know what we mean, in a rough and ready way, and so we do not ask whether that is in fact the case. However, when we look at the ordinary, everyday uses of the terms "authenticity" or "authentic", we will quickly see how slippery these words really are. "She has an authentic East Texas accent" – that is, she is in fact a woman from Dallas, or perhaps she speaks just like a woman from Dallas even though she grew up in Boston. "That novel is an authentic work of genius" – not just a skilfully contrived tale, but rather a story that communicates human experience in a powerful, convincing and enduring manner. "An authentic performance of Handel's *Messiah*" – presumably, a performance which we believe would sound much like those staged by the composer himself 250 years ago, in spite of the enormous difference between the instruments and vocal styles of his time and ours. An authentic diamond necklace is made from real diamonds, but what shall we say about an "authentic replica" of a necklace worn by the Duchess of Windsor? We mean, I suppose, that it is meant to look like one she would have worn, though she would not have been fooled. In short, authenticity might refer either to reality, or to the illusion of reality, or to the recollection (real or imagined) of reality. More broadly, authenticity seems to mean something like "conforming to a certain defined pattern, adhering to an ideal type".

In light of these remarks, we should not be surprised to learn that the notion of authenticity may have different meanings – more properly, ranges of meaning – when it is applied to different classes of texts. Taxonomies are always problematic, fuzzy at the edges and contestable, whether we are talking about texts or turtles. However, for the purposes of this discussion, I will proceed from the premise that both Muslim and non-Muslim constructions of early Islam rest on five categories of texts. Each of these serves different purposes in Muslim discourse; each opens a different window onto the beginnings and early development of Islam. They should reinforce one another, and they sometimes overlap, but they are very different in their putative authorship, in intended purpose, in literary and rhetorical construction, in manner of transmission, in the uses to which they were put. In order of the level of religious authority they carry, and the degree to which they embody and reveal the divine purpose, they are as follows:

1. prophetic revelation (the Qur'an),
2. the teaching by word and example of Muhammad (hadith),
3. narratives which recount the events of the Prophet's life (*sira*),
4. narratives which recount the words and deeds of his successors and followers after his death (*ta'rikh, akhbar*), and finally
5. poetry (*shi'r*) from his lifetime and the decades immediately thereafter.

In this paper I will focus on the first three categories, since they embody by far the most sensitive religious issues. Moreover, the historical *akhbar* that address the early caliphate and the first conquests – that is, the three decades following the death of Muhammad – retain many of the core characteristics of the *sira* narratives and pose very similar methodological problems. Only with the reign of Mu'awiya after 661, and even more with the rise of the

Marwanids, do we see a gradual shift to a markedly different narrative register. As for poetry, though forgery and suspicion of forgery abound, much of it is widely regarded among modern scholars as archaic – that is, actually composed during the period to which it is attributed. However, poetry is normally imbedded in prose texts as a witness to or commentary upon events and persons already presented there. Only in the Umayyad era (most famously in the persons of al-Akhtal, Farazdaq and Jarir) does poetry begin to constitute an independent witness to the ideological currents and factional quarrels which beset Muslim society.

It will immediately be apparent that authenticity must mean quite different things for each category (namely, the Qur'an, hadith and *sira*). If, for example, the Qur'an is held to be God's own eternal and uncreated speech, transmitted verbatim by His chosen prophet, as Sunni dogma ultimately declared it to be, then each and every *aya* must contain precisely the words voiced by Muhammad in a state of inspiration, neither more nor less. On the other hand, a narrative (*khabar*) about the Battle of Qadisiyya faces a more forgiving standard. Here, authenticity is a very fluid concept. It might refer to an issue of substance: that is, whether the *khabar* reports more or less accurately an event that really did happen. Or it might refer to the *khabar* as a text: whether it actually does transmit verbatim or at least paraphrase the statements made by its purported original narrator, no matter if he was a scrupulous truth-teller, a bold-faced liar or a spinner of fables. Moreover, such a *khabar* need not have a fixed verbal form; there is some room for editorial intervention in the course of transmission. It is even permissible to have contradictory *akhbar* about one and the same incident, since different reporters will have had different information. In terms of sanctity and doctrinal significance, the hadith and *sira* represent an intermediate status between the Qur'an and post-prophetic history, but as we shall see, the hadith is subject to a far more rigorous level of scrutiny than the *sira*.

This simple typology of sacred or quasi-sacred texts is clear and appealing, but it reflects the frame of reference developed among Muslim scholars of the ninth century and later. As such it has an obvious problem – it begs the question, and in fact many questions. To begin with, it presupposes that all these texts are stable (though not necessarily fixed) from the time they were composed and put into circulation. It presupposes also that we can determine with some certainty which texts actually do originate in the time and place that they claim to represent, and which represent later iterations or fabrications. Finally, it presupposes that the earliest generations of Muslims regarded a given text in the same way as did their successors in the ninth and tenth centuries, and assigned to it the same level of sanctity and value. All these presuppositions are demonstrably false.

The texts which emerged out of early Islam evolved continuously until well into the ninth century, when they were more or less crystallised. (In saying this I make a substantial but not complete exception for the text of the Qur'an.) This fluidity has made it extremely difficult for scholars to date the texts that have come down to us, to isolate archaic elements within them and track the strata of editorial reshapings and interpolations. If scholars had developed precise, agreed-upon criteria – the equivalent of well-established archaeological pottery sequences – there would be a lot more consensus than we now observe, but such criteria are still a work in progress.

The problem is complicated by the fact that early Muslims engaged in intense and even vitriolic debate about everything, and that the nature of this debate changed markedly over time. To name only a few points at issue: the precise text of the Qur'an and how it was recorded and transmitted; the sources of religious authority within the Community after the death of Muhammad; and the political significance of certain critical events (for example, the "election" of Abu Bakr, the revolt against 'Uthman, the battles of Siffin and Karbala'). Was some limited degree of variation in the text of revelation to be tolerated or not? Who if anyone had final authority to establish a Qur'anic text *ne varietur*? Did the authority to teach and guide the Community after Muhammad rest with the caliphs, with charismatic imams in the lineage of 'Ali, with the consensus of learned and pious Muslims, or with the Prophet himself through his recorded statements? Were the actual rulers of the Community its lawful heads, and in what arenas (if any) did they have the right to demand obedience from the Muslims? If so, by what criteria, and what authority should they wield over the specifically religious beliefs and practices of Muslims? These debates were of course never settled (apart from the need for a fixed text of the Qur'an), but by the mid to late ninth century they were at least flowing in regular channels. In contrast to the chaotic arguments of the first two hundred years, there had come to be a well-defined, indeed stubbornly durable discourse on each major point of contention.

All of this tells us that we need to re-examine the concept of Qur'anic authenticity as it applies to the different classes of early Islamic texts, this time from a historical perspective – for, like all objects of human action, texts are constantly being recreated or at least reimagined.

We begin, as one must, with the Qur'an. For historians (though of course not for the believer) one issue should be perfectly irrelevant: a historian need not ask whether the Qur'an is authentic in the sense of being literally God's own speech. That is a question first of faith and secondly of theology. In historical thought, the concept of authenticity refers to other problems. One is obvious: whether the Qur'an in its present form is wholly constituted of statements proclaimed by Muhammad b. 'Abdallah in Mecca and Medina between 610 and 632. Do we have the words, and only the words, pronounced by Muhammad himself? How confident can we be that his proclamations were accurately collected and transmitted? Are textual variants (such as those apparently preserved in the Yemeni fragments) merely testimony to the fallibility of human memory and the rather haphazard way the primitive texts were first recorded? Or do they signal a real fluidity and instability in this text? In either case, did such variants substantially affect the way the Qur'an was taught and understood during the first two or three generations of Islam? Whatever our answer to these questions, I would argue that we can properly affirm that the Qur'an is fully "authentic", at least in the sense that it contains the earliest memories and records of what Muhammad had presented as revelation. That is, we can still rely on it to tell us what Islam looked like as it first emerged in the first half of the seventh century.

This conclusion would not be affected by the argument proposed most recently by Christoph Luxenberg[11] that the Qur'an was at bottom an assemblage of materials already quite familiar among the oasis settlers of West Arabia – apocalyptic imagery and ritual texts derived more or less directly from Syriac prototypes, Christian preaching and Jewish *midrash*, combined with some scattered pronouncements of Muhammad himself. From this perspective the Qur'an would be primarily a repository of the religious currents criss-crossing early seventh-century Arabia; only the contingencies of time and place would have made it a powerful, even transformative religious vision. However, *if* the established canonical text goes back to the time of Muhammad and his earliest followers, then however it came into being, it would still be fully authentic in this sense: that it is a true witness to the beginnings of Islam.

It is worth remarking that neither of these ways of seeing the Qur'an is peculiarly modern; both go back to at least the early eighth century. By then, Muslims were insisting that the Qur'an was precisely and literally God's word revealed through His chosen prophet Muhammad. Among Christian observers, in contrast, the Qur'an was presented as a farrago of recycled Jewish and Christian teaching, with some peculiar distortions added to the mix. We can trace these perspectives further back into the late seventh century. The famous inscription in the Qubbat al-Sakhra (692) explicitly links Muhammad with a new dispensation, with several passages that are citations or a very close paraphrase of Qur'anic verses as we know them. On the other side, Christian writers like Sebeos of Armenia (c. 660) and John Bar Penkaye (c. 690) portray Muhammad as drawing freely on Jewish and Christian teachings, though they do not explicitly ascribe a book or scripture to him.

Now, suppose we adopt Wansbrough's argument – whatever we might be able to say about Muhammad (very little, in fact), the Qur'an as we now have it certainly does not date back to him. It would have taken its present form as much as two centuries later. Is there some meaningful sense in which we could claim authenticity for the text? I would say that there is, though no Muslim (and few non-Muslims) would find it at all satisfying. Under this hypothesis, the Qur'an could not stand as a record of Muhammad's prophetic speech, but it would be an unambiguously authentic record of what Muslims of the late eighth and early ninth centuries had established and accepted as the revelation brought by him. As such, it would continue to be the foundational text of all later Muslim religious thought and practice. Scholarship based on the premise of a "late Qur'an" would have to ask how such a long, complex text was moulded out of disparate elements, and (far more importantly) how Muslims had been persuaded to accept this text as the revelation vouchsafed to Muhammad two centuries earlier. On the other hand, our understanding of how the Muslims of the ninth and later centuries interpreted and used the Qur'an would – at least in principle – hardly be affected. One might compare this (admittedly hypothetical) situation to the one confronted by historians of Christianity. For students of the first and second Christian centuries, it is crucial to ask when and how the Gospels were composed and put into circulation. For students of the third and later centuries, the Gospels are a fact; the point is what they meant to those who read them.

Hadith and *sira* pose a radically different set of problems; here the concept of authenticity cannot mean what it does with the Qur'an. Both hadith and *sira* are sacred texts, albeit in different ways and on different levels, but they represent human speech rather than *wahy* or *tanzil* – namely the speech of Muhammad himself, and the speech of those who observed and recorded his career. As such, their contents are sacred, but their words per se are much less so. Sanctity and religious authority inhere in what they say, not how they say it.

Moreover, hadith and sira are far more fluid than the Qur'an in both content and language, and they have been far more subject to challenge by both Muslim and non-Muslim scholars. The Qur'an became a closed corpus very early on – at the death of Muhammad, in the 'Uthmanic compilation, or in the Marwanid recension, depending on how one reconstructs the history of the text. Once it was fixed in content and language, its status as divine speech meant that no one could alter it via emendation, inserted glosses, the harmonisation of contradictory passages or the deletion of repetitions. In contrast, neither hadith nor sira have ever constituted a genuinely closed corpus, though great efforts were certainly expended by al-Bukhari, Muslim and other scholars in the late ninth century to place hadith in precisely this category.

On the other hand, though they appear to overlap in subject matter (the words and acts of Muhammad), the two genres of text are really very different in character and purpose. Some of the same anecdotes and dicta do find a place in both, but they serve quite different functions. Put simply (perhaps too simply), hadith constitutes formal doctrine: it is meant to yield principles of belief ('aqida) or rules of conduct (ahkam). In terms of formal structure, hadith is fragmented into disjunct statements and anecdotes, and these are typically decontextualised from particulars of time and place – "Once the Prophet was seated in the marketplace, when a certain man approached him and said...". *Sira,* in contrast, provides a historical context, a *Sitz im Leben*, for the Qur'an and hadith – texts which, taken by themselves, are quite devoid of concrete references to time and place. (A colleague of mine once commented that for the life of Jesus, we have a context but no text; for the life of Muhammad, we have a text but no context: a neat if aphoristic way of putting the matter.) By grounding these sometimes gnomic texts in the life and struggles of the Prophet, sira makes them intelligible and meaningful to those striving to follow in the path the Prophet laid down. More broadly, sira portrays the world in which he lived and which he strove to bring into obedience to God. Its fundamental purpose is to inspire reverence and emulation; or, to paraphrase Bolingbroke, it is religion teaching by examples. It might have suggested models of action to both later Muslim rulers and their opponents, but it never constituted a formal source for *kalam* and *fiqh*.

In view of these fundamental distinctions in structure and purpose, it is obvious that hadith and sira have each posed very distinct issues of authenticity, both for medieval Muslims and for modern Muslim and non-Muslim scholars. In regard to sira, there was always something new to say about the Prophet's life and career, and the criteria for admitting new material into the sira were generous, to say the least. Medieval Muslim scholars did not bar new material, as long as it was reasonably consonant (doctrinally as well as factually) with what had already been accepted. In this sense, the corpus of sira was open-ended. Indeed, from the tenth century on, a great deal of new material, albeit mostly of the *dala'il al-nubuwwa* genre, was continually added to the foundational narratives laid down in the century and a half between Ibn Ishaq (d. 767) and al-Tabari (d. 923).

In the early sira compilations, scholars focused on recovering the facts of Muhammad's life, and on establishing the *asbab al-nuzul* through which these facts were linked to the highly allusive statements of the Qur'an. In the eyes of these scholars, such narratives could be very plastic in structure and rhetoric without forfeiting a claim to authenticity. They needed only to be what they claimed to be – statements about the Prophet's words and actions which could be reliably attributed to the reporter who first put them into circulation. Moreover, this first reporter did not need to be an eyewitness or contemporary of the events in question; he could well be a collector-compiler from a much later generation. Recall that much of the material in Ibn Ishaq is reported without explicit attribution, or simply on the authority of "one whose testimony I do not doubt".

These fluid criteria for admitting material into the corpus of sira mean that modern scholars cannot always be certain on just what grounds a particular item was thought worthy of inclusion. For example, when Ibn Ishaq states, without citing any source, that a certain *aya* of the Qur'an was revealed on the occasion of such-and-such an event, we cannot really know whether this statement represents an opinion of the earliest Muslims, or an opinion widely held among his own contemporaries, or just an idea of Ibn Ishaq's own.

For the early compilers of *sira* narratives, then, authenticity meant the exclusion of forgeries (that is, statements falsely attributed to a given reporter) and narratives wilfully distorted in the course of transmission. Authenticity did not necessarily imply that a story was factually accurate, though it goes without saying that the compilers tried to exclude material they regarded as unreliable or mendacious. Likewise, a rigorously fixed text was of no importance; a story could be told in various ways and still constitute authentic testimony. Conflicting versions of an event were the inevitable result of the frailties of human perception and memory. This inclusive criterion of authenticity was acceptable because sira did not lay down binding precedents or generate authoritative doctrine or rules of conduct. Its purpose – serious enough in its own right – was to provide a compelling myth of origins for the Community of Believers, and to encourage reverence for the Prophet and his unique place in human history.

What then should authenticity mean for modern students of sira? Surely we have something more in mind than did these early Muslim scholars, even if we share their concern to identify forgeries and spurious lines of transmission. The meaning of authenticity depends on what we are trying to achieve. If we are seeking a "historical Muhammad" in the manner of a historical Abraham Lincoln or Gamal 'Abd al-Nasir, this goal poses specific kinds of problems. We have a rich fund of material to work with – our medieval Muslim predecessors saw to that – but this material only began to crystallise in something like its present form roughly a century and a half after the death of Muhammad. However archaic some of it may be, it has been heavily redacted to fit the religious expectations and political concerns, the linguistic and literary models, and the scholarly criteria, of a late eighth-century audience, with further redaction and reshaping as we move into the generations succeeding Ibn Ishaq. We will all have our own instincts about what adheres closely to the testimony of early witnesses and what is a late forgery, about what reflects actual events and what is legend. But I am not convinced that we have developed reliable and uniform criteria for sorting all this out. Just about the only text in Ibn Ishaq that (almost) everyone agrees has been transmitted in its primitive form is the so-called Constitution of Medina, and it is so utterly different in language, content and formal characteristics from everything else in his compilation that it cannot be used as a template for other *sira* texts. A hallmark of good science is that experiments and the results they yield can be replicated. Modern students of sira have not yet worked out how to do this; our arguments and conclusions overlap to some extent, but they do not concur across the board.

Most modern scholars would agree that "authenticity" in sira does not require that a given narrative be told just as it originally was. Paraphrasing, abridging and blending originally separate narratives, and emphasising elements that speak to the compiler's own concerns are all legitimate aspects of transmission. We can only insist that the transmitter not alter a story so as to change its meaning or invent things that never happened. But even as we agree on this self-evident point, we seem unable to apply it to specific cases in any consistent manner.

Early sira materials contain much that is miraculous (albeit not so much as later increments do – such as the *siras* influenced by the model of Dala'il al-Khayrat, that is, miraculous signs of prophethood) and this fact creates another set of problems for modern readers, especially non-Muslims. However, things that appear fantastic or legendary to a modern consciousness would not have seemed so among the people of early Islamic times. For them, miraculous events were an integral and even indispensable element in the life and work of any prophet. For that reason we need to take such stories seriously and not dismiss them out of hand. They may of course be inventions intended to assimilate Muhammad to earlier prophets or to the Syrian and Egyptian holy men of his era, but they may just as well reflect the way his followers experienced his presence, however we may wish to explain that experience. The problem is whether we can develop usable criteria for testing miracle stories and legend-like narratives, and thereby determine whether they embody some element of contemporary experience or are merely conventional topoi. Without such criteria, these stories are opaque and unusable; a stumbling block to our efforts to understand the changing thought-world of early Islam.

In seeking for the "historical Muhammad", therefore, we are forced to take a minimalist approach. Rather than expanding the story, we find ourselves reducing it to its barest structural elements. Ibn Ishaq and his successors have given us a well-honed plot line, which we are constrained to follow because we have no other. They have done this by selecting *akhbar* which focus on what they regarded as the crisis points of Muhammad's life and the earliest community: the call to prophethood, the resistance and hostility of the dominant lineages of Quraysh to him and his message, the Hijra and the founding of the new *umma,* the three great battles which secured the future of this *umma,* the struggle with the Jewish clans in Yathrib, and so on. However, the stories and poetry which coalesced around these crisis points may well be much later inventions or at best epic elaborations of the primitive accounts. The fact that a given event really did happen does not guarantee that the stories told about that event are truthful in any sense. As a result, most modern scholarship on the life of Muhammad is simply a process of thinning out this material; of deciding which of its elements might reflect a factual reality rather than an imagined past.

More important, perhaps, is that these crisis points represent a specifically Muslim way of remembering and reconstructing Muhammad's life. We might expect that his Qurashi opponents in Mecca or the Jews of Yathrib would have chosen quite a different set of crisis points. Likewise, there were certainly alternative Muslim grand narratives about Muhammad's life that have simply disappeared. We can discern traces of such competing narratives in accounts of the succession to Muhammad – the Ghadir Khumm story in its fervent Shi'i and anodyne Sunni versions, the acclamation of Abu Bakr, the odd and very ambivalent role ascribed to 'Ali in the days following the Prophet's death, and so on. And of course the competing narratives which portray slightly later moments – such as the caliphate of 'Uthman and the 'Ali-Mu'awiya conflict – demonstrate just how bitter these debates over the past could be.

Perhaps, then, we cannot reconstruct a verifiably documented historical Muhammad, but only a hypothetical (albeit plausible) one. We cannot paint a portrait from life, so to speak, but instead must fashion an image based on uncertain and often contradictory second-hand memories. If that is so, the criteria of authenticity that guided the early collectors and editors of sira, even as modified to fit the methods of modern textual criticism, will not quite work for us. We know what an authentic report about the life of Muhammad would be according to these criteria, and there may well be many such reports in the mass of material that has come down to us, but we cannot be certain precisely which ones they are. Objective authenticity in this sense is real and meaningful, but finding it is like chasing shadows at twilight.

This conclusion does not mean that authenticity of a different kind is unattainable, however. On the simplest and most obvious level, the sira texts are incontestably authentic statements of how Muslims in the late eighth and ninth centuries had come to think about the (multiple) meanings of Muhammad's life for their own society. Moreover, this era's construction of Muhammad continues to have powerful resonance, since it has provided a durable template for Muslim thought and feeling about the Prophet throughout the last twelve centuries. That is, it is in the simplest and most literal sense an authentic witness to the ways in which contemporary Muslims think about who they are and how they ought to direct their lives. (The power and durability – indeed, the unassailable sanctity – of this ninth-century template are also formidable obstacles to any serious effort among Muslim scholars to re-study Muhammad's life. But that is a question for another paper.)

From this perspective, the very fact that the sira narratives are full of both subtle and blatant contradictions, of puzzling gaps, of topoi skipping from one report to the next, is not a problem. On the contrary, these anomalies are direct testimony to the religious and ideological tensions of this period. Sira texts embody the memory (properly, the many cross-cutting memories) which Muslims constructed of their beginnings. Those memories were to some degree grounded in the actual events, persons, conflicts and ideas of

Muhammad's time, but they were also constructed memories of an imagined past – a past that was not conceived all at once, but rather had been built up layer upon layer as Muslims in each generation tried to make sense of what was happening to them, and to preserve (or revitalise) the ties between their own lives and the sacred origins of the *umma*.

When we look at sira texts in this manner, as continuously generated and reshaped through time, we need to think about authenticity in a third sense. Sira texts are neither a direct record of Muhammad's time nor (an equally simplistic view) a snapshot of the several decades when they crystallised in a stable and semi-definitive form – c. 760–840. Rather, sira texts embody the long process by which they came into being. The metaphors of an archaeological dig or geological strata come to mind, and these can be very useful if one explores them seriously. In the sira, as in an archaeological site or a complex geological formation, there are many layers. However, these layers do not appear in any simple chronological sequence. In a geological formation, strata are twisted and inverted; archaic strata wind up on top of recent ones, and old rocks are transformed by the very processes that create new ones. Likewise in archaeology, recent construction penetrates and disturbs the earliest layers, while elements of the earliest settlements remain imbedded in and shape the new ones in the most unexpected ways.

In this context, authenticity means bearing reliable witness to the multiple layers imbedded in the sira corpus. A report (*khabar*) would be authentic insofar as it was generated as part of one of those layers. The question is whether these layers can be identified and recovered. We know they must exist, but is there any method of analysis by which we can discern them with some degree of consistency and confidence? In attempting this we confront two problems. First, there is the need to deconstruct the existing texts – to unpeel accretions, restore redacted passages to a more primitive form, weed out partisan or sectarian interpolations, and so on. Second, and even more challenging, the layers imbedded in the sira narratives are not clearly separated; it is not a matter of red, yellow, blue and orange stripes. On the contrary: these layers bleed into and contaminate one another.

Deconstruction – in the present context, the effort to recover progressively earlier forms of the sira material – is an exceedingly delicate task, and the further back we try to go, the less confidence we can claim for our results. However, if we regard sira not as an isolated literary genre, but rather as part of a highly integrated cultural discourse, we might discover certain characteristics – of grammar, vocabulary, rhetoric, ways of constructing an argument, topics of debate, and so on – that would allow us to situate such deconstructed texts in concrete times and places. We could thereby claim, at some level of probability, that they were authentic representations of a given phase in the development of sira. To be precise, our reconstructed texts could not claim to recover the actual originals, but we could plausibly argue that they constituted a reasonable facsimile of those originals. To return to an example from the beginning of this paper, the situation would be much the same as an "authentic performance" of Handel's *Messiah* in contemporary London.

One would begin this endeavour with the mid and late ninth century, because we possess a rich body of contemporary evidence (not only literary texts, but also coins and inscriptions) with which to reconstruct the religio-political discourse of those decades. Because we also have a stable and highly developed sira literature from this period, we can see sira texts in their full cultural contexts and determine just how they functioned within the broader discourse. Obviously the evidence (or at least reliable contemporary evidence) for the shape of religio-political debate as well as the broader cultural milieu becomes progressively thinner as we move back in time into the early Abbasid, late Marwanid and early Marwanid periods. Thus our efforts to recover earlier versions of now-existing sira texts will inevitably become more and more provisional and hypothetical. But once we have defined how sira texts fit into the cultural discourse of the ninth century, we should be able to apply the same method to earlier periods and thereby work our way as far back (perhaps even to the age of 'Abd al-Malik and al-Walid I) as we have some reliable independent evidence to guide us.

We turn at last to hadith. It is a very different matter from sira, although a great many of the above remarks apply. To begin with, hadith quickly came to have (no later than the third quarter of the eighth century) a distinctive purpose of its own. Hadith does not exist primarily to exalt the Prophet, although of course it does that by its very nature. Nor does it portray the origins of the *umma* in a broad historical sense, though it certainly does claim to articulate and fix the pure, original doctrines and practices of Islam. The fundamental purpose of hadith is to give concrete, detailed guidance to Muslims, to tell them how they should lead their lives, how they should think and act. In a technical legal sense, it is a material source (*asl*) in *fiqh*; as such it lays down authoritative cases and binding directives. Because hadith is imbedded in a systematic scholarly discourse, and because so much is at stake, authenticity must be far more rigorously defined than with sira. Or to follow the argument of al-Shafi'i, if Muhammad's words were divinely guided, though not divinely inspired in the full sense, then these words possessed a tremendous weight and sanctity; the flexibility (not to say laxness) allowed in sira was not permissible here. Moreover, two competing objectives had to be met: scholars should strive to recover the Prophet's dicta as completely as possible – ideally, the totality of the guidance he had provided to his followers – even as these dicta had to be rigorously winnowed and sifted in order to rid the corpus of anything spurious or doubtful. While hadith scholars in the late eighth and early ninth centuries focused on the mandate to collect as much as possible, those of the late ninth century stressed the need to fix an indisputably reliable corpus. Later on, as hadith became widely used for general moral guidance, practical standards were loosened a bit – sometimes more than a bit – even as the critical methods of specialists became ever more rigorous.

Ideally, hadith should have become a closed corpus constituted of precise, unvarying texts, solidly attested all the way back to the Prophet's Companions who first reported his words. In reality that was never possible, and medieval hadith scholars reluctantly recognised this fact. There were too many uncertainties about lines of transmission, too much human fallibility, too much disagreement as to which hadith actually met the criteria for reliability that they struggled so hard to establish. Even to them, the origins of hadith collection were murky and hard to document convincingly. (Obviously these doubts have blossomed into full-blown scepticism among most, though not all, modern non-Muslim scholars of the subject.) In the end, the study and criticism of hadith represented an informed "best guess" about what the Prophet had actually said and what he had meant. Even with these reservations, however, medieval and most modern Muslim scholars did build up a body of material which they believed they could use with confidence. In the long run, a well-defined corpus of reliable hadith, along with more apocryphal dicta that were useful as general doctrinal and moral guidance for ordinary believers, was confirmed by almost universal consensus, and this corpus remains normative down to the present. For the overwhelming majority of Muslims over the last eleven hundred years, the reliable hadith collections (the "Six Books") unquestionably represent the actual words and actions of the Prophet – or at least as close to those words as it is humanly possible to get.

For non-Muslim scholars the matter is rather different. There is, to begin with, no consensus among them as to the authenticity of the hadith literature, or even as to what "authenticity" might mean. Some, following the implications of Joseph Schacht, would deny any demonstrable historical connection between hadith and the actual teachings of Muhammad. For these scholars, hadith is at bottom an invention of the mid-eighth century: the statements of early pietists and proto-jurists retrojected back onto the Companions and ultimately the Prophet himself. Since this interpretation posits a radical disjuncture between the life of Muhammad and the historical *umma*, it makes the question of authenticity almost meaningless unless one wishes to restrict this concept to the discourse of the late eighth century and later. That is, following Goldziher's analysis, we could say that hadith is an authentic statement of the ideas and values of this period, and of how these ideas and values were understood to be part of the true original essence of Islam. An interesting consequence of this perspective is that all hadith are equal – that every hadith is an authentic statement of the doctrine held by one group or another. The only issue is to discover which group it should be attached to.

Schacht's approach has not gone uncontested. More recently, some scholars (most notably Harald Motzki [12]) have argued that there is in fact an authentically archaic core in this material, and that we can determine at least some elements of it. Without being able to claim that any given words were indeed the words spoken by Muhammad himself, we can re-establish a meaningful connection between the hadith compiled in the late eighth century and the doctrines and practices of the earliest Muslims. In effect, this approach claims an authenticity of substance (though not necessarily strict verbatim authenticity) for at least some parts of the hadith corpus. As a matter of historical logic, this claim seems more satisfying than the almost Pyrrhonean scepticism of some of Schacht's followers, but still the argument must be rigorously articulated on a case-by-case basis.

In spite of these fundamental disagreements, most non-Muslim scholars would concur on a few points. First, all of the classical hadith collections, even the revered *Sahihayn* of al-Bukhari and Muslim ibn al-Hajjaj, contain a considerable quantity of spurious material. By the criteria of ordinary textual criticism (as opposed to the criteria of faith), a great many hadith cannot possibly date from Muhammad's time. Second, even those hadith which might faithfully reflect the Prophet's teaching should be considered paraphrases rather than verbatim reproductions of his actual statements. The frame stories are too stylised, the diction too "modern", to represent actual encounters between Muhammad and his followers. Third, Muslim scholars should summon the courage to revisit the canonical corpus of hadith, either to validate it or to try to build a new, more reliable corpus on the basis of modern critical methods. This would admittedly pose very serious problems for any number of long-established theological and legal doctrines, but it would be a crucial step towards rethinking Islam.

The preceding discussion demonstrates how fluid a concept authenticity really is. Indeed, this concept is only meaningful and usable when it is deployed in a precisely defined literary-historical context. Only rarely can it mean that we have direct, unmediated access to words actually produced by the supposed original speaker. At the same time, authenticity is not a vacuous term. The statements we find in our texts were in fact spoken by someone, and most often they represent a decades- or centuries-long process of statement and restatement, of transmission, revision and redaction. For the contemporary scholar – Muslim as well as non-Muslim – the search for authenticity thus lies less in an often vain struggle to recover an original form of words than in the effort to uncover and elucidate the process by which the words we actually possess took shape and came down to us. In this search we will never attain anything like irrefutable certainty. However, a carefully articulated understanding of authenticity's many meanings will do much to guide our analysis. Such an understanding might also provide some common ground, or at least points of constructive debate, for scholars of very different religious and intellectual perspectives as they examine the sacred texts of early Islam.

Notes

1. I. Goldziher, *Muslim Studies*, ed. S. M. Stern, trans. S. M. Stern and C. R. Barber, 2 vols. (Chicago: Aldine, 1973; originally published in German as *Muhammedanische Studien*, 1889–90).

2. J. Wellhausen, *Prolegomena zur ältischen Geschicte des Islams* in *Skizzen und Vorarbeiten* (Berlin: De Gruyter, 1985; originally published 1899), vol. 6.

3. L. Caetani, *Annali dell'Islam*, 10 vols. (Milan, 1905–26).

4. H. Lammens, *Le berceau de l'Islam* (1914) among many publications.

5. J. Schacht, *Origins of Muhammadan Jurisprudence* (Mich: ACLS Humanities, 2001; originally published 1950).

6. A. Noth and L. I. Conrad, *The Early Arabic Historical Tradition: A Source-Critical Study* (Princeton, NJ: Darwin Press, 1994; originally published in German, 1972).

7. F. Donner, *Narratives of Islamic Origins: The Beginnings of Islamic Historical Writing* (Princeton, NJ: Darwin Press, 1998).

8. R. G. Hoyland, *Seeing Islam as Others Saw It: A Survey and Evaluation of Christian, Jewish and Zoroastrian Writings on Early Islam* (Princeton, NJ: Darwin Press, 1998).

9. See *The Biography of Muhammad: The Issue of the Sources*, ed. H. Motzki (Leiden: Brill, 2000) and H. Motzki, *The Origins of Islamic Jurisprudence: Meccan Fiqh before the Classical Schools*, trans. Marion H. Katz (Leiden: Brill, 2002).

10. See F. Donner, *Narratives of Islamic Origins* and "Notes" and "Guide to Further Reading" in F. Donner, *Muhammad and the Believers: At the Origins of Islam* (Cambridge: Belknap Press of Harvard University Press, 2010).

11. The pseudonym of the author of *The Syro-Aramaic Reading of the Koran: A Contribution to the Decoding of the Language of the Qur'an* (Berlin: Verlad Hans Schiler, 2007). Originally published in German, 2000.

12. See footnote 9.

Constructing Islam in the "Classical" Period: *Maqalat* Literature and the Seventy-Two Sects[1]

Josef van Ess

"Le mahométisme est divisé en plus de soixante et dix sects." ("Mohammedanism is divided into more than seventy sects.") This is what we are told under the entry "Philosophie des Sarrasins" in the *Encyclopédie*, a document of the French Enlightenment edited by Denis Diderot and Jean de Rond d'Alembert shortly before the French Revolution. Islam was presented here by way of a Muslim source – a prophetic hadith to be exact. However, the French reader was not informed of this. He was left alone with his associations, and he must have thought that Islam was torn by innumerable schisms, especially in contrast to Europe which had meanwhile entered the Age of Reason. This was the way Europeans liked to see themselves at that time: as heirs of the *siècle des Lumières*, living in the light as it were, unlike the Muslims living in darkness. But religious wars had been rare in the Islamic world, and most of the few "sects" mentioned in the article by name were in reality juridical schools: the Hanafites, the Malikites, the Shafi'ites. In their French incarnation they were all misspelled; the author of the article "Philosophie des Sarrasins", the Chevalier de Jaucourt, seems not to have been sufficiently familiar with the topic. He relied on a German source, for he spelled Shafi'ites with *sch*-, a peculiarity found only in German orthography, and he dared not change it because he did not know how the names sounded in Arabic.

As a matter of fact, Martin Crusius, a Protestant theologian from the university of Tuebingen, had already written in his *Turcograeciae libri octo* (1587) – which witnessed to his good, though provincial relations with Orthodox Christianity and the Patriarchate in Constantinople – "Superstitio Mohametana est in septuaginta duas principales sectas divisa, quarum una sola in Paradisum dux est, reliquae vero in inferos". ("The Mohammedan superstition is divided into seventy-two principal sects, of which one alone leads into Paradise and the others indeed to hell".) This is not exactly what the Chevalier later said. We now have seventy-two sects instead of seventy, and the Shafi'ites are not mentioned; instead, the *Turcograeciae libri octo* confront us with the somewhat disturbing affirmation that all seventy-two will go to hell except for one. This was the discourse of people who believed in a Realm of Evil; paradise only belonged to those who followed the correct path or doctrine. The underlying dictum of the Prophet is the same, but the conclusion is different.[2]

If there is "orthodoxy", why then the great number of aberrations? Let us first have recourse to philology: the word which stands for Latin *secta* in the Arabic original, *firqa*, simply means "group" and is not necessarily pejorative. It seems that the Muslims realised early on that their Islam was not a plain phenomenon which looked alike everywhere, but rather consisted of a plurality of nuclei and communities. On the one hand, they behaved like a chosen people who had been given a new and ultimate revelation; this is why some influential groups among them called themselves *ahl al-janna*.[3] On the other hand, by their military success and the rapid expansion of their movement, they acquired new and various identities in the highly cultured areas of the Ancient World which they had conquered. What held them together were two things: 1. an ethnic criterion – they were all Arabs, and Muhammad was the Prophet sent to the Arabs, and 2. a symbolic act, namely their peculiar and unmistakable way of praying. Over the centuries, their expression for "all of us" or "the Muslims as such, irrespective of their different denominations" was *ahl al-salat* or *ahl al-qibla*.[4] In contrast to this, the Qur'an did not yet serve as an entity. The text of the Scripture was not yet fully available, and there was no single, reliable version. During the campaigns under the first caliphs, the soldiers sometimes only had a few verses which could be recited,[5] and there were certainly not enough *qurra'* to accompany them and to serve as their imam. As far as doctrine was concerned, they had to construct their identity, and later generations would admit that the ensuing constructs had not always been the same. The Muslims prayed in their Islamic way, but they had not yet defined where this should be done. *Masjid* did not yet mean "mosque" but simply "a place fit for prostration". Sometimes the Muslims even prayed in churches, as Suliman Bashear has described.[6]

The diversity could seem disconcerting and frightening. *Firqa* was very close to *furqa*, meaning "schism, dissension". In fact, the numbers seventy or seventy-two, which marked the breadth of the split inside the community, had been taken, by analogy, from a paradigmatic event which was widely known in salvation history: the erection of the Tower of Babel which humanity had failed to complete.[7] Speech had been confused ever since, and the languages which had sprung up had been connected, in early exegesis, with the peoples mentioned in the preceding chapter of the book of Genesis. These "nations" of the Ancient World, each of which spoke its own idiom, had been counted as seventy or, following the Church fathers, as seventy-two. Both numbers were symbolic, denoting plenitude and perfection, and seventy-two occupied (as six times twelve) a special rank in the sexagesimal system. In Arabic, the "peoples" had been translated as *milal*, and under the influence of Ancient Syriac, the word *milla* had become equivocal; in the Qur'an it could also mean "creed, religion".[8] This created a new situation. As long as one had talked about a multitude of languages, this could be accepted, without emotion, as a mere fact of life. The diversity of religious doctrines, however, aroused strong feelings, for not only did it provoke misunderstandings but also polemics and strife. It is true that the Christians believed that the linguistic confusion was not irreversible, thanks to their experience of Pentecost. But the Muslims noticed that the miracle had not resulted in harmony; instead of finding a common language, the Christian churches had continued quarrelling.[9] In contrast to languages, creeds and denominations multiplied. They throve on an inherent claim of "truth"; this made them dangerous. Two reactions were possible: one could accept religious diversity as an inexplicable decree of God's will (today we would call this tolerance). Or one could view it as a product of Satan to be fought because it obscured the "truth", a truth which could only be one. In both cases it seemed advisable to learn more about the various factions. This is the origin of what was once termed "heresiography", originally a kind of "Listenwissenschaft",[10] which under favourable circumstances could develop into doxography – a compilation of philosophical doctrines.

Early Muslims seem to have reacted more with realism and resignation than with interfactional aggression. Mu'awiya is said to have asked 'Abid b. Sharya, the old wise man from the Yaman,[11] about the *tabalbul* of mankind – their lack of "dialogue" as we might say today – and their "babylonisation" because of the confusion of languages or ideologies.[12] And the preachers of his time, the *qussās*, began to talk in a typological way about the division of the Children of Israel into seventy groups[13]. What they wanted to say was that hoping for union and harmony had already deceived the Jews and the Christians; it had turned out to be an illusion which had emerged everywhere in salvation history. Nevertheless, there was no doubt that Islam was special. What was happening was simply that the Muslims made their own mistakes due to their military strength and their rapid expansion. The third caliph was murdered, and it was said that 'Uthman had been killed by the "Egyptians". In the same way, the followers of 'Ali who had not supported him were the "Kufans" (*ahl Kufa*). They were not yet known as Shi'i – this term appeared later. The regional differences were the focus of the trauma.

This is at least how our first witness explained the situation, when he spoke about the dramatic event in terms of *firaq*. Maymun b. Mihran was an Umayyad bureaucrat who lived in Upper Mesopotamia and died around 734.[14] After this political disaster, which to him was a kind of "Urkatastrophe" – similar to the First World War – Mihran says we encounter firstly the adherents of 'Uthman, who consisted of the people from Syria and Basra, secondly the adherents of 'Ali, who were from Kufa, and lastly the Murji'ites, who had not wanted to side with either. The latter group is not explicitly located because, according to Mihran, the Murji'ites had been on a campaign and when they returned to Medina where 'Uthman had been assassinated, they saw that the old unity had ceased to exist.[15] From what we know about the community of the original "believers", we might assume that they were Yemenites rather than Medinans, for the Hijazis (at least those who were wealthy enough) had not joined the campaigns but had stayed at home to enjoy or administer the revenues of the unexpected expansion.[16] The *fitna* had brought the underlying tensions to the surface. Before the *fitna*, Maymun diagnosed only one faction: the Kharijites, the first great challenge of the community. However, they had dispersed and therefore remained locally undefined.

Apart from these four groups, Mihran identifies a fifth group which he names the *fi'at al-islam*, using a new key, as it were: religious rather than geographical. We are reminded of our modern Islamists, but in fact we do not find this term again during the entire Middle Ages. What we find instead is an expression similar in meaning though not yet used by Maymun: *al-firqa al-najiya*. Maymun leaves no doubt that, like a *firqa najiya*, his *fi'at al-islam* followed the right path. They may appear similar to the Murji'ites, but there is one notable difference: whereas the Murji'ites took a negative stance and "doubted" (that is, they did not side with anyone), the *ahl al-islam* declared their solidarity with 'Uthman as well as 'Ali. They left the matter of guilt open and avoided any discussion. What they wanted was *jamaa*, to live in harmony, almost as in a modern democracy. However, we do not know for sure how they understood their *jamaa*: as "concord" (that is, an abstract ideal), or as "majority" (the concrete demographic realisation of this ideal, in the sense of *al-sawad al-a'zam* as one would later say in Iraq and especially in Central Asia).[17] Behind the term *jamaa*, we discover Mu'awiya's policy and the ideology of the Umayyads. In an empire no longer ruled from what had become the periphery (Medina) but from an old power centre (Damascus), it was expedient to promote concord under the pretension of representing the majority of the Muslims. The year in which Mu'awiya hoped to assemble the adherents of both 'Uthman and 'Ali behind him (by having bribed Hasan b. Ali) was aptly called *'am al-jamaa*.[18]

Maymun had belonged to the circle of 'Umar b. 'Abdal'aziz. But in his old age he knew that the plan for *jamaa* had not worked. It is true that, among the factions or "sects", Maymun did not yet mention the Qadarites who emerged under Hisham (and in the army at that), but we can guess that politically and religiously the concord did not reach far beyond Syria. Mu'awiya was said to have equated the *jamaa* with the *firqa al-najiya*, but in the context of the same apocryphal saying of the Prophet which predicted the split of the community. This allowed for the question of how a group that goes to Paradise could be the majority when seventy or seventy-two other groups existed alongside it. Mu'awiya had allegedly solved the contradiction by adding one more prediction of the Prophet: "There will arise people in my community in whom there is a frenzy as if from rabies" (*"Yatajara bihim kama yatajara l-kalab"*).[19]

This was a clear allusion to the Kharijites. Although few in number, they had split endlessly. They were the seventy-two then; the rest was the *jamaa*. But this interpretation could not be retained, for the Shi'ites also split, and when the Qadarite doctrine was taken over by the Mu'tazilites they also founded numerous individual schools. This was not necessarily a negative experience. The development could be seen as an example of plurality, a plurality that was tolerated because it was not fostered by the government (which meanwhile had become Abbasid).

One could say, of course, that such diversity is based merely on theology; that it is useless and misleading, just idle talk, *kalam*. Outside the intellectual world, theology was widely considered a rather dubious art discredited by the Christians. In Christianity, theology was protected by an institution, and some churches were on uneasy terms with one another because of their differing views on the subject. In contrast, Islam treated theology as a matter of the market – people could simply boycott it. But they also had the freedom to choose the variety they preferred, at least in the big towns. The "schools", many of which were rather like debating clubs (and not only so among the Mu'tazilites), advertised themselves by issuing an 'aqida (creed).[20] A considerable number of these texts (symbola or Bekenntnisschriften) still exist, especially for the second and third centuries AH. They were carefully preserved and documented, but none of them lasted forever as the Christian dogma did, which is still recited in every divine service. One of our oldest theological treatises, Dirar b. 'Amr's K. al-Tahrish (which has recently been discovered in Yemen), deals with these schools as a fact of the author's world. Dirar wrote his treatise because somebody had complained about the ikhtilaf (the difference of opinions), and as a matter of fact, Dirar himself was unhappy with the situation. He quotes the saying "bada'a ghariban wa-saya'udu ghariban" ("[true] Islam is a stranger in this world"). But he does not deny that the phenomenon exists. Rather, he undertakes to simplify matters by showing that certain groups which had different names were nevertheless identical and merely distributed regionally. For instance, the Murji'a was known as "Jahmiyya" in Khorasan, "Ghaylaniyya" in Syria, "Shamiriyya" in Basra and "Waddahiyya" in Kufa, without any notable doctrinal difference.[21] Even Abu al-Qasim al-Ka'bi, the first great Mu'tazili heresiographer, who lived a century after Dirar, did not yet deal with religious reality in terms of true and false. Rather, he collected the opinions and doctrines out of professional curiosity; he noted where his earlier Mu'tazili colleagues cultivated their idiosyncrasies and "stood apart" (tafarradu) from them,[22] but did not attack them for their differences. These idiosyncrasies did not become heresies or "objects of abomination" (fada'ih) until a century later, in 'Abdalqahir al-Baghdadi's Farq bayna l-firaq.

The understanding of the lists depended on how Islam was construed. The Mu'tazilites knew the hadith about the seventy-two sects; it is quoted in a heresiographical work probably composed by Ja'far b. Harb.[23] But they did not use the hadith as a guideline, nor did they talk in terms of jama'a or the firqa al-najiya. This was done elsewhere, not so much in Iraq as Iran, among the disciples of 'Abdallah b. al-Mubarak (d. 797). We also notice the consequences of this phenomenon in some early texts of Iranian origin, such as Khushaysh b. Asram's (d. 867) K. al-Istiqama, parts of which were later included in Malati's K. al-Tanbih wal-radd. Khushaysh is one of the first authors to count the sects in order to get seventy-two of them; he then refutes them with a flood of Qur'anic quotations in the name of the *firqa al-najiya*.[24] The author who brings this method to perfection is Abu Muti' Makhul al-Nasafi (d. 930), an Iranian contemporary of Abu l-Qasim al-Ka'bi. He managed, in his *K. al-Radd 'ala ahl al-bida* to arrange the seventy-two sects so as to illustrate an underlying "orthodox" *'aqida*. Each sect was then connected with only one heresy, so that rejecting these seventy-two aberrations amounted to defining the true creed. The sects themselves, their names as well as their doctrines, were a product of the author's imagination rather than of a living reality, but whoever had read Nasafi's book or taken an introductory course on its basis knew henceforth how to understand Islam.[25] The text did not help in learning about events outside Central Asia, but it was apt as a cicerone to the virtual world of orthodox belief, and as such enjoyed an enormous reputation. Its nomenclature survived for a millennium, both in Iran and in India, and was included in modern encyclopedias such as Dehkhuda's *Lughatname*.[26]

The region where *K. al-Radd 'ala ahl al-bida* had emerged, the town of Nakhshab (or Nasaf as it was known by the Arabs), was in certain ways a backwater, devoid of historical information about the wide range of Islam. This was different in Iraq, where Abu l-Qasim al-Ka'bi had studied, who came from the same area. Instead of learning the seventy-two sects by heart, the students there were taught how to engage in disputations. This produced a kind of academic literature characterised by the term *maqalat*. The genre is best represented by Ash'ari's *Maqalat al-islamiyyin*. Note the expression *islamiyyin*, which has nothing to do with Maymun b. Mihran's *fi'at al-islam*, but means "the Muslims in their entirety", the *ahl al-salat*; this is why the title continues with *wa-khtilaf al-musallin*.

Maqalat books did not aim at a creed. They were the leftovers of prior and perhaps forgotten speculations; theological ideas of the past that it was helpful to know (and perhaps better to avoid) when discussing matters with a rival of one's own school. The theologians, known as *mutakallimun*, acquired their name from their attempts to push their ideas through by way of dialectics (*kalam*, derived from *takallama*). Today we would speak of "dialogue" in this respect, but in Ash'ari's time, the way of achieving *kalam* was not by loose dialogue but by more or less disciplined disputation (*munazara*). In order to prepare for this intellectual exercise, the participants seem to have memorised the arguments and positions they might expect from the opponent. During the public exercise, the "talk show" as it were, it was also expedient to keep in mind all the errors which had been committed in the past. The goal of the endeavour consisted, of course, in attaining the truth, but in contrast to the *'aqa'id*, the *maqalat* had a historical dimension, and the participants were perhaps still aware of the fact that even when victorious they had not yet reached a result that would withstand all criticism.

This was another way of construing Islam, equally as successful as the former. In its own way, it lasted as long as Abu Muti' al-Nasafi's approach, especially due to the work of Shahrastani. Shahrastani intended to be objective, as had Ash'ari. Neither kept to their promise consistently, but this was as at least what the literary genre demanded. Shahrastani could not explicitly state his personal conviction anyway – he was an Isma'ili who had managed to pose as an Ash'arite.[27] Nevertheless, his presentation was taken up by countries from Iraq to Spain, and especially by Egypt. Most people did not realise his non-orthodox connection; they liked the way he merged Islamic denominations with pagan schools, especially of Greek philosophy. The Isma'ilis had been doing this for generations.

In addition to that, however, Shahrastani had something else to offer that seems unusual – at least to us, if not so much so to his contemporaries. When organising his material, he used a system derived from the practice of Iranian bureaucracy. He describes the system in the last of his five introductions, and Daniel Gimaret was the first to furnish us with an astute interpretation of the relevant passage.[28] Shahrastani was familiar with the *hisab diwani* in Iran – that is, the way the revenue was administered and calculated in the chanceries – and he distributed the denominations in the same way. A feature of the "construction" was its reference to bureaucracy. At all times, bureaucracies produced classifications; classification was the only way to grasp the confusing plenitude of living reality. The Christians owed their name "Christ people" in contrast to the ordinary Jews.[29] Sasanid practice of the same kind seems to survive in the way the Muslims categorised the dualist "sects", for when enumerating the Manicheans, the Mazdakites, and so on, they usually forgot the Zoroastrians – probably because the Muslims had taken over a system which dated from the time when Mazdaism was the dominant religion in pre-Islamic Iran and had defined who was a heretic and who was not.[30] In the second half of the third century AH, a certain Misma'i, a nephew of the Mu'tazili theologian and heresiographer Zurqan, produced the book *K. Ma'rifat ma yahtaju l-muluk ila ma'rifatihi fi usul al-din wa-aqawil firaq al-umma*, a kind of manual for the government which contained, besides a catechism, a survey of the Islamic denominations.[31] Our best example is Khwarazmi with his *Mafatih al-'ulum*, for in his endeavour to serve the needs of secretarial organisation he made use of the tradition of the seventy-two sects.[32] The list he incorporated into his manual corresponds to the list we find in a contemporary Isma'ili text, the *Bab al-shaytan* from Abu Tammam's *K. al-Shajara* (recently edited by Paul Walker and Wilferd Madelung). The list can perhaps be retraced to Abu Zayd al-Balkhi, another contemporary of Abu l-Qasim al-Ka'bi and Abu Muti' al-Nasafi. Shahrastani, however, did not take it up; perhaps he did not know it.

In these administrative manuals the system showed its useful side. It did not aim at coercion; it aimed at tax-paying. Even when a *firqa* pushed its doctrine or its social behaviour to the point at which it transgressed the borderline between sectarianism and unbelief, the officials in the chanceries mainly thought about money; they made "the sectarians" pay *jizya* instead of *kharaj*. The adherents of the Muqanna', a man who had been persecuted as a rebel and an unbeliever, were not extinguished; they were found centuries later as peasants living in the mountains of Central Asia paying the *jizya* just as the Zoroastrians had, and travellers such as Muqaddasi boasted of having visited them.[33] The Nusayris, again peasants but also retailers in remote places, survived in Syria.[34] Today, due to their denominational *'asabiyya*, they lead the government. There are, of course, groups and communities who were less fortunate, and I abstain from making further statements about the modern period. But in general, and up to the nineteenth century, divergent religious convictions were, in spite of all criticism and polemics, ultimately treated as *maqalat*. Generally speaking, with regard to religion, the Islamic world remained more peaceful than Europe before the Enlightenment.

What I have discussed until this point are simply virtual realities; when we say "Islam" we use a construct. This is true for the past as well as for the present. These constructs have expanded enormously due to ideological pollution and the media's influence. On the other hand, constructs are fragile; they can lose their persuasiveness from one moment to the next. We know this from our economy and from our politics. As historians, our dilemma is that we are constantly dealing with constructs (all of our written sources are constructs), yet we want to know the reality. We should never pretend to have discovered it; we are able only to present constructs ourselves. But we can develop theories that help to explain these constructs. Is there any theory that explains what I have described in this paper? I have not elaborated any theories myself, but one in contemporary religious studies seems to fit: denominationalism.

This is how I imagine early Islam. Islam did not present itself as a union then, and neither does it do so today. Religion always exists in small communities. When you walk through a North American town, it seems as though you find a church at every second corner, but Christian belief may be presented differently from church to church. Similarly, when we want to interpret the situation in early Kufa according to our heresiographical sources, we find all kinds of people trying to explain Islam to themselves under certain assumptions, everybody in his own way, and probably in his own mosque. None of them lacked a community, for without an audience their ideas would not have been recorded. The reports were collected and publicised as a catalogue of idiosyncrasies. This is how the talk about *ikhtilaf* came up, with or without resentment concerning the phenomenon. At the end of this process we get a literary genre, heresiography, or rather a whole gamut of genres: *maqalat* literature, creeds, administrative manuals, polemical pamphlets, and so on. Each of these points to the plurality of Islam (though not to its pluralism, since pluralism was not yet the habit of the age). There was, however, no institution which endeavoured to stand for them all (no "Church"), and on the fringe there was syncretism, transculturation and liminality.[35] People noticed the differences either with curiosity or with exasperation. Specialists prepared lists of groups: "sects" or "heresies". However elaborate the lists, they did not last forever, and became obsolete after some time. In contrast, the phenomenon itself survived; a man like Muqaddasi took plurality for granted. Even today, Moroccan Islam differs from the Saudi or Iranian variety, and there is no indication that this will change.

Notes

1. This essay takes up some ideas which I develop in my book *Der Eine und das Andere: Beobachtungen an islamischen häresiographischen Texten* (1–2, Berlin: De Gruyter, 2011). For brevity's sake I have not repeated the documentation collected there; I simply refer the reader to the corresponding page numbers of the book.
2. *Der Eine*, p. 7.
3. For references, see my book *Der Fehltritt des Gelehrten* (Heidelberg: Winter, 2001), p. 97f. and index.
4. *Der Eine*, p. 1270.
5. Cf. Sukayna al-Shihabi (ed), *Ta'rikh Dimashq*, vol. 38, 1986, p. 13, mentioned in *Der Fehltritt des Gelehrten*, p. 72; also ib (= *Fehltritt*), p. 171.
6. Suliman Bashear, "Qibla musharriqa and Early Muslim Prayer in Churches", *The Muslim World*, 81 (3–4), October 1991, pp. 267–292.
7. *Der Eine*, p. 15ff.
8. "Religion" is A. J. Arberry's rendering (Qur'an 2:120). "Creed" is that given by U. V. R. Paret ("Bekenntnis"), (Qur'an 2:114).
9. The Qur'an alludes to this (5:14): "So We have stirred up among them [the Christians] enmity and hatred, till the day of Resurrection" (trs. A. J. Arberry). Using a common language in a multilingual world is extremely rare; imagine the Europeans speaking Esperanto in the Parliament of Brussels!
10. This term is mentioned by the German Old Testament scholar Albrecht Alt. See also J. Z. Smith, *Imagining Religion: From Babylon to Jonestone* (Chicago: University of Chicago Press, 1982), p. 47f., and J. Neusner, *The Twentieth Century Construction of "Judaism": Essays on the religion of Torah in the history of religion* (Atlanta: Scholars Press, 1991), p. 83f.
11. F. Rosenthal (ed), *Encyclopedia of Islam*, 2nd ed., vol. 3, "Ibn Sharya", p. 937.
12. R. Tajaddud (ed), *Ibn al-Nadim's Fihrist* (Teheran: Marvi, 1973), p. 102, lines 3–4. Abdesselam Cheddadi stresses the paradigmatic character of this story in his *Les Arabes et l'appropriation de l'histoire* (Paris: Sindbad, 2004), p. 55f.
13. *Der Eine*, p. 12ff.
14. F. Rosenthal (ed), *Encyclopedia of Islam* 2, vol. 6, p. 916f. (F. M. Donner).
15. *Der Eine*, p. 26ff.
16. *Der Fehltritt des Gelehrten*, p. 402f.
17. Cf. al-Hakim al-Samarqandi's (died 453 CE) catechism *K. al-Sawad al-a'zam*, composed for the Samanid prince Isma'il b. Ahmad (ruled 892–907).
18. *Encyclopedia of Islam* 2, vol. 7, "Mu'awiya" (M. Hinds), p. 265; cf. *Der Eine*, p. 21f.
19. Transmitted in several hadith collections; cf. *Der Eine*, p. 24.
20. *Der Eine* p. 1208ff.
21. *Der Eine*, p. 133ff.
22. *Der Eine,* p. 340 and 342.
23. Died 850. Cf. my *Frühe mu'tazilitische Häresiographie* ("Early Mu'tazilite heresiography"), (Beirut: In Kommission bei F. Steiner, 1971), Ar. text, p. 20, line 12ff.
24. *Der Eine*, 310ff.
25. *Der Eine*, p. 428ff.
26. *Der Eine*, p. 1148.
27. Cf. now, as the last contribution to this topic, T. Mayer's introduction to his *Keys to the Arcana: Shahrastani's Esoteric Commentary on the Qur'an* (Oxford: Oxford University Press in association with the Institute of Ismaili Studies, 2009), p. 3f.

28. Shahrastani, *Livre des Religions et des Sectes*, vol. 1 (Leuven: Peeters/UNESCO, 1986), p. 149f.; cf. *Der Eine*, p. 873ff.

29. *Der Eine*, p. 1213.

30. *Der Eine*, p. 186.

31. *Der Eine*, p. 184.

32. *Der Eine*, p. 553ff.

33. *Der Eine*, p. 1326f.

34. *Der Eine*, p. 1328.

35. Cf. now, with respect to India, D. S. Khan, *Crossing the Threshold: Understanding Religious Identities in South Asia* (London: Institute for Ismaili Studies, 2004). India under British rule is a good example of the part that bureaucracy played in this process. The urge on classifying led to the creation of the term "Hinduism" derived from British jurisdiction under Warren Hastings.

Modern Discourses of Superiority: Muslims and Christians in Contact

Stefan Wild

In order to honour a globally acknowledged scholar of Mohammed Arkoun's standing, it is tempting to take a cue from one of his major and most recent study, *The Unthought in Contemporary Islamic Thought*.[1] I freely admit that I have succumbed to this temptation. One of the most important chapters in Arkoun's book deals with authority and power in Islamic thought. My paper is an attempt to analyse an aspect of the power structure inherent in inter-religious polemics. Part one will deal with Christian and Muslim discourses of superiority. I will compare the role of reason in and for religion as seen by Pope Benedict XVI and the nineteenth-century Egyptian reformist, Muhammad ʿAbduh. In part two, I will attempt to point to subtle but significant changes of attitude in inter-religious dialogues between Muslims and Christians in modern times. Here we find first attempts to transcend the discourse of superiority and to overcome what has been called "exclusivism". How does the introduction of the "religious Other" into theological discourse affect the construction of belief? There are not many theologians or intellectuals on either side of the Christian–Muslim divide who deal with these questions. And it has to be admitted that the ideas and proposals that I will discuss may at present interest only a small minority of believers. Nevertheless, the "theology of the religious Other" in a globalised, multicultural and multi-religious world is a new concept that may provide a possibility for overcoming the fairly worn-out discourses of superiority.

1. Discourses of Superiority: Pope Benedict XVI, Muhammad 'Abduh and the Role of Reason in Religion

Christianity and Islam claim to have privileged, if not exclusive, access to transcendental truth.[2] Without this claim, and the concomitant claim that this truth is of crucial importance for the well-being of the individual and his or her community both in this world and the hereafter, these religions would lose their meaning. Religious belief as seen from the inside is, therefore, to some extent irreducible, incommensurable and beyond rational comparative evaluation. In multi-religious societies, however, no religion can enforce any longer what it considers its superior and exclusive claim to truth. As globalisation spreads religions across the world, the multi-religious factor in many societies will most probably become more visible. The staunchest atheist will have to live beside the most pious religious literalist, be they Christian or Muslim, Buddhist or Hindu. The constant confrontation with a multitude of religious possibilities may in the long run blunt the edges of exclusivism. One aspect of religious reality, overlooked at times, is that the average individual did not and does not choose a religion, but was born into a religion. History and geography are in this respect often as important as or even more important than theological doctrine and individual choice.[3]

Early and medieval Muslim societies enjoyed a living experience of pluralism that was stronger than that in parallel Christian societies.[4] Under Muslim rule, several communities (Jews, Christians, Zoroastrians) could exist side by side – at least in principle. They had scriptures in different languages that were nevertheless acknowledged to contain similar messages. Three important Sunni legal schools taught that even non-Arab pagans had a protected status under Islam.[5] Under medieval Christian rule, however, the fact that Jewish scripture was also part of Christian scripture usually did nothing to alleviate the mostly deplorable reality of Jewish life under Christian rule. For Muslims under medieval Christian rule, prospects were even dimmer.

The inter-religious competition over whose religion was the true one, has marked religious and social life through the ages wherever different religions have come into contact. Christianity and Islam are to this day caught up in these discourses of superiority, and are linked to or maybe even trapped in this competition. This rivalry shows itself in missionary activities, in Christian *tabshīr* and Muslim *da'wa*. Many theologians on both sides, true to their universalist claims, agree that giving up *tabshīr* or *da'wa* would betray their most cherished values. For mainstream theology, proselytising as a principle is in both cases not negotiable. The missionary competition between Muslims and Christians in many parts of the world, notably on the African continent, is very much alive. In Europe, where conversions between Islam and Christianity are a growing phenomenon, this competition is widely seen as an unsolved religious problem. In the course of history, blood has been shed by the adherents of both religions in order to prove their point – less on the Muslim side than on the Christian side, at least until the advent of modernity. One cannot overlook the fact that just as much blood has been shed *within* Christianity and less blood *within* Islam to make "religious truth" prevail and "heresy" or "error" disappear. Nor should one forget that militant anti-religious movements and regimes have produced no fewer victims among the religious either. In Central Europe, the concept of the freedom of religion, including the right to change one's religion or to profess no religion at all, has been successfully implemented, by and large, even where there is a Christian state religion. In countries dominated by a Muslim majority, the issue of this type of full religious freedom is often seen either as marginal or as artificial. The Muslim diaspora, however, disagree. The most important Muslim organisations in Germany accept the principle of full freedom of religion, without reservation.

In any case, religious truth in Christianity and Islam was and is still tied up with the idea that there is only one true religion and that all other religions are wrong. "Exclusivism" consists of the idea that only one religion, Christianity or Islam, is true or even that only one particular brand of Christianity (such as Roman Catholicism) or of Islam (such as Sunni Islam) is true. "Inclusivism" means that while there may be elements of truth in other religions, only one religion possesses truth in a singular and unsurpassable way. Inclusivism, however, while seeming generous, may actually co-opt other faiths without their leave.[6] Finally, "pluralism" theologically allows for different religious accesses to truth. For unsophisticated mainstream Christianity and Islam, missing the true religion and adhering to a wrong one is punishable, if not already in this world then certainly in the world to come.

Within Christianity and Islam, the conviction that the religious "Other" will be eternally punished and burn in hell was for a long time the dominant paradigm, and it is still fairly widespread. Conversely, many Christians and Muslims are convinced that on the strength of their beliefs and their behaviour they stand a fairly good chance of entering paradise, even if they can never be completely sure of eternal salvation and bliss. This stance is not mitigated by the fact that in the eyes neither of Christians nor of Muslims is the other religion completely false. But in spite of large areas of overlapping, Christianity and Islam encapsulate a particularly strong antithesis between true and false religion. Many Christians still fear Islam; many Muslims still fear Christianity. My thesis is that in modern religious discourse and in its construction of belief, the opposition between a completely true and a partially false religion is gradually being replaced by the opposition between a culturally superior religion and a culturally inferior one. Thereby, hegemonic aspects are introduced: which religion is the more vibrant, the more modern, or the more successful in converting others? Such aspects tend to be superimposed on the question of mere truth. Mohammed Arkoun has already pointed out the way an "Islamic reason" and a "Western secularised reason" oppose each other.[7] He argued for an anti-hegemonic critique of both. Islam is feared in many parts of Europe because it contests the hegemony of the Christian Churches and/or of secularism. Christianity and secularism are feared in many parts of the Muslim world because they are perceived as hegemonic doctrines. It is often, therefore, not so much the truth of competing religions that is at stake today, but their attractiveness, their vitality and their power. Numerous Muslim scholars consider a powerful Islam inextricably linked to an Islamic state. They act as though even the fundamental rituals of Islam are not "practices Muslims must undertake because they are an irreducible part of being a believer, but rather because they are socially useful in inculcating the habits and the discipline that assist in the project of striving for an Islamic state".[8] On the other hand, a diaspora situation leads many Muslims, silently or openly, to renounce the idea of a universal Islamic state.

What I mean by "discourse of superiority" is best explained by a comparison that may seem far-fetched: that of Muhammad 'Abduh and Pope Benedict XVI, and how both construct the role of reason in their religions.

Pope Benedict XVI, in his famous lecture in Regensburg of 12 September 2006 on "belief and reason" (*Glaube und Vernunft*), discusses the role of reason in Islam. He quotes a public religious discussion between the Byzantine emperor Manuel II and a learned Muslim in 1391. Among other issues, this dialogue deals with jihad, and the Pope quotes Manuel II with the words, "Show me what Muhammad taught as new and you will find only evil and inhumanity – such as Muhammad's command to spread the faith which he preached by the sword." Muslim troops at the time stood not far from Constantinople. Even if the Pope called this quotation "unacceptably gruff in form", the damage was done. According to the Pope, Islam taught that religion should be spread by the sword. This is why, in his view, the religion of Islam cannot be said to be built on reason. Christian theology, on the other hand, teaches that "not to act with the logos" (that is, with reason) is incompatible with God's essence. And the Pope links this position with the fact "that Christianity, in spite of its origin and in spite of important developments in the Orient, received its historically decisive imprint in Europe".[9]

In Islam, and to a lesser extent in parts of Protestantism, Pope Benedict tells us, this amalgamation of revelation and Greek reason is weak or absent. Pope Benedict compared (Catholic) Christianity with Islam (and Protestantism), and few people were surprised when he found (Catholic) Christianity to be superior. The question of how revealed religion relates to human reason is, of course, one of the oldest questions of philosophy and theology in both cultures. And the kind of comparison that the Pope uses has a long polemical history on both sides.

We find analogous statements of comparison in many modern Muslim treatises dealing with Islam – of course, invariably in favour of Islam. Islam, in this view, is superior to all other religions, and in particular to Christianity. A main argument is that Islam is the most "reasonable" of all religions, and that it is in particular more reasonable than Christianity. This is already manifest in Muhammad 'Abduh's (1849–1905) well-known apologetic polemic against Christianity, "Islam and Christianity, in relation to science and culture".[10] Farah Antun (1874–1922), a Greek Orthodox Christian and Egyptian nationalist, had espoused Ernest Renan's (1823–92) idea that Islam as such was inimical to science and reason, and had written about it in the learned Egyptian journal *al-Jami'ah*. Renan had based this view on a mainly racist anti-Arabic paradigm of history. Muhammad 'Abduh, and after him numerous Muslim scholars, rose to defend Islam. Many of them claimed and claim that the tension between reason and belief so often invoked in different Christian theologies simply does not exist in Islam. And the argument was reversed: Christianity, according to 'Abduh, rests on belief in the irrational. 'Abduh did admit a possible divergence of religion and reason in Islam. But according to him, any potential conflict was easily resolved: "The adherents to the Islamic faith – except for a negligible few – agree that if reason and (religious) tradition conflict one should follow reason."[11]

So according to an overwhelming majority of Muslim scholars, the central tenets of Islam are "more reasonable" than those of Christianity. Here 'Abduh probably underrated or downplayed the number of the "negligible few" dissenters. In any case, for him reason was embodied in the first place in the natural sciences. But reason also had to reign in metaphysics. The unity of God is a more reasonable proposition than the dogma of the Trinity; the dogma that God's son had died on the cross defies human reason. Furthermore, 'Abduh criticised the fact that Christian doctrine is based on Christ's miracles and that it teaches its adherents to keep aloof from worldly things – both stances contradict reason. So we find that Pope Benedict XVI and Muhammad 'Abduh – more than a hundred years apart – take contradictory but symmetrical positions. Each finds his own religion superior because it can be shown to be more "reasonable".

In both cases, the main addressee is not the "religious Other". When Muhammad 'Abduh, the mufti of Egypt, wrote his treatise, there were very few non-Muslims who read him. One of these must have been Ignaz Goldziher (1850–1921), secretary of the Israelitish community of Budapest, and the foremost European authority on Islam at the time. Goldziher's relation to Judaism was problematic, and his view of Christianity even more sceptical. He had met 'Abduh personally in Cairo in 1873–74. He wrote very much in Abduh's line of thought:

> During these weeks, I so much assimilated the Mohammedan spirit, that in the end I was convinced that I was myself a Mohammedan. I found that this was the only religion, which even in its official doctrinal shape and formulation could satisfy philosophical brains. My ideal was to elevate Judaism to a similar level. Islam, I learnt by experience, was the only religion, in which superstition and pagan rudiments are not countered by rationalism but by orthodox doctrine.[12]

But Muhammad 'Abduh's message addressed neither a European public nor the Coptic reader in Egypt. The implied recipient was the enlightened Muslim intellectual inside and outside Egypt, who spoke Arabic. This type of discourse is normally in the first place self-assertive: it addresses the community of co-believers, and it is designed to strengthen their belief and their cohesion. This, in my opinion, is also true for Pope Benedict's lecture. However, with the latter – more than a hundred years after Muhammad 'Abduh's death – globalism had struck, and the more polemical parts of a lecture delivered in the provincial German town of Regensburg reached a Muslim public worldwide within hours. We all know the consequences: Muslims reacted with a remarkable *Open Letter to the Pope* (signed by thirty-eight Muslim scholars, dated 13 October 2006), and a second letter called

A Common Word Between Us and You, signed by 138 Muslim scholars and directed not only to the Pope but also to twenty-two Orthodox patriarchs, archbishops and metropolitans; to four Protestant and Anglican bishops; to the Secretary General of the World Council of Churches; and to the "leaders of all Christian Churches" (13 October 2007 = 'Id al-Fitr 1428).

There are numerous other discursive devices to "prove" religious superiority. Let me add one other instance. Religious superiority is often invoked by claiming to have a better, meaning superior, idea of who or what God really is. This is often expressed in endless discussions – mostly amongst Christians, I think – of whether Muslims, Christians and Jews believe in the same God or not. Post-Holocaust Christian theology in Europe was eager to emphasise the dependence of Christianity on Judaism, the relative autarchy of the Jewish religion, and the privileged closeness of Christianity to Judaism. In this vein, the German Jesuit, Felix Körner, argued that whereas Christians and Muslims cannot be said to believe in the same God, it is appropriate to say that Christians and Jews do.[13] The aspect of superiority is clearly visible: Jews and Christians have the better, the "truer" image of God, which they share, and which Islam prevents Muslims from attaining.

2. Beyond Superiority and Exclusivism: the "Religious Other"

Whereas in Islam and Christianity there are and have always been strong currents that insist on the superior character of their own truths, in modern times, there are growing tendencies to assure the "religious Other" of a partial overlapping of truths and to stress this partial agreement in a gesture of inclusivism. Differences are not denied but recalibrated. This also has a dialectic of its own: it is admitted that the teachings of the "other religion", the wrong one, are not completely false, especially if interpreted in the light of the tenets of the speaker's religion. This often works in a retroactive way. Christianity could not but accept parts of Judaism; Islam could not but share parts of Judaism and Christianity. But Christianity for a long time accepted Jewish scripture only if it was interpreted in a Christological way. Similarly, many contemporary Muslim religious scholars judge the validity of Christian and Jewish scripture by the measure of their compatibility with the Qur'an and hadith.

This official inclusivist emphasis on a partial inter-religious agreement usually serves a dialogical aim. A good example is the concept of an "Abrahamic tradition". The construction of an Abrahamic unity between Islam, Christianity and Judaism was foreshadowed by the Qur'anic concept of the "religion of Ibrahim" (*millat Ibrahim*, for example, sura 2:130) as well as by the concept of Ibrahim as a *hanif* Muslim (for example, sura 3:65–70). Ibrahim's monotheist religion was in a way an Islam before the term existed. Ibrahim's religion existed before the Qur'an had been revealed and before the Prophet Muhammad was born. This had its legal consequences in the concept of *dhimma* (covenant of protection) in Islam. It was taken up or reinvented much later, mainly by Christians and was, as far as I know, only unfolded as a possible starting point for dialogue between Muslims, Christians and Jews in the twentieth century. Names like Louis Massignon (1883–1962) and Youakim Mubarac (1924–95) come to mind. The best-known modern proponent of the construction of an "Abrahamic" bond between the monotheist religions is possibly Pope John XXIII in Vatican II with his famous statement on Abraham in *Nostra Aetate*:

> The Church regards with esteem also the Moslems. They adore the one God, living and subsisting in Himself; merciful and all-powerful, the Creator of heaven and earth, who has spoken to men; they take pains to submit wholeheartedly to even His inscrutable decrees, just as Abraham, with whom the faith of Islam takes pleasure in linking itself, submitted to God. Though they do not acknowledge Jesus as God, they revere Him as a prophet. They also honour Mary, His virgin Mother; at times they even call on her with devotion. In addition, they await the Day of Judgement, when God will render their deserts to all those who have been raised up from the dead. Finally, they value the moral life and worship God especially through prayer, almsgiving and fasting.
>
> Since in the course of centuries not a few quarrels and hostilities have arisen between Christians and Moslems, this sacred synod urges all to forget the past and to work sincerely for mutual understanding and to preserve as well as to promote together for the benefit of all mankind social justice and moral welfare, as well as peace and freedom.[14]

In this statement, the Pope acknowledged for the first time that the free choice of religion was a fundamental human right – even in the Roman Catholic Church. There was salvation outside the Church; there was even salvation outside Christianity.

There is a certain analogy between this "Abrahamic tradition" and what in modern Muslim terminology are often called the three "heavenly religions" (*al-adyan al-samawiyya*), a term that stresses the similarities more than the differences between the three monotheist religions. I must confess that I do not know how old this term is, but it seems to me to be fairly modern.

A further element of constructing an inter-religious monotheist bond was and is the fight against a common enemy. This enemy was, for a certain period, militant communism. After the downfall of state-controlled socialism, the perceived ideological positions of the common enemy were mainly agnosticism, materialism and atheism. To this triad, secularism very often has to be added. While it has to be admitted that a common enemy can be a powerful element in forging a unified front, it is less clear whether a pluralist approach to religion will gain anything by marginalising and vilifying these positions. Be this as it may, it is pleasing to see that at a time when dialogue has become a byword for tolerance and peace, there are specialised learned journals from both sides of the religious divide that deal exclusively with questions of Muslim–Christian dialogue: *Islamochristiana* (Rome) and the *Bulletin of the Royal Institute for Inter-Faith Studies* (Amman) are just two examples. The "religious Other" – a term which would have been incomprehensible a hundred years ago – is on its way to becoming part of Christian and Muslim theology.

There are many theological initiatives from both sides to transcend the discourse of superiority and to replace or at least complement it with a different approach.[15] I will not go into the obvious similarities between Muslim *tasawwuf* and Christian mysticism. That would be too vast a subject. Instead, I have selected four of the lesser-known attempts to bridge the inter-religious gap:

1. The *anima naturaliter Christiana* and the *fitra,* that is, the concept of Islam as encompassing all monotheist religions.
2. The concept of an "anonymous Christian" in Vatican II theology, and the *muslim / mu'min* difference in modernist Muslim exegesis.
3. The call for a Christian recognition of Muhammad as a prophet.
4. The self-view of Muslims as an *umma wasat* ("a moderate community") and Muslim pluralism.

i. The *anima naturaliter Christiana* and the *fitra*

Church father Tertullianus (d. after 220 CE) developed the doctrine of a "naturally Christian soul" (*anima naturaliter Christiana*). According to

Tertullianus, some pagans show by their behaviour that deep in their hearts they believe in God's unity, in the immortality of the soul and in the existence of evil spirits. They share, therefore, major Christian tenets. Their soul is, as it were, naturally Christian, independent of their professed religion. In the Middle Ages in Europe, some saw in the Roman pagan poet Vergilius (d. 19 BC) an example of just such a "naturally Christian soul". This concept was taken much further in the twentieth century by Karl Rahner's development of the idea of an "anonymous Christian" (see point 2).

I see in the Islamic concept of *fitra* a certain analogy with Tertullianus's "naturally Christian soul". According to a well-known hadith, every human being is born in the *fitra*: the inborn religious predisposition of every child. Al-Ghazali (d. 1111 CE) explains:

> I saw that the Christian children grow up in Christianity, and that the Jewish children grow up in Judaism and that the Muslim children grow up in Islam. Every child is born in the *fitra*, then his parents make him a Jew or a Christian or a Magian. And my innermost feeling reached out to find the truth of the original *fitra*.[16]

Such texts imply that every child's predisposition or inborn nature is Muslim; every child has an *anima naturaliter Islamica,* so to speak. It is only the environment, that is, the parents, who imbue it with a deviant belief.

ii. The Concept of an "Anonymous Christian" in Vatican II Theology, and the *Muslim / mu'min* Difference in Modernist Muslim Exegesis

The concept of an "anonymous Christian" was developed by the German Jesuit, Karl Rahner (1904–84). All salvation is through Christ. However, people who have never heard the Gospel or even rejected it might still be saved through Christ, and could therefore be called "anonymous Christians", Rahner suggested. This concept became part of the declarations of the Vatican II (1964), which stated:

> Those also can attain to everlasting salvation who through no fault of their own do not know the gospel of Christ of his Church, yet sincerely seek God and, moved by grace, strive by their deeds to do His will as it is known to them through the dictates of conscience (*Lumen Gentium*).[17]

This inclusivism is at present a widespread inter-religious position in

Europe. Non-Christians "can have the salvific grace of God, through Christ, although they may never have heard of the Christian revelation", nor of the cross, the Trinity, incarnation or resurrection.

This doctrine came under fire from two directions. Firstly, there was the traditional Catholic view, protesting that "biblical Christianity is true and other religions are not". After Vatican II, some groups even separated from the Catholic Church, and often gave this very inclusivism as one of their reasons. Secondly, there was the liberal voice from inside and outside the Catholic Church that found this idea possibly well-meant but paternalistic in the extreme. Hans Küng stated, "It would be impossible to find anywhere in the world a sincere Jew, Muslim or atheist who would not regard the assertion that he is an 'anonymous Christian' as presumptuous."[18] John Hick agreed with him by criticising Karl Rahner's notion of an "anonymous Christian" as "an honorary status granted unilaterally to people who have not expressed any desire for it".

The Syrian scholar, Mohamad Shahrour (b. 1938) developed an idea somewhat analogous to Karl Rahner's concept, in his book *al-Islam wa-l-iman*.[19] This book – famous in the eyes of some Muslims, notorious in the eyes of others – distinguishes between the notions of *islam* and *iman*, of *Muslim* and *mu'min*. He vigorously contests the widely accepted position that the word *islam* in the Qur'anic text more or less equals *iman*. For Mohamad Shahrour, these are two radically different concepts: *islam* designates the universal religion of mankind in which Muslims, Christians, Jews and other peoples of good faith are united. All mankind of good will is *muslim*, all are members of this all-embracing one religion (*din*) called Islam. This is true not only for Jews and Christians, but also valid for most (or all?) other religions, such as Buddhism and Hinduism.[20] Rahner's "anonymous Christian" seems close to Shahrour's concept of being Muslim without realising it. It would be possible to speak of an "anonymous Muslim", though Shahrour never does so. Still, the reasoning behind Rahner's and Shahrour's concepts is rather similar: many Christians limit paradise to Christians only; all others go to hell. In the same way, most Muslims confine paradise to their own religion while all others are condemned to the eternal fire. In reality, for Shahrour, all people of good will who follow their natural universal religion have to be called "Muslims" and therefore can enter paradise.[21] On the other hand, what people call "Islam" today should, according to Shahrour's understanding of the Qur'anic text, be called "Iman". The "five pillars of Islam", in the sense of the five religious duties of the followers of the Prophet Muhammad, should be called the "five pillars of Iman", and the specificity of him who was heretofore called a Muslim is guaranteed in that he is a Mu'min. Islam consists of the belief in God and in the Day of Judgement and thus comes close to the concept of an Abrahamic monotheism.

An early predecessor of Shahrour was al-Ghazali. In his book *The Decisive Criterion for Distinguishing Islam from Clandestine Apostasy*[22] he speaks of non-Muslims who can be excused for not adopting Islam:

> Those whom the call i.e. to Islam, SW has not reached are of three kinds. The first kind are those who have never heard the name of Muhammad, they are excused; the second kind are those who have heard his name and his virtue and his miracles and who live close to the Muslim land and have contact with them, they are the unbelievers and the heretics; and there is a third group between them. They have heard the name Muhammad and have not heard of his qualities and traits, but they have from their earliest youth heard that a treacherous liar named Muhammad claimed to be a prophet. Those belong in my view to the first kind. Because they have heard his name and at the same time the opposite of his qualities and that does not motivate them to further enquiries. That means that most Christians from the Rum and of the land of the Turks will be covered by God's mercy.[23]

The first and the third group can in the hereafter expect God's mercy without professing Islam.

Shahrour's method was criticised by many – the best-known and most competent among his critics was probably the Egyptian, Nasr Hamid Abu Zayd (b. 1943).[24] Nevertheless, Shahrour can serve as an example for a bold revisionism. He certainly is one of a new brand of Muslim intellectuals in the public sphere who have led to a "collapse of earlier, hierarchical notions of religious authority based on claims to the mastery of fixed bodies of religious texts".[25]

iii. The Call for a Christian Recognition of Muhammad as a Prophet

There is a long-standing complaint among Muslim theologians that Christianity did not and does not acknowledge the prophethood of Muhammad, while the Qur'an does recognise the prophethood of Jesus. In recent times, some Protestant theologians have argued that Christians should acknowledge Muhammad's prophethood. One of them is the

German theologian Reinhard Leuze in his book *Christianity and Islam*.[26] Another, Wilfred Cantwell Smith, wrote:

> I myself – after studying the history of the Islamic and the Christian movements and having friends in both groups – am not able to think of any reason that one might reasonably have for denying that God has played in human history a role in and through the Qur'an, in the Muslim case, comparable to the role of Christ in the Christian case in and through Christ.[27]

The most famous proponent of such a view, however, seems to be the controversial Swiss Catholic theologian, Hans Küng (b.1928), whose authority to teach Catholic theology was revoked by the Vatican. Since 1995 he has been President of the Foundation for a Global Ethic ("Stiftung Weltethos"). He wrote:

> If the Catholic Church after the declaration on the non-Christian religions in Vatican II (1964) ... 'also sees the Muslims with great respect who pray to the one and only God ... who spoke to mankind' – then the same Church – and all Christian Churches – should ... see the one person with great respect whose name is not mentioned in that declaration out of embarrassment, although he and he alone led the Muslims to worship this one God and although God spoke through him, Muhammad the Prophet.[28]

We all know that Hans Küng does not represent Catholic mainstream theology – but I find it difficult to contradict him.

iv. The Self-View of Muslims as an *umma wasat* ("a Moderate Community") and Muslim Pluralism

A complete pluralism is reached when some modern Muslim exegetes offer a new interpretation of Qur'anic verses, such as 2:143 and 5:66 that describe righteous Muslims as constituting a "moderate community" (*umma wasat*) and righteous Jews and Christians as a "balanced community" (*umma muqtasida*). "Taken together, these verses clearly suggest that it is subscription to some common standard of righteousness and ethical conduct that determines the salvific nature of a religious community and not the denominational label it chooses to wear".[29] The Indonesian scholar Nurcholish Madjid (1939–2005) used to stress in his exegesis the importance of sura 2:62: "Surely they that believe, and those of Jewry, and the Christians, and those Sabeans, whoso believes in God and the Last Day, and works righteousness – their wage awaits them with their Lord, and no fear shall be on them, neither shall they sorrow."[30] In his view, this and other Qur'anic verses show that all non-Muslims who believe in God could be recompensed by paradise. He was convinced that not only Jews, Christians and the mysterious "Sabeans", but also Hindus, Buddhists and adherents of other religions would find grace with God. He thus comes close to Mohamad Shahrour's interpretation of the Qur'anic word "Mu'min".[31] This in some way reflects the reality of Indonesian society. Hamka (Haji Abdulmalik ibn Abdulkarim Amrullah, d. 1981), also an Indonesian exegete, emphasises in his commentary that religious sectarianism, exclusion of other religious groups and attitudes of superiority are far removed from the original aim of religion to attain truth. Those who believe that only they possess the truth and that all others err, will only create strife and will not achieve any good for others. Sura 2:62 aims above all for a peaceful coexistence of all religions.[32]

Sura 2:62 has for some time been interpreted in a fairly inclusivist or even pluralist way. The Bombay-born scholar Abdullah Yusuf Ali (1872–1953) commented on this verse in his translation *The Holy Qur'an. Text, Translation and Commentary* (Sh. Muhammad Ashraf Publishers: Lahore, 1938):

> The point of the verse is that Islam does not teach an exclusivist doctrine, and it is not meant exclusively for one people... Even the modern organized Christian churches, though they have been, consciously or unconsciously, influenced by the 'Zeitgeist', including the historical fact of Islam, yet cling to the idea of Vicarious Atonement which means that all who do not believe in it or who lived previously to the death of Christ are at a disadvantage spiritually before the throne of Allah. The attitude of Islam is entirely different. Islam existed before the preaching of Muhammad on this earth... Its teaching (submission to Allah's will) has been and will be the teaching of Religion for all time and for all peoples.[33]

The official Saudi Qur'an text, along with an English version, was prepared by the King Fahd Complex in Medina in 1990. It used Abdullah Yusuf Ali's translation as well as his commentary with the fairly inclusivist exegesis of sura 2:62. However, the revised edition of the Qur'an, printed in Medina by the same King Fahd Complex in 2009, chose two translators from

Medina and radically changed the explicative commentary. In a staunchly traditionalist and exclusivist note to sura 2:62, the reader was warned that this verse had been abrogated.

A well-known Catholic theologian, Christian W. Troll, comes to a sceptical judgement on the overall merits of Yusuf Ali's stance versus Judaism and Christianity, in spite of the latter's inclusivist tendency:

> What many readers may well object to is that Yusuf Ali repeatedly attributes the fact that Christians did or do not accept key teachings of Islam proposed to them to morally reprehensible motives on their part. Little room is made for honest dissent. In this respect, Abdullah Yusuf Ali's notes remain pre-modern in a negative sense.[34]

Finally, the South African Muslim Farid Esack is determined "to find a space in my own theology for those who are not Muslim, yet are deeply committed to seeing the grace and compassion of an All-loving Creator expressed in the righteous and caring works of ordinary men and women". He also criticises some Muslim movements as "anti-everyone-other-than-ourselves".[35] My impression is that, in general, contemporary Muslim commentators who write in Arabic are much less inclined to admit that Jews and Christians have a chance of salvation than those who write in Turkish, Persian or Indonesian. In the eyes of many Arab mainstream exegetes, the link between the exclusive superiority of Islam, on the one hand, and the certitude that non-Muslims are doomed to eternal damnation, on the other, is obvious. There is also a link between a militant exegesis and *takfir* (charge of unbelief). The comparatively inclusivist position of Muhammad 'Abduh and Rashid Rida toward sura 2:62 was and is, in the eyes of the Academy of Islamic research of al-Azhar, a "deformation" for which only "some heretics" can be responsible.[36]

Let me close this paper with a prediction: new Muslim approaches toward their religion and toward the religions of others will come mainly from Islam in the periphery (India, Indonesia or Malaysia) or from the Muslim diaspora. They will probably not come from Cairo or Rabat, let alone from Mecca or Medina. The person in whose honour we have assembled here and the institution that hosts us both seem to confirm this point.

Notes

1. M. Arkoun, *The Unthought in Contemporary Islamic Thought* (London: Saqi Books, 2002).
2. For a general introduction to the topic, see J. Hick, *Problems of Religious Pluralism*, (London: Macmillan, 1985) and J. Hick and P. F. Knitter (eds), *The Myth of Christian Uniqueness: Toward a Pluralistic Religious Theology of Religion* (Eugene, Oregon: Wipf and Stock, 1987).
3. J. Hick, "Religious Pluralism and Islam" [Lecture delivered to the Institute for Islamic Culture and Thought, Teheran], February 2005. Available at: www.johnhick.org.uk/article11.html (Accessed: 4 February 2011).
4. Y. Friedmann, *Tolerance and Coercion in Islam: Interfaith Relations in the Muslim Tradition* (Cambridge: Cambridge University Press, 2003).
5. I have to thank my student, Dr Jens Bakker (University of Bonn), for pointing out to me the relevant passages in *fiqh* literature.
6. S. J. Samartha, "The Cross and the Rainbow: Christ in a Multireligious Culture", in J. Hick and P. F. Knitter (eds), *The Myth of Christian Uniqueness* (Eugene, Oregon: Wipf and Stock, 1987).
7. U. Günther, *Mohammed Arkoun: Ein moderner Kritiker der islamischen Vernunft* (Würzburg: Ergon Verlag 2004) p. 72; M. Arkoun, "Du Dialogue inter-religieux à la reconnaissance du fait religieux", *Diogène*, 162, 1998, pp. 103–26.
8. M. Q. Zaman, *The Ulama in Contemporary History: Custodians of Change* (Princeton and Oxford: Princeton University Press, 2002), p. 104.
9. Benedikt XVI, *Glaube und Vernunft. Die Regensburger Vorlesung. Vollständige Ausgabe. Kommentiert von Gesine Schwan, Adel Theodor Khoury, Karl Kardinal Lehmann* (Freiburg: Herder, 2006), pp. 20, 70.
10. G. Hasselblatt, *Herkunft und Auswirkungen der Apologetik Muhammad Abduhs (1844–1905) Untersucht an seiner Schrift: Islam und Christentum im Verhältnis zu Wissenschaft und Zivilisation* (Göttingen: Dissertation, 1968).
11. Ibid. p. 44.
12. I. Goldziher, *Tagebuch: Herausgegeben von Alexander Scheiber* (Leiden: Brill, 1978), p. 59. The English translation is R. Patai's.
13. F. Körner, *Kirche im Angesicht des Islams: Theologie des interreligiösen Zeugnisses* (Stuttgart: Kohlhammer, 2008), p. 175.
14. E. I. C. Cassidy, *Ecumenism and Interreligious Dialogue: Unitatis Redintegratio, Nostra Aetate* (Paulist Press: New Jersey, 2005).
15. J. Lumbard, "Qur'anic inclusivism in an age of globalization", in Muhammad Suheyl Umar (ed.), *The Religious Other: Towards a Muslim Theology of Other Religions in a Post-Prophetic Age* (Lahore: Iqbal Academy Pakistan, 2008), pp. 151–162; A. Filali-Ansary and S. Karmali Ahmed (eds), *The Challenge of Pluralism: Paradigms from Muslim Contexts* (Edinburgh: Edinburgh University Press, 2009); J. Hick, *Problems of Religious Pluralism* (London: Macmillan, 1985).
16. D. B. Macdonald, "fitra" in *Encyclopaedia of Islam* 2nd edn, vol. 2, pp. 931–32. Hadith scholars disagree on the meaning of this hadith as well as on the meaning of the word *fitra* in the Qur'an. In 30:30, the Prophet Muhammad is admonished to adhere to a religion, which is God's *fitra*, the primeval and original religion of mankind, the innate and unchangeable monotheistic disposition of mankind. See also M. Yasien, *Fitrah: The Islamic Concept of Human Nature* (London: Ta-Ha Publishers, 1996).
17. R. Gaillardetz, *The Church in the Making: Lumen Gentium, Christus Dominus, Orientalium Ecclesiarum* (New Jersey: Paulist Press, 2006).

18. "Anonymous Christian" (2010), *Wikipedia*, available at: http://en.wikipedia.org/wiki/Anonymous_Christian (Accessed: 4 February 2011).

19. M. Shahreur, *Al-Islam wa-l-iman. Manzumat al-qiyam* (Damascus: al-Ahali, 1996).

20. Ibid. p. 38.

21. Ibid. p. 33f.

22. This book is primarily "about who should *not* be accused of unbelief and clandestine apostasy", cf. F. Griffel, *Al-Ghazali's Philosophical Theology* (Oxford: Oxford University Press, 2009), p. 105.

23. H. J. Runge, *Über Ghazalis Faysal al-tafriqa bayna l-Islam wa-l-zandaqa. Untersuchung über die Unterscheidung von Islam und Ketzerei* (Kiel: Dissertation, 1938), pp. 55–58; F. Griffel, *Apostasie und Toleranz im Islam: Die Entwicklung zu al-Ghazali's Urteil gegen die Philosophie und die Reaktionen der Philosophen* (Leiden: Brill, 2000).

24. A. Christmann, "'The Form is Permanent, but the Content Moves': The Qur'anic text and its interpretation(s) in Mohamad Shahrour's *Al-Kitab wa-l-Qur'an*", *Die Welt des Islams*, 43, 2003, pp. 143–172. On p. 148, footnote 27, A. Zayd's relevant articles in *al-Hilal* (Cairo) are quoted.

25. D. F. Eickelman, "Islam and the Languages of Modernity", *Daedalus* 129, 2000, pp. 129–30, quoted by A. Christmann in "'73 Proofs of Dilettantism': The construction of Norm and Deviancy in the Responses to Mohamad Shahrour's book *Al-Kitab wa-l-Qur'an: qira'a mu'asira*", *Die Welt des Islams*, 44, 2004, pp. 20–73.

26. R. Leuze, *Christentum und Islam* (Tübingen: Mohr, 1994).

27. W. C. Smith, "Idolatry in Comparative Perspective" in J. Hick and P. F. Knitter (eds.), *The Myth of Christian Uniqueness* (Eugene, OR: Wipf and Stock, 1987), p. 64.

28. H. Küng, J. van Ess, H. von Stietencron, H. Bechert (eds), *Christentum und Weltreligionen* (Tübingen: Mohr, 1994).

29. A. Afsaruddin, "The Hermeneutics of Inter-Faith Relations: Retrieving Moderation and Pluralism as Universal Principles in Qur'anic Exegesis", *Journal of Religions and Ethics*, 37, 2009, pp. 331–354.

30. Translation by A. J. Arberry.

31. Johanna Pink, *Sunnitischer* tafsir *in der modernen arabischen Welt: Akademische Traditionen, Popularisierung und nationalstaaatliche Interessen* (Leiden: Brill, 2011).

32. Ibid. pp. 210–11.

33. *The Holy Qur'an* (King Fahd Complex: Medina, 1990), p. 27, footnote 77.

34. C. W. Troll, "Jesus Christ and Christianity in Abdullah Yusuf Ali's English Interpretation of the Qur'an", *Islamochristiana*, 24, 1998, pp. 77–101.

35. F. Esack, *On Being a Muslim: Finding a Religious Path in the World Today* (Oxford: Oneworld Publications, 1999), p. 5.

36. J. Pink, *Sunnitischer* tafsir *in der modernen arabischen Welt* (Leiden: Brill, 2011), p. 209.

The Political, Social and Technological Construction of Understanding: An Essay in Analysis of the Disruptive

Mark Sedgwick

Understandings of religions, like many other understandings, can be analysed in terms of their production and in terms of their reception. The analysis of the production of understandings of Islam is relatively well advanced. Scholars working in the ancient Muslim tradition have been studying the relevant texts for centuries, and scholars working in the contemporary Western tradition have been studying many of the relevant texts, histories and biographies since the nineteenth century. The study of the reception of understandings of Islam is far less advanced. Its contrast with the study of understandings of Christianity in Europe is striking. The study of the work and biography of the Protestant theologians of the Reformation, for example, was really the enterprise of the nineteenth century; modern studies generally focus not on the production of Protestantism but on its reception.

This essay examines the reception of one particular understanding of Islam: that typified by the name of Muhammad 'Abduh. At one point in the nineteenth century, this understanding of Islam appeared to be in the ascendant in Egypt. Today, this is no longer the case. Similar understandings persist and have become more sophisticated but are not in the ascendant. Taking a historical approach and focusing on political, social and technological factors, this essay attempts to explain why.

This essay's inspiration is the work of François Guizot, now remembered principally as a nineteenth-century French prime minister, but also one of Europe's greatest historians. Guizot's work was an inspiration not only for European thinkers such as Karl Marx,[1] but also for 'Abduh, and it is strange that so little attention is paid to it today.

In his *Histoire Générale de la Civilisation en Europe*, published in 1838, Guizot challenged the then standard focus on political history by demonstrating the interrelation between three varieties of history: the political, the intellectual – which he saw as being partly determined by the political but also as helping to determine the political – and the social, which he saw as both determining and being determined by the other two. Marx and his followers emphasised the impact of the social (and especially of the social's economic element) on the political and the intellectual.

This essay retains both Guizot's emphasis on the political as an independent variable and a somewhat Marxist emphasis on the economic element of the social. It does not, however, understand class in purely economic terms. Instead, class is understood in the broader sense of a social group defined both "horizontally" (by economic and occupational factors) and "vertically" (by social and cultural criteria). Among others, Mattei Dogan has argued for this approach, pointing out that most societies are structured in this way:

> A country in which there were only vertical cleavages would lose its unity. If a large number of horizontal cleavages were superimposed without counterbalancing vertical cleavages, the society would experience social unrest. The fabric of a well-established democracy is formed by the weave of cleavages.[2]

Dogan was especially interested in well-established democracies, but his argument holds true for other types of polity.

In addition to looking at the political and socio-economic aspects of the reception of 'Abduh's understanding of Islam, this essay will look at a further variable that neither Guizot nor Marx saw as having much independent importance, but which many recent studies have emphasised in various contexts: media of communication.

The Political

The relationship between 'Abduh's understanding of Islam and political history is relatively easy to explain. Initially, 'Abduh and his understandings were promoted by the political – by the khedive who appointed 'Abduh to his post as mufti, and by Lord Cromer, who sponsored 'Abduh after he lost the support of the khedive. The khedive's exact motives for appointing 'Abduh are not known, but were probably more political than intellectual: an expectation that 'Abduh would be a reliable and efficient administrator. There must also have been, however, an intellectual element, since the khedive can hardly have been ignorant of 'Abduh's general intellectual position. Cromer's support was certainly also politically motivated, but there was evidently an intellectual sympathy between the two men.[3]

Political patronage did not last. First the khedive turned against 'Abduh, as it was felt that he was too close to Cromer, and then Cromer's successor, Sir Eldon Gorst, sought a rapprochement with the khedive and so turned against 'Abduh's former associates, who themselves became opponents of English influence. After a brief period during which some of those former associates and their sympathisers held powerful positions, political power promoted other forms of Islam: nationalist, mobilisational, revivalist. 'Abduh's understanding of Islam, then, has not enjoyed political support in the Arab world for a century. However, variations on those understandings are now beginning to attract some political support in Europe, as well as in Tunisia and, perhaps, Syria.

The political aspect of the story, then, is well known and easily told.[4]

The Social

A similar approach to the one taken below was used in a short article in *MERIP Reports* in 1977 by Judith Gran, to explain two very different attitudes towards women in Egypt: the "pro-emancipationist" and the conservative. Gran proposed that these two attitudes were "associated with a particular social class and a particular nationalist ideology". The "pro-emancipationist" was "associated with the upper classes and upper-middle classes", with the Hizb al-Umma and the Wafd. "Conservative attitudes", on the other hand, were associated with the lower-middle class, with the Hizb al-Watani, the Society of the Muslim Brothers and the Free Officers.[5]

Although Gran was careful to use the word "associated" (and needed to, since Tala't Harb was an opponent of Qasim Amin in so far as questions of gender were concerned), she also suggested explanations for the associations she had observed. Men of the upper classes and upper-middle classes benefitted from Egypt's trade links with the West, Gran suggested, and as such they were especially receptive to Western values; as time passed, the sphere of their wives' activities expanded. The men of the lower-middle class, in contrast, suffered economically from those same links, and became more hostile to the West and to Western values. As they moved from household-based artisanal production to employment outside the home, the sphere of their wives' activities decreased.[6]

Gran's economic explanation is interesting but not wholly convincing, and may be open to the charge of "crude materialism" made in another context by Eric Davis. In the context of studies of radical Islamism, Davis has described Gran's type of approach as "anaemic":

> Ideology is either viewed in terms of crude materialism or in terms of psycho-social needs. In one instance, it is a reflection of class interests ... and in another, a reflection of ... social strains ... This means that the internal structure of Islamic radical thought, causes underlying its changes over time, its emotive power, and the political constraints and advantages it bestows on its adherents are never fully discussed.[7]

The present essay, however, is limited in its ambitions. It does not aim to investigate the ideology or understandings of 'Abduh or of his heirs, on which much work has already been done. It does not aim to investigate the emotive power of those understandings, which might be an interesting project. It does not examine the relationship between ideology, economic interests and psycho-social need. It merely assumes that such a relationship exists, and looks at socio-economic factors underlying changes in ideology over time by establishing a correlation between changes in classes and changes in predominant understandings of Islam.

The Classes that Welcomed Muhammad 'Abduh

Initially, 'Abduh's work appealed to at least two groups, one in Egypt and one in Syria. These groups can be seen as a single class and understood as a social group defined both vertically and horizontally. Why 'Abduh's work appealed to these two groups is not difficult to see, but it falls beyond the scope of this essay, which is more interested in the fact of the association of particular understandings with particular classes, and in the consequences (not the causes) of that fact.

One of the groups to which 'Abduh's work evidently appealed was the group to which he himself belonged, along with his closest associate, Sa'd Zaghlul, and other members of the Muslim Benevolent Society to which both 'Abduh and Zaghlul devoted much time in the 1890s.[8] The second group was that for which 'Abduh initially composed his *Risalat al-tawhid* ("The theology of unity"): young men studying at the Sultaniyya, an ambitious modern school in Beirut that aimed to rival the European and American schools that had recently proved so successful.[9] 'Abduh's understandings may also have appealed to other groups: he was, for example, clearly appreciated by that section of the Egyptian general public which attended his Azhar lectures. We know little about this public, however, save that it was numerous, educated and included Christians.[10] This does not give us enough to go much further.

The class in Egypt to which 'Abduh and Zaghlul and their friends on the board of the Muslim Benevolent Society belonged was associated more with the ṭarbush than the turban. Its typical member was a lawyer or a judge – and 'Abduh had of course been a senior judge in the National Court system before becoming mufti. Vertically, it was defined by its familiarity with European languages, thought and culture on the one hand, and by its attachment to Egypt on the other. Horizontally, it was defined by its growing prosperity: this was the small Egyptian professional class that had emerged to serve the modern state that had been established during the nineteenth century. The social origins of its members were often modest, but their rise put them in touch with the highest horizontal levels, as Zaghlul's marriage to Safiyya Fahmi (daughter of Prime Minister Mustafa Fahmi) indicated.

The group found at the Sultaniyya was similar. It was defined vertically in exactly the same way that the Egyptian group was: on the one hand, by familiarity with European languages, thought and culture. This familiarity was one of the main objectives of the Sultaniyya. On the other hand, the group was defined by its attachment to the Syrian version of the Ottoman order: this, again, was one of the main objectives of the school, and the main reason for establishing an alternative to the foreign schools in the first place. It was, in 'Abduh's own words, the group that, having learned modern European science and philosophy, might look at the ignorance of the Muslim 'ulama' and turn away from Islam, regarding it as "a kind of old *thawb* [garment] in which it is embarrassing to appear".[11] The horizontal definition of the group is less clear. The school educated some children of the Syrian elite, including seven members of Jerusalem's Husayni family,[12] but cannot have been a purely elite school, as the children of the elite were hardly numerous enough to fill an entire school.

The two groups, then, seem to belong to the same class: the modern but patriotic professional upper-middle class. This conclusion is similar to that reached by Gran. In fact, Gran traced the "pro-emancipationist" attitude to women via this class, from 'Abduh to graduates of the American University in Cairo during the 1970s.[13]

The Disruptive Class

The professional upper-middle class is important in any society, save, perhaps, in extremely authoritarian states of the sort established in some places during the twentieth century, which did not really have such a class. It was especially important in Egypt at the end of the nineteenth century because it was a rising class, increasing in numbers, wealth and power. In other words, it was a "disruptive" class. The adjective is borrowed from economics, where it is commonly applied to technology; for example, a "disruptive technology" is a new invention that dramatically undercuts or destroys the market for an existing product.[14] Classic examples include the railway and the motorcar, which destroyed the stage-coach business and made riding horses a leisure activity; the digital watch, which made mechanical watches a luxury item; and the personal computer, which entirely destroyed the typewriter. A disruptive technology makes waves in a way that other technologies do not. Likewise, the new professional upper-middle class made waves in the late nineteenth-century Egyptian and Arab world. Most importantly, it disrupted the 'ulama', destroying their former semi-monopoly of intellectual life, and taking over many of their sources of income and prestige. As a disruptive class, it was in a position that allowed it easily to take the initiative. Faced with disruption, established classes (like established technologies) are, by definition, on the defensive: weakened, and with little room for manoeuvre.

Conceived horizontally, the Egyptian upper-middle class also included, in the words of Juan Cole, "government officials, large landowners, foreign investors, and large-scale entrepreneurs".[15] Of these, the professional upper-middle class and the class of foreign investors were the most disruptive. Large landowners were important but not disruptive, as they had been important since the days of Mehmet 'Ali Pasha, or perhaps since the eighteenth century.[16] Foreign investors, though disruptive, were not of great importance for Islam. Large-scale entrepreneurs – for whatever reason – do not feature in any accounts of the intellectual life of the period, save occasionally as donors.

The disruptive class of 'Abduh's time was closely allied with the then disruptive medium of communications: the newspaper. As the work of Ami

Ayalon and others has shown, there was a remarkable overlap between the group that had gathered around Jamal al-Din al-Afghani in the 1870s and the creation of an independent political press in Egypt.[17] In later years too, the newspaper was important to 'Abduh: not just *Al-Manar*, but also *Al-Mu'ayyad*, edited by 'Abduh's friend, 'Ali Yusuf.[18] Why a disruptive class is often associated with a disruptive medium (today's such class is associated with the new media, including social media) is a question that falls beyond the scope of this essay. It does, however, often seem to be the case. Newspapers were the perfect medium for the transmission of 'Abduh's work – they reached other members of his class, and they encouraged relatively thoughtful, non-professional reading.

The Rise of the Urban Working Class and of the Lower-Middle Class

The professional upper-middle class and the newspaper remained important in Egypt after 1921, but neither remained disruptive. The early twentieth century saw the emergence of two new disruptive classes as the urbanisation of Egypt began. Slightly more than a third of the population of Cairo in 1907 had been born elsewhere, presumably in the countryside.[19] An urban working class, though small in comparison with the industrial proletariats of European capitals, was developing. The 1907 census reported 280 thousand Egyptians engaged in manufacturing; that of 1917 reported 420 thousand.[20] This presumably reflected the impact of British demand during the First World War. At the same time, a lower-middle class was emerging: school teachers, minor officials and university students. Primary-school enrolment increased from 193 thousand in 1926 to 1.08 million in 1941,[21] and numbers of school teachers increased accordingly. By 1941, there were nine thousand university students in Cairo.[22] Although this was not a substantial number in itself, it was disruptive in a society that had only recently acquired a modern university. Students were especially prominent in later years in the Muslim Brothers, comprising a remarkable 24 per cent of those arrested in 1954.[23]

This lower-middle class was the new disruptive class, sometimes joined by the new urban working class: demonstrations and strikes became a regular part of Egyptian political life after 1919, and especially from the 1930s onwards, led by the lower-middle class (including students) which was sometimes joined by the small urban working class. Joel Beinin and

Zachary Lockman have shown the disruptive impact of these classes on the society and politics of the period.[24]

These new disruptive classes both differed from the professional upper-middle class horizontally, in terms of their economic position and their relationship to political power. They also differed vertically. They were familiar with European languages, thought, and culture, but superficially so, having in general been educated in Arabic-language schools rather than the French- and English-language schools favoured by the upper-middle classes. They knew of European culture and thought, but only in outline.

The work of 'Abduh and his immediate heirs was evidently not particularly attractive to either of these new disruptive classes. The question of why this should be, once again, falls beyond the scope of this essay. We can deduce that it was the case partly from the fact that the most vocal and destructive opposition to 'Abduh during his final years as mufti had come from *Himarat Munyati* ("Donkey of my desire"),[25] a newspaper whose readership probably came from precisely these classes. That 'Abduh's work did not appeal to them can be deduced by looking at the understanding of Islam that they clearly *did* find attractive: that of the Muslim Brothers. The Muslim Brothers are sometimes seen as linked to 'Abduh through Rashid Rida, but the analysis of Muhammad Haddad – that Rida's claim to be 'Abduh's successor served to legitimise him but lacked much real basis – is entirely convincing.[26] 'Abduh and the Muslim Brothers had some points in common, of course, but the differences between them are surely more significant.

Hasan al-Banna was a school teacher, and thus of the lower-middle class. The leadership of the mature Society of the Muslim Brothers had a similar profile: that of what Richard Mitchell has called "an emergent and self-conscious Muslim middle class".[27] The Muslim Brothers was not, however, just a lower-middle class organisation. Its first members in Ismailia were workers, and in later years the Muslim Brothers emphasised that most of its members came from the working class.[28] The nascent workers' movement, where the Muslim Brothers competed with the Communists, was one of the Muslim Brothers' major fields of activity.[29] However, in Cairo it was reported to be "the student, the civil servant, the teacher, the clerk and office worker" that predominated, as well as "the professional in their Western suit".[30] Since the quality of the suits is not described, it is hard to say whether their wearers came from the older upper-middle class or the newer lower-middle class – most sources fail to make a distinction between the two. Although there were probably some members of the upper-middle class in the higher ranks of the Muslim Brothers, the lower-middle class seems to have been the most important group, just as the urban workers were the most important group in the active base. Certainly some members of the Muslim Brothers were from rural areas, but though they were of some significance numerically, peasants were almost impossible to organise, and so were not of major importance.

The Muslim Brothers were not, of course, equally attractive to all: some members of the lower-middle and working classes also evidently contented themselves with conventional Islamic practice, while others adopted the relaxed understanding of religion that modernisation theory would predict.[31] The Muslim Brothers, however, were the new and notable expression of the understanding of Islam favoured by the disruptive classes of the period, just as the Islam of 'Abduh had been a new and notable expression in the earlier period. In a sense, the Muslim Brothers' understanding of Islam was in itself disruptive. And one of the established features of life it could not help but disrupt was the understanding of Islam typified by 'Abduh.

During this second period, additional media emerged. Egyptian Radio started broadcasting in 1934 and Studio Misr was established in 1936, marking the beginning of a major Egyptian film industry. The Muslim Brothers themselves may be considered a sort of medium of communication: the mass movement is also a communications network. These new media are, once again, associated with the new disruptive classes. The case of the Muslim Brothers has already been considered. Radio audiences came predominantly from the same classes, with the urban working class listening to the radio in cafés, and the lower-middle class perhaps even affording to buy a radio set for use at home.[32] The low price of cinema tickets also placed film within the reach of the urban working class.[33]

The Muslim Brothers' communications network promoted understandings of Islam very different from those proposed by 'Abduh. Unlike the newspaper, the mass movement did not encourage reflection; rather, it encouraged conformity. The other two media were probably neutral. The black-and-white musical is not a suitable medium for intellectual or religious purposes; Egyptian Radio remained under British control until 1947,[34] and its religious broadcasting was presumably conservative.

The changed class and media configurations in Egypt during the first half of the twentieth century explain the changed status of 'Abduh's understanding of Islam during that period. Whatever else happened, 'Abduh's understanding could hardly have maintained its ascendency against the rise of the new disruptive classes. Heirs of 'Abduh such as Taha

Husayn and 'Ali 'Abd al-Raziq were active in this period, but their voices were in competition with new voices: not just the old voices of the 'ulama' that 'Abduh's voice had competed with, but the new and powerful voices of the Muslim Brothers.

The Late Twentieth Century

Two further class shifts during the twentieth century may be identified. One of these is the period of Arab nationalism typified by the presidency of Gamal Abdel Nasser; the other is the period of the Islamic resurgence.

The greatest difference between the period of Arab nationalism and the periods that preceded it was political, not social. The Nasserite state established a monopoly on information and the public sphere, giving little scope for dissenting voices. This was not so much a period in which a new disruptive class appeared, then, as one in which earlier socio-economic developments reached a political conclusion. The two disruptive classes of the early twentieth century finally replaced the dominant classes of 'Abduh's time, the lower-middle class leading and the urban working class following. The urban working class had continued to expand, growing significantly during the Second World War in response to the needs of the British war effort as well as to the decline in imports,[35] though this expansion was in some ways temporary: the end of the Second World War brought mass unemployment to those whom the war effort had employed.[36]

The class origin of Nasser's army officers and senior officials is unclear, but this group did not represent a new class. They portrayed themselves as lower-middle class – in order to "solidify their populist base", according to Joel Gordon – but may not always have been as lower-middle class as they seemed. They were not of the upper-class and upper-middle-class backgrounds that had dominated the military academy before 1937, but some were the sons of architects, engineers or judges.[37] In horizontal terms, they formed a new class as they established control over Egypt and began to enjoy the fruits of that control, but in vertical terms there was less change. Such change was delayed until subsequent generations. Power and prosperity did not make the dominant class of Nasser's Egypt any more interested in European thought, unless Soviet ideology can be considered European.

Whatever understanding of Islam was attractive to the urban working class of the 1960s, the Nasserite state's monopoly on information in the public sphere meant that the Islam that mattered was that of the section of the lower-middle class that had taken power. As is well known, this might almost have been the understandings of the Muslim Brothers, to whom many of the Free Officers had once been close. In the event, however, politics intervened: the logic of the consolidation of power led to the suppression of the Muslim Brothers, and thus to a silence in which the voices of the 'ulama' unexpectedly re-emerged.

The period of Arab nationalism was a continuation of the first period of the twentieth century. The period of the Islamic resurgence that succeeded it marked a new discontinuity, and coincided with the emergence of new disruptive classes and of a new medium. It coincided also with the weakening of the Nasserite state.

The new disruptive classes in Egypt were public-sector employees and the urban poor. The urban poor had always existed, but the size of this class increased dramatically during the last decades of the twentieth century, as the total population of Egypt grew dramatically, driving urbanisation. Cairo grew from about three million inhabitants in 1947 to about eight million in 1976,[38] and then to probably more than fifteen million by the end of the century. Some of this increase reflected natural growth, but much – perhaps most – came from rural migration. Reliable statistics do not exist, but it is clear that many or most of these new Cairenes lived in poverty.

By many measures, Nasser's industrialisation programme was not a success, but it did create a massive new class of public-sector employees, to which university students can be added. The nine thousand university students of 1941 were in the lower-middle class; the three and a half million Egyptians who graduated from universities and technical and vocational institutes during the eight years between 1983 and 1991[39] were in a different class, both horizontally and vertically.

As a result of employment guarantees dating from the 1960s, government and public sector employment, as well as the tertiary education certificates that gave access to them, grew steadily until, during the 1980s and '90s, about a third of Egypt's labour force was working for the state in one way or another.[40] As the drain on the state budget of paying the salaries of so many unproductive employees grew, inflation was allowed to erode the real value of wages, which had never been high, and which fell by some 60 per cent between 1981 and 1986, and continued to fall thereafter.[41]

Horizontally, these two disruptive classes differ: public-sector employees and students enjoyed slightly more economic security and social status than the urban poor. Vertically, however, they are more uniform, characterised by poor education and, probably, an inherited religious practice and piety, often of rural origin. That their education was poor is clear. It was the result of a dramatic increase in enrolments without commensurate increases in funding, and of a shortage of qualified teachers – the pre-existing educational system was relatively recent and not without its own problems in the first place. The millions of university graduates, let alone the others, had in most cases only limited knowledge of their own thought and culture, and minimal familiarity with European languages, thought and culture. The inherited religious practice and piety are harder to establish, but are suggested by casual observation.

Again, the work of 'Abduh and his successors was not attractive to the new disruptive classes, and again, this can be seen by examining what understanding of Islam *was* attractive. The Islam of the Muslim Brothers clearly retained some appeal, though of course the Muslim Brothers of the 1990s differed in many ways from the Muslim Brothers of the 1930s. This time, the most striking development was the spread of public piety. Congregations at Friday prayers spread beyond the mosque into the street. For women, the hijab became almost universal. The period also saw the rise of radical Islamism, but it was the hijab, not the suicide bomb, that became the norm.

Like the Muslim Brothers of the earlier period, public piety during this period only represents a particular understanding of Islam – that is, it is a "proxy" for that understanding, not the essence of that understanding. And like the Muslim Brothers themselves, it was not universal. Given human diversity, an essence might be hard to find, and no understanding is universal. Like the understanding of Islam of the Muslim Brothers, however, the understanding of Islam for which public piety is a proxy was disruptive, and was hardly compatible with the understanding of Islam typified by 'Abduh.

Two new media are associated with this period. One, appearing towards the end of the twentieth century, was satellite television. Its impact was delayed. The other, appearing at the beginning of this period, was the cassette tape: this, as in Iran, was highly disruptive, circumventing the state's media monopoly, and proving a highly efficient medium for the circulation of revivalist preaching. Recorded preaching, like the communications network of the mass movement, encourages conformity more than reflection.

The Islamic resurgence in Egypt was part of a global pattern of religious resurgence which went beyond the Muslim world. This global religious resurgence is a matter for another essay, but it will be noticed in passing that it too may have a class basis. In Turkey, it is associated with the emergence of new disruptive classes that successfully challenged the established secularist elite; in Israel, it is associated with the end of the dominance of the Ashkenazi socialist elite; it may be associated with similar developments in India and in the United States.

Conclusion

This essay reveals some fundamental reasons for the continuing limited enthusiasm for the understandings of Islam which 'Abduh's name typifies; understandings which had once been in the ascendant, encouraged by the political, the disruptive classes, and the disruptive media of the late nineteenth century. This does not mean, of course, that no other factors were at work. Lest this essay seem overly deterministic or even simplistic, it should be emphasised that its purpose is not to advance a complete explanation of the waning of receptivity to 'Abduh's variety of understanding, but rather to draw attention to certain factors which have had a significant impact on Egyptian intellectual history.

Before 'Abduh, the understandings of the 'ulama' reigned almost unchallenged. What challenges there were – from the Wahhabis or the Senussis, for example – came from the periphery and had little impact and no political support in places such as Cairo. The rise of a new professional upper-middle class, familiar with nineteenth-century European culture and thought, was associated with the ascendency of new understandings of Islam. These also received some political support, first from the khedive and then from Lord Cromer.

During the first half of the twentieth century, as Cairo's working class and lower-middle class grew, it was the Islam of the Muslim Brothers that was ascendant: not universal, but certainly disruptive, as were the classes with which it was associated. This understanding did not receive political support, but neither did the understanding of 'Abduh receive the political support it had once received. During the second half of the century, political changes resulting from the establishment of the Nasserite state suppressed all dissenting voices, whether those of the Muslim Brothers or of the remaining advocates of the understandings typified by the name of 'Abduh.

By the end of the twentieth century, it was no longer the industrial working class and the lower-middle class that were growing, but the urban poor and the class of underpaid public-sector employees. Although there is no proxy for the understanding of Islam of these disruptive classes as obvious as the Muslim Brothers was for that of the second period, public piety seems the best proxy, and again this was disruptive, and again the disruptive understanding was very different from the understandings typified by 'Abduh. Public piety was not promoted by the Egyptian state, but it did receive some political support in the sense that the state was careful not to affront the pious. For example, the state's failure to intervene in support of Nasr Abu Zayd was, in a sense, a form of political support for his opponents.

Whatever the merits of 'Abduh's understanding of Islam, an understanding that appealed to the newspaper-reading upper-middle class of the 1890s could hardly be expected to appeal to the industrial worker listening to a member of the lower-middle class at a meeting of the Muslim Brothers in 1941, nor to a member of the urban poor listening to a cassette tape of a revivalist preacher in 1991.

Notes

1. L. Siedentop, Introduction to François Guizot, *The History of Civilisation in Europe* (1864) trans. W. Hazlitt (London: Penguin Books, 1997).

2. M. Dogan, "From Social Class and Religious Identity to Status Incongruence in Post-Industrial Societies", *Comparative Sociology* 3, no. 2 (2004), pp. 166–67.

3. This section and the following paragraph are distilled from my book *Muhammad Abduh* (Oxford: Oneworld, 2009).

4. Those interested in pursuing this aspect further should consult K. Dalacoura, *Islam, Liberalism and Human Rights* (London: I. B. Tauris, 1998), pp. 76–106, where an argument similar to that made in this essay is developed, placing somewhat greater emphasis on the political. I read Dalacoura only as this essay was about to go to press.

5. J. Gran, "Impact of the World Market on Egyptian Women", *MERIP Reports* 58 (June 1977), p. 3.

6. Ibid. pp. 3–7.

7. E. Davis, "Islamic Radicalism in Modern Egypt", in *From Nationalism to Revolutionary Islam*, ed. Said Amir Arjomand (Albany: SUNY, 1985), p. 138.

8. L. Herrera, "Overlapping Modernities: From Christian Missionary to Muslim Reform Schooling in Egypt", *CIAO Working Paper*, 2001. Available at: http://www.ciaonet.org/conf/mei01/hel01.html (Accessed: 8 February 2011).

9. J. Hanssen, *Fin de siècle Beirut: The Making of an Ottoman Provincial Capital* (Oxford: Oxford University Press, 2005), p. 174.

10. M. Sedgwick, *Muhammad Abduh* (Oxford: Oneworld, 2009), p. 84.

11. Muhammad 'Abduh, *Risala al-tawhid* (Cairo: Matba'a al-kubra al-amiriyya, 1897), p. 153.

12. J. Hanssen, *Fin de siècle Beirut* (Oxford: Oxford University Press, 2005), p. 175.

13. J. Gran, "Impact of the World Market", *MERIP Reports* 58 (June 1977), pp. 4 and 6.

14. The term derives from J. L. Bower and C. M. Christensen, "Disruptive Technologies: Catching the Wave" in *Harvard Business Review* 73, no. 1 (January–February 1995), pp. 43–53.

15. J. R. Cole, "Feminism, Class, and Islam in Turn-of-the-Century Egypt", *International Journal of Middle East Studies* 13 (1981), p. 389.

16. P. Gran, *Islamic Roots of Capitalism, Egypt 1760–1840* (Austin: University of Texas Press, 1979).

17. A. Ayalon, *The Press in the Arab Middle East: A History* (New York: Oxford University Press, 1995).

18. It was *Al-Mu'ayyad* who published Muhammad 'Abduh's response to Gabriel Hanotaux.

19. N. Hanna, "The Urban History of Cairo around 1900", in *Historians in Cairo: Essays in Honor of George Scanlon* ed. J. Edwards (Cairo: AUC Press, 2002), p. 196.

20. Z. Lockman and J. Beinin, *Workers on the Nile: Nationalism, Communism, Islam, and the Egyptian Working Class, 1882–1954* (Princeton: Princeton University Press, 1988), p. 38.

21. D. M. Reid, *Cairo University and the Making of Modern Egypt* (Cambridge: Cambridge University Press, 2002), p. 112.

22. Ibid. p. 119.

23. Davis, "Islamic Radicalism in Modern Egypt", in *From Nationalism to Revolutionary Islam* ed. Said Amir Arjomand (Albany: SUNY, 1985), p. 142.

24. Z. Lockman and J. Beinin, *Workers on the Nile* (Princeton: Princeton University Press, 1988).

25. I. F. Gesink, "Beyond Modernism: Opposition and Negotiation in the Azhar Reform Movement, 1870–1911" (unpublished Ph.D. thesis, Washington University, St. Louis, 2000).

26. M. Haddad, "Les oeuvres de 'Abduh : histoire d'une manipulation", *Institut de Belles Lettres Arabes* (Tunis) 60 (1997), pp. 197–222; and M. Haddad, "'Abduh et ses lecteurs: pour une histoire critique des lectures de M. 'Abduh'", *Arabica* 45 (1998), pp. 22–49.

27. R. P. Mitchell, *The Society of the Muslim Brothers* (New York: Oxford University Press, 1993), p. 330.

28. Ibid. pp. 277–78.

29. Z. Lockman and J. Beinin, *Workers on the Nile* (Princeton: Princeton University Press, 1988), pp. 364–65.

30. R. P. Mitchell, *The Society of the Muslim Brothers* (New York: Oxford University Press, 1993), p. 330.

31. "Evidently" because this comment is based on informal recollections of family history by contemporary Egyptians.

32. See, for example, discussion in V. Danielson, *The Voice of Egypt: Umm Kulthum, Arabic Song, and Egyptian Society in the Twentieth Century* (Chicago: University of Chicago Press, 1997), p. 85.

33. Until 1941, when falling real wages made them difficult to afford, and arrangements for cheaper access to *Gone with the Wind* were demanded on behalf of the workers. Z. Lockman and J. Beinin, *Workers on the Nile*, p. 248, note 28.

34. P. Starkey, "Modern Egyptian Culture in the Arab World" in *The Cambridge History of Egypt*, ed. M. W. Daly and C. F. Petry (Cambridge: Cambridge University Press, 1998) vol. 2, p. 424.

35. Z. Lockman and J. Beinin, *Workers on the Nile* (Princeton: Princeton University Press, 1988), pp. 259–62.

36. Ibid. pp. 260–62.

37. J. Gordon, *Nasser's Blessed Movement: Egypt's Free Officers and the July Revolution* (New York: Oxford University Press, 1992), p. 42.

38. Census figures taken from the Institution of Civil Engineers, *Greater Cairo Wastewater Project* (1993), p. 5.

39. R. Assaad, "The Effects of Public Sector Hiring and Compensation Policies on the Egyptian Labor Market", *The World Bank Economic Review* 11, no. 1 (1997), p. 88.

40. Ibid. pp. 86–95.

41. Ibid. p. 92.

Believing and Belonging: The Impact of Religion for "Muslim" Adolescents in a Pluralistic Society – Empirical Findings from Hamburg, Germany

Ursula Günther

> Oddly enough, the paradox is one of our most valuable spiritual possessions, while uniformity of meaning is a sign of weakness. Hence, a religion becomes inwardly impoverished when it loses or waters down its paradoxes; but their multiplication enriches it because only the paradox comes anywhere near to comprehending the fullness of life.
>
> C. G. Jung[1]

Introduction

"Reflexive modernity" or – speaking with Jürgen Habermas – "the post-secular situation" confronts the individual with a radical plurality of meaning, including the challenge of living with the paradox and the end of security-providing certainties presented by a central perspective. In other words: certainties are replaced by possibilities. Polyphony turns out to be the magic word. Unfortunately it does not endow individuals with the necessary tools to deal with plurality in terms of decision-making. The individual is compelled to engage in negotiations, which are accompanied by a permanent balancing, coordination and integration of conflicting interests, loyalties, value and norm systems, and meanings. Processes of reflexive questioning are often innovative since any loss of meaning is accompanied by the development of new visions and patterns of action. The field of religion and religiosity is not excluded from this development – quite the contrary. Processes of pluralisation, among other things, give rise to the questioning of religious or theological monopolies of interpretation, while new perspectives, interpretations and concepts of religious worldviews are negotiated and again put up for negotiation according to the context they face. These processes can often be interpreted as educational (*Bildungsprozesse*) in the sense of a profound transformation of how one perceives the world and the self.

These challenges of modernity – albeit very condensed – are particularly significant for the findings elucidated below. Since the paper is relatively short, two perspectives provide a focus: the first aims to clarify the concepts of religion and religiosity. This will be embedded in the current debates concerning the secularisation thesis and the possibilities offered by the individualisation thesis, since it is in this context that the notions of believing and belonging have been introduced in the last two decades, namely by Grace Davie. However, applying these terms in a "Muslim" context, at least with regard to "Muslim" minorities in "non-Muslim" countries – that is, the context of the study referred to – necessitates some modifications. The second perspective concentrates on the relationship between believing and belonging, still considered two major indicators for religiosity. For that purpose the adolescents I interviewed and their statements will take centre stage. There will also be a brief outline of the research project, accompanied by some insights into the particular context of Germany's "Muslims", illustrated with prominent elements of the discourse.

At this point, the use of the term "Muslim" in quotation marks deserves an explanation: I make the emphasis in order to point out that the notion "Muslim" provides information neither about a person's religiosity (let alone its degree), nor about their adherence to a particular denomination or dogma. "Muslim" includes both practising believers and numerous individuals "who make claims upon a culture, a sensitivity, a spirituality, in other words an Islamic ethos without confining their thought to the dogmatic closure of a single orthodoxy".[2]

Religious Education among "Muslim" Adolescents:
Outline of a Research Project

The findings elucidated below relate to an empirical research project conducted in Hamburg under the current working title of "Religious education among 'Muslim' adolescents in the fields of school and mosque". The approach is an interdisciplinary one: theoretical and methodological prerequisites established by empirical research in the social sciences (the qualitative approach) are applied in order to transform questions that originate in religious studies and the sociology of religion into a research project located at the nexus of education and Islamic Studies. Keeping in mind the ongoing debate about dominant discourses and past and present Western hegemonic ambitions, a temptation that neither intellectuals nor scholars are entirely proof against, especially where "Other" cultures or religions are the subject of their study, post-colonial critique can be deployed to adjust perspectives through critically questioning the implicit and explicit systems and frames of reference. Gender as a research perspective provides an additional analytical framework.

It is beyond the scope of this paper to unfold the entire research project as well as the research process in its methodological details. The following pointers should suffice for depicting the broader context of the project: on the one hand, it is based on thirty-nine interviews with "Muslim" adolescents between the ages of seventeen and twenty-four; on the other hand, twenty interviews with professionals mainly in the field of education, theology, sociology of religion and related areas, both "Muslim" and non-"Muslim". Thirteen of the adolescents are migrants, though only six could recall the experience of migration. The others were either infants or toddlers when their parents fled or left their country of origin. The rest are regarded to have a "family migration background". The importance of this distinction is evident in the following explication. The adolescents represent a wide range of cultures of origin, such as Albanian, Afghan, Algerian, Bosnian, Iranian, Kurdish, Lebanese, Syrian, Tunisian and Turkish, as well as some of bi-cultural origin. Their voices are polyphonic. They offer impressive insights into religious experiences and approaches to religion. Their religiosity varies between rather orthodox readings of Islam, indifference to or outright renunciation of religious issues, agnostic positions, and positions detached from either orthodoxy or dogmatic readings, or outside the bounds of religious institutions. Of particular interest for this paper is the diversity of approaches to religion and/or religiosity beyond dogmatic closure.

The findings of the interviews are counterbalanced with participant observation during Religious Education classes both at school and in the mosque. Furthermore, I will consider the broader context on a national and international level as reflected in the manifold discourses concerning "Muslims" and Islam in Germany/Europe, religion and religiosity in the post-secular situation, as well as the impact on educational concepts. Interviewees were selected using the method of "theoretical sampling", combined subsequently with the "snowball sampling" method.

The research project does not aim to present a typology of religiosity or of approaches to Islam. It focuses on decisive aspects concerning religious education in two fields of education, namely school and mosque, and the approaches to religion for young people that result from this constellation. The second focus consists of the pedagogical priorities in terms of religious education and whether they are innovative or not. Thirdly, the needs and desires that the adolescents articulate themselves are of particular interest. Though this point comes last, its central importance needs to be emphasised: on the one hand, the findings offer a valuable corrective to one-sided or even wrong assumptions about "Muslims" in Germany, while on the other hand the findings illustrate how ideas about Religious Education need to take account of the changing situation of the main stakeholders: the young people themselves. Therefore it is important to investigate whether or not these needs were integrated in the schools' and mosques' concepts, and why. This is necessary for finding out whether they answer the demands of modernity as they are present in Germany while meeting the requirements of a pluriform society.[3] Furthermore, the research project should provide indications concerning the impact of Religious Education by dealing with tradition and "orthodoxy", since for the parents' generation the religious community corresponded to a "place to save the Turkish-Islamic way of life in Germany".[4] This is no longer the case for the third or fourth generations, such as the interviewed adolescents. They are looking for other approaches to religion. This is due to the changing socio-political context as well as their migration background and their ways of dealing with this heritage. All these elements lead to the issue of changing discourses reflecting a different way of searching for meaning in a pluriform society.

It is evident that the findings of qualitative research are not representative. However, they outline tendencies. In our case they provide insights into "Muslim" life in Germany. Although the interviewees do not form a homogenous group, they have a lot in common: at the very least they have to deal with ascriptions and perceptions, and balance conflicting interests, loyalties and multiple forms of belonging in order to find their place in German society.

Religion and Religiosity: Conceptual Remarks

There have been many attempts, theological and sociological, to define the term "religion", and no consensus has been reached. A satisfying definition would address the term in its complete plurality, a demand that appears impossible to meet. Nonetheless, defining the concepts of religion and religiosity must be an indispensable part of any research project, even if the definition falls short of full inclusivity. Its suitability will ultimately be judged in the light of the data generated.

Anyone working with current definitions of religion and religiosity will have to enter the controversial debate surrounding what is known as the secularisation thesis. Detlev Pollack shows that despite massive criticism of this thesis, the empirical data for Europe does not contradict it. Furthermore, he emphasises that secularisation in terms of a universal and global phenomenon due to processes of modernisation has almost been disproven.[5] However, the shift of religiosity into the private sphere does not – at least in Europe – mean a decline in the social significance of religion. This phenomenon is addressed in a further development, namely the individualisation thesis:

> This thesis more or less accepts the theoretical framework of the secularization theory by arguing that the social status or religion within modernity is determined by processes of industrialization, urbanisation, cultural pluralisation, economic growth, rising levels of education and functional differentiation, but it describes other consequences for the role of religion in modernity. While the secularization theory predicts the inevitable stable decline in the social significance of religion as a consequence of processes of modernization, the religious individualization thesis concedes that the traditional churches and church-related behaviours in modern societies have been affected by an obvious decline but they contend that this does not mean a loss of religiousness of the individual. On the contrary, the decline of the established religious institutions goes hand in hand with a rise of individual religiosity.[6]

The individualisation thesis allows us to demonstrate empirically that individual processes of emancipation and a distancing from institutionalised forms of religiosity are taking place in connection to religious orientation today. This is, among other things, the result of individual decisions in the course of the negotiation processes that are part of all pluriform cultural and religious orientations, and the broadening of horizons that modernisation brings. Simultaneously, this reflexive modernity is invariably accompanied by a loss of established certainties. Fixed points of orientation seem irretrievably lost, forcing the individual to make decisions.

Many authors, amongst them again Detlev Pollack, state that the secularisation thesis and the individualisation thesis are the most appropriate ways of describing the religious changes in Europe.[7] One should point out here, though, that when experts in the field speak of religious changes in Europe, they are usually referring to developments in Christian churches. The dimensions of religion and religiosity that Charles Glock developed in 1962 and that are still widely applied, refer to Christianity as well as the corresponding model of an institutionalised and established religion, which also implies a degree of dogmatic rigour.[8] We can assume that each implicit frame of reference is equally based on a Christian model. Comparable studies of "Muslims" are very rare, be they of majority- or minority-"Muslim" societies. In those that do exist, such as Germany's 2008 *Religionsmonitor* which was followed by a representative study dedicated to "Muslims" in Germany as the second largest religious group in the country, religious change is not the focus of attention.[9] Needless to say, a focus on change would question the dominant discourse about Islam and "Muslims" still considered to be a homogenous entity with a high degree of religiosity.[10] Research with regard to religion and "Muslims" usually concentrates on the importance of traditional religious settings and formal aspects of religiosity. The German *Religionsmonitor* also refers to the five dimensions of religiosity as developed and defined by Glock:

1. The subjective dimension, which describes religious experience.
2. The ideological dimension, corresponding to agreement with specific tenets of faith.
3. The ritual dimension, relating to adherence to certain religious practices and strictures.
4. The intellectual dimension that corresponds to basic knowledge.
5. The dimension of social consequences that is equivalent to the impact of religiosity on social relationships and interactions.

This approach can be characterised as rather normative and orientated towards formal aspects of religiosity, and it has an immediate impact both on questionnaires and on expected results. However, it is still the prevailing basis for studies of religiosity, regardless of the above-mentioned processes of reflexive questioning also observed in religious matters. To what degree the proponents of this understanding of religiosity should face the reproach of perpetuating rather than productively deconstructing orthodoxies – be it consciously or unconsciously – remains to be seen. The importance this approach is accorded in empirical research mirrors the implicit frame of reference of Western scholars, namely the "Christian Occident", as well as the need for theoretical and conceptual shifts, particularly in the context of "Muslim" approaches to religion and religiosity. In other words: the context of institutionalised or organised religious communities needs to look more closely at individuals claiming to be religious without a particular affiliation to a specific religious community, organisation or dogma. And this does not necessarily mean that these individuals do not articulate any feeling of belonging at all. Such a shift of perspective will reveal that institution is not a *sine qua non* of a sense of belonging. This at least is expressed implicitly by many of the adolescents interviewed in the study referred to in this paper.

Institutionalised or organised religion – particularly in the societal context of a religious minority – implies in most cases readings within dogmatic closures that claim to represent the majority of the supposed adherents. Research projects that adopt this claim of monopoly of definition without questioning it risk being one-sided and more descriptive than analytical, quite beside the fact that a huge part of the religious reality of "Muslims" is not taken into consideration. This is true not only of Germany and societies where "Muslims" represent a minority, but also of societies where "Muslims" form the majority. An inclusive approach is promising, since it both reflects dominant discourses, and broaches the issue of the secularisation dilemma and changes of attitudes and approaches responding to socio-cultural change. Simultaneously, it tries to explain current trends in religiosity and religious consciousness outside the context of organised religious communities and therefore outside the bounds of religious institutions.

The challenge to be faced when leaving the institutional or organised context of religion or religious communities is to develop a wider understanding of religion and religiosity that embraces the two major principles of belonging: firstly, belonging to a concrete religion, religious institution and community offers elements of prescribed belief and formalised patterns of behaviour. Secondly, and generally neglected in research dealing with religious phenomena, a sense of belonging without prescribed paradigms and the support of a religious institution or community, but with the support of belonging to a particular culture, spirituality or ethos, as mentioned above.[11] This element of belonging refers to individual approaches, forms and realisations of religiosity.

The adjective "religious" can refer to both religion and religiosity.[12] John Cumpsty's broad understanding of religion provides a helpful incentive while searching for different approaches, taking into consideration the changing elements concerning believing and belonging, since his focus leaves open whether religion takes place within or without the bounds of religious institutions:

> Religion is the quest for, maintenance or realization of belonging to an ultimate-real. The ultimate-real being that to which the individual most feels the need to belong in order to secure, give meaning to, or otherwise enrich his or her existence.[13]

Introducing the notion of belonging leads us to a broader understanding of religiosity taking into consideration different layers of meaning. Religiosity can refer to a fundamental ability:

> to arrive at an integrative meaning relation of your own life and the world in such a way that both your own personality and the world are experienced and interpreted in the awareness of a transcendent reality, which we usually refer to as God.[14]

Religiosity can also refer to the individual realisation of the way in which religious elements are integrated into the life of an individual. This is closely related to the development of the personality of an individual and must be understood as a dynamic process. This dynamism and flexibility extend to all the dimensions of this religiosity that develop over time. Hemel's approach does not follow the rather normative and formal dimensions developed by Glock. Instead, he takes into consideration current trends concerning religiosity and religious consciousness outside the context of religious communities. This leads us to the following dimensions of religiosity that can be connected with learning tasks from an educational perspective:

1.   Religious sensitivity that ties into the task of religious perception.
2.   Religious content that ties into the task of religious education in the

sense of a differentiated religious view. Here, the cognitive level is addressed.

3. Religious communication that ties into the ability to express and communicate religious content.

4. Religious expression that ties into the task of finding and assuming your individual religious role.

These four dimensions give no indication of the relevance that religious issues have in an individual's life. He or she may well possess considerable religious sensitivity and communicative competence without necessarily according religion a central role in his or her life. It is the dimension of the religiously motivated life that indicates the individual relevance of religion.

By raising the question of the difference between religiosity and faith, Hemel touches on a crucial, current issue, especially as it is becoming increasingly clear that this difference does not lie in content but in identification, that is, the expressed sense of belonging to a defined faith community. The idea of faith then takes on a dual reference of its own: it refers to individual beliefs as well as social belonging. According to Hemel, the impact of the context of and the identification with a religious community is important for "believing religiosity" (his phrase) or a concrete religiosity, without neglecting the individual features of this religiosity. Although the notion of religiosity mainly covers the relation to transcendence, it is not necessarily linked to a particular religious denomination. Obviously, this interpretation can easily apply to religions other than Christianity. However, my data proves that some modifications concerning the understanding of believing are necessary, particularly bearing in mind the approach of the individualisation thesis. The notion of believing should not equate a believer's identification with a concrete religious community. This aspect will be covered by the notion of belonging. This is the moment to mention Grace Davie, since it was she who coined the phrase "believing without belonging" (BWB).[15] The necessity of such a modification is evident when we are comparing the adolescents beyond dogmatic closure with those who strongly identify with a religious community affiliated with a mosque and who emphasise the necessity of following all obligations. This is the major feature of their self-image of being a "Muslim" or being religious. Most of these adolescents were rather shocked by other "Muslim" peers, as well as Christians, professing to be religious without practising or respecting religious obligations. Many of them even showed tendencies to condemn such behaviour. Understanding the notion of believing as Hemel does would mean for the "Muslim" context that a rather orthodox perspective is projected onto the "rest". Furthermore, the understanding of belonging should be enlarged, since many adolescents mention the feeling of belonging. They do not refer to a particular community or mosque association but to the aspect I mentioned earlier, quoting Mohammed Arkoun: they refer to a culture, a sensitivity, a spirituality; in other words, an Islamic ethos. However, before we shift our attention to the adolescents themselves, we should outline the German context in order to conceive of the reality – including the one hidden in discourses – that these youths face.

"Muslims" in Germany

In 2011, about 3.6 million "Muslims" live in Germany, representing approximately 4 per cent of the total population. More than 2 million of them are of Turkish descent. Of the Germans from "Muslim" families, 35.5 per cent were born in the country (679 thousand), with the number of German converts, many of them through marriage, accounting for an estimated additional 100–120 thousand.[16] German citizens with a migration background from "Muslim" countries, estimated at around 1 million, are not counted in official statistics. It is illuminating how statistics on "Muslims" in Germany (or other European countries) are generated: they are based on immigration statistics which take the country of origin for a presumed religious orientation. Numbers of adherents of other religions immigrating from "Muslim" countries, naturalised German citizens from "Muslim" countries, and conversions to Islam taking place in Germany are estimated.[17] Thus, descent, not religious practice or belief, is used as the statistical reference. Nonetheless, "Muslims" as a group are assumed to be unusually religious and observant.

This quotation from a "Muslim" working professional regards the realities of "Muslim" life in Germany:

> I think I got the epithet 'Muslim' on 9/11. Before that day, I was all kinds of things: the Austrian in Germany, the Persian in Bavaria, the Bavarian, the Indian in Bavaria, all kinds of things people imagined I might be. But I became a Muslim in people's eyes on 9/11, everybody asked me about it afterwards. [...] After 9/11 being 'Muslim' is more important. When I was invited to a conference as an expert of the Max-Planck-Institute, I never was perceived in the past as: 'She is telling this because she is "Muslim"'. They never asked me questions

like 'you as "Muslim", what do you think?' I don't like these questions since I think which part of my speech did invite you to ask my religion. As if as 'Muslim' you have to feel different. Yes, I feel things because I am 'Muslim', or because my parents are 'Muslims', or because I have the impression Islam is attacked by 'Muslims' and non-'Muslims' and I have to protect it somehow. The impression that you have to defend this part of identity, I think this is something many people of 'Muslim' societies share. That their reactions are not really due to the fact that they are 'Muslims' but that they are immigrants, and as such part of a minority. It is an awareness of minorities. They always remind you that you are different, that you don't belong to them.[18]

These words aptly illustrate a sense of discomfort expressed either explicitly or implicitly by many interviewees, and not just by young people. This discomfort goes hand in hand with a sense of the need to justify themselves for having a "Muslim" identity. Two examples show this: firstly, the increasing tendency of "Muslim" organisations in Germany to formally distance themselves from terrorist actions through public statements; secondly, the question of what "the Muslims" think of Germany's Basic Constitutional Law is gaining greater prominence in the public arena. At the same time, these words – just like the quotation marks around the word "Muslim" – indicate the effect of ascribed identities and labels on the continuities, fractures and reconstructions of self-constructed identity.

The trend in discourses on "Muslims" is also an important indicator of opinions in mainstream society. Here, one must bear in mind that, however paradoxical it may seem, no matter how detached from reality many discourses on "Muslims" may be, they are nonetheless real, even if they are located outside the reality of "Muslims'" lives and often at odds with their state of mind and environment. The importance of the social and socio-political context as a matrix for self-definition and the reformulation of self-images must not be underestimated. If we look more closely at the development of the public discourse that labelled those arriving in Germany as "Muslims", we get the following picture: the term "guest worker" (*Gastarbeiter*) was coined after 1955, when religious affiliation was still off the radar. In the 1970s, the expression was replaced by "foreign worker" (*ausländischer Arbeitnehmer*) or "foreigner" (*Ausländer*). Here, too, the actual origin and religion of the worker in question are irrelevant, most likely due to the prevailing assumption at the time that they would return home after a number of years. In the course of the 1990s, the focus shifted away from the status of worker to that of religious affiliation. "Muslims" became the centre of attention. This shift went alongside a broadening of focus that moved "Muslim" women into the realm of public debate. They entered the picture in a very real sense. At the same time, a newly vigorous discourse on integration – connected with changes to citizenship law that culminated in the immigration law of 2004 – focused on migrants and especially "Muslims".[19] Rising numbers of naturalisations meant that "Muslims" increasingly took part in the discourse themselves, as newly German former foreigners, Turks, migrants or fellow citizens of foreign nationality (*ausländische Mitbürger*) – a contradiction in terms that nicely mirrors the internal contradiction of German attitudes; and could no longer simply be categorised as "other". What nevertheless made them "other" was their religion. Overall, we can state that the power of the public discourse on "Muslims" in Germany that views them as observant adherents of a strictly normative reading of Islam goes almost unchallenged. Even German citizenship offers no protection from being labelled with the stigma of the cultural and religious "other". The power to assign this definition lies with the majority, which keenly guards this presumed right. This seems to be one explanation of why citizenship alone does not make German "Muslims" equals.

Believing and Belonging: the Adolescents' Voices

The opening question in the interviews was, "What does it mean for you to be a 'Muslim' today?" It goes without saying that the findings do not provide answers, but they might deliver insights into "Muslim" adolescents' realities, and at best they will contribute to a better or different understanding of recent dynamics regarding religion and religiosity, particularly believing and belonging, two of the most important indicators for religiosity.

The following quotations represent only a selection of the adolescents interviewed, namely those whose access to religion and religiosity lies beyond the bounds of dogmatic closure and outside the bounds of religious institutions. Interestingly, this group includes many who have experienced migration. This differentiation between migration experience and a family migration background has already been touched upon. The data indicates the importance for changes in the relationship between believing and belonging as it refers to both a changed context and a horizon of experience not shared by German-born "Muslims". Migration not only changes the social context but also the terms of belonging. Social pressures to conform and control are decreased, and this fosters a more individual religiosity and private faith. This phenomenon is not limited to Germany and "Muslims". It has been observed by Grace Davie in the UK for the Christian context.[20] Belonging no longer consists of social considerations and the balance of advantage and disadvantage, but expresses individual acceptance of the fundamental beliefs of a concrete community arrived at by personal choice.

This kind of development is exemplified by the statement of twenty-one-year-old Faiz. He was strictly observant when he came to Germany from Afghanistan aged fourteen, and considered himself very religious during his first two years in the country:

> My parents did not force me, but the environment did. When I didn't go to mosque, it was not my father who asked me about it but the neighbour or the teacher. These are things I don't like, now. Now it's totally different for me, I live in an open society, nobody can force me to do something I don't want to do [...] At some point I read my second book, I became a little more critical, I struggled with myself about what faith and religion really is. Why does religion exist? What is it good for? Why should we be religious? Why do I pray and for whom? Why should I get up at five in the morning and pray? If you are 'Muslim' and take religion seriously, you get up. I also got up for two years and then I stopped, I didn't see the sense any more and I said to myself: 'You're still a "Muslim", but you stay critical, you can critically address Islam and religion as a whole, you don't need to take the one way prescribed by Mohammed or another prophet, i.e. you must find your own faith that you can stand up for and that fulfils you. You don't need to follow anyone.' My father allowed me to think the way I want to. I am free to think that this religion has those advantages and that one those and to choose the third. That is my affair. I can't say whether I am religious, I can't say whether I have a religion, I can't say whether I'm an atheist.[21]

Faiz, like many other youths with a migration background, speaks of an experience that second- or third-generation immigrant children did not have: that of a social presence of Islam, an Islamic lifestyle and a social "normality" of Islam, in which almost everyone is "Muslim". In this case, the change in social context created new opportunities. This also applies at the mental level, where a consciousness opens new spaces and leaves behind the idea that religion, tradition, faith and habit need be conterminous.

In many cases this consciousness results in changes in believing, which is now characterised by a more individual approach to religion and a new critical perspective. Belonging, too, is changed in the course of this process of negotiation and individual decision. Finally, the relationship between believing and belonging shifts. However, there are differences from the findings of studies that investigated processes of religious changes unfolding in Europe, particularly religious changes concerning Christianity, such as the one described by Grace Davie. In the interviews, it emerged that belonging refers not only to a specific religious community, usually a mosque association in the German context, but also to a broader sense of being "Muslim" and belonging to a community of persons who share a common culture and spirituality without a concrete adherence to a specific orthodoxy. In Faiz's case, the decision of how to position himself in terms of believing and belonging is not yet complete.

Kali, an eighteen-year-old Tunisian who came to Germany at the age of sixteen, provides an example of belonging in the sense of belonging to a common culture, without believing in concrete tenets of faith. She says:

> I really don't know whether I'm a 'Muslim', but I am – as my father puts it – culturally 'Muslim'. I don't practise any religion, but I observe Ramadan, that is more out of habit. Tradition is something else. I don't know if that means much but I know I would never convert. It's the religion I have. Despite everything that has happened recently, even if I'm not observant, it is still my religion.[22]

Kali expresses a particular aspect of belonging by fasting during the month of Ramadan, although her fasting does not refer to the tenets of faith. Obviously she does not feel the ambivalence an outside person might perceive. On the contrary, she copes very well with it. Later she states vigorously, albeit with regret, that she will never enter a mosque, since she would be obliged to wear a headscarf: something which she finds unacceptable.

Many of the youths used expressions such as "if you believe it in your heart" or "if your heart is pure" to describe their "Muslimity". They distance themselves from notions of orthodoxy and orthopraxy and are highly critical of the mosque associations that structure religious practice in Germany. This type of community and this form of belonging seem to be of no importance for their faith or their experience of a "Muslim" normality. They re-appropriate the Qur'an and the traditions and, in the process, reinterpret them to fit their specific context. Their reinterpretations can take on different shapes, though as a rule without recourse to the religious authorities present in mosques. Instead, they use modern communication media to access information on religious questions, to research literature and to exchange views. They meet to read the Qur'an together in the spirit of a *halqa*, and many of them, especially women, consciously practise positively modern forms of *ijtihad*. It is interesting that they do not allow polarities and paradoxes to disconcert them, but instead use the potential that they find in their position between two simultaneous systems of reference, which they do not experience as contradictory.

"If you believe it in your heart, you don't need to prove to anyone that you are a faithful 'Muslim', because as a believer I know that God sees it," as nineteen-year-old Hamburg-born Tyson puts it.[23] Such a position can be helpful when you are trying to understand inner conflicts such as the question of whether to wear a headscarf and risk losing an apprenticeship or whether to delay this choice and ensure yourself a better education. Another matter is adherence to prayer hours as well as school work despite the fatigue this entails. In most cases, religious considerations take second place to other concerns, and are frequently put off until later in good conscience.

I will close this section with a statement from twenty-two-year-old Leyla, who comes from a mixed German–Turkish family and was socialised in both cultures and religions. I choose this example not least because the number of people from bicultural and bi-religious families is on the increase in Europe's pluriform societies, and we should expect interesting developments in terms of believing and belonging. Leyla represents a specific form of hybrid identity emerging through cultural and religious cross-interferences in the immediate environment, holding considerable transgressive potential that goes hand in hand with a renewal of established structures.

> Well, part of my identity may be that I think of it as equally valid because I feel I somehow always feel bicultural, bilingual, that everything has two sides, that may be part of my identity. Maybe that is also the reason why I can always fit it together, somehow, that gives me a bit of freedom maybe, just to say I can believe this way [...] Yes, that is my freedom in a way. [...] But it has always been like that, I wasn't aware of it, but it gives you a good feeling to somehow be comfortable with yourself.[24]

This approach to believing and belonging should hold quite a few challenges to theologians and other guardians of orthodoxy.

Conclusion

The selected adolescents' voices are almost self-explanatory. They point out simultaneously that an intensive empirical study of young "Muslims", who are sadly neglected in many academic contexts, can contribute to an overdue shift in perspective on the importance of Islam in the context of reflexive modernity, and the changing needs of believing and belonging. The few examples presented above show that it is not only religion that influences people, but that people also shape religion and believing. Even though the frame of reference might be unclear or does not correspond to what would be expected from "Muslims", we should take the phenomenon into consideration.

Furthermore, the data proves that in many cases educational processes are taking place, a concept introduced and developed by empirical research on education that might open up a horizon for further research:

> Education (*Bildung*), (i.e. what educational action should enable and promote) can be understood as a process of basic transformation of the way persons behave with regard to the world and to themselves. *Bildung* in terms of such transformations always then takes place (or better: can take place) when humans make experiences that cannot be coped with using the existing means and options. Formulated differently: *Bildungs*-processes exist in the emergence of new forms, new figures of world views and self concepts in dealing with issues that cannot be processed by the existing figures of world views and self concepts.[25]

This kind of transformation also affects forms of believing and belonging, and reveals dynamics which could be interpreted as an individual integration of the achievements of intellectual modernity as well as a way of coping with a radical plurality of meaning. This kind of integrative effort is often experienced as emancipatory by the adolescents themselves.

The ultimate consequences this will have on theological and educational issues are as of now impossible to predict. One thing is certain, however: even though secularisation processes will not displace individual religiosity, we must expect significant changes that both Islamic theology and "Muslim" associations and organisations will need to react to; ideally, in the spirit of modernity, in a multi-perspective approach that will put an end to the shadowy existence of the paradox and that will lead us to a more comprehensive vision of religious change.

Notes

1. C. G. Jung, *Psychologie und Alchemie* (Olten: Walter Verlag, 1972), 7th ed., trans. R. F. C. Hull and B. Hannah as *Psychology and Alchemy* (London: Routledge, 1953) vol. 12, p. 18.

2. M. Arkoun, "Contemporary Critical Practices and the Qur'ān", in J. Dammen and McAuliffe (eds.), *Encyclopaedia of the Qur'ān* (Leiden & Boston: Brill, 2001), vol. 1, pp. 412–431.

3. Using the Dutch term *pluriform* and its derivatives like *pluriformity* instead of *plural* and *pluralism* follows a new trend within the social sciences. Instead of referring to the diversity of certain systems, such as religious communities, it refers to a general diversity extending even to within these systems, such as the coexistence of members of a religion with a secular attitude and members with a rather orthodox one. With the term *pluriform*, one avoids emphasising the implicit homogeneity of systems that are not genuinely homogeneous.

4. G. Klinkhammer, *Moderne Formen islamischer Lebensführung. Eine qualitativ-empirische Untersuchung zur Religiosität sunnitisch geprägter Türkinnen der zweiten Generation in Deutschland* (Marburg: Diagonal-Verlag, 2000), p. 283f.

5. See, for example, D. Pollack, "Religious Change in Europe: Theoretical Considerations and Empirical Findings", *Social Compass*, 55 (2), 2008, pp. 168–186.

6. D. Pollack and G. Pickel, "Religious individualization or secularization: an attempt to evaluate the thesis of religious individualization in Eastern and Western Germany", in D. Pollack and D. Olson (eds.), *The Role of Religion in Modern Societies* (New York, London: Routledge, 2008), pp. 191–220, here p. 191.

7. D. Pollack, "Religious Change in Europe: Theoretical Considerations and Empirical Findings", *Social Compass*, 55 (2), 2008, pp. 168–186.

8. C. Y. Glock, "On the Study of Religious Commitment", *Religious Education* (Research Supplement), 42 (July–Aug), 1962, pp. 98–110. See also chapter two in C. Y. Glock and R. Stark, *Religion and Society in Tension* (Chicago: Rand McNally, 1965).

9. M. Rieger (ed.), *Religionsmonitor 2008: Muslimische Religiosität in Deutschland* (Gütersloh: Verlag Bertelsmann Stiftung, 2008).

10. This corresponds exactly to the findings presented in the survey: "Muslims" in Germany are religious and practising to a very high degree in contrast to their Christian fellows. For further details see Rieger, *Religionsmonitor 2008*.

11. J. S. Cumpsty elaborated on religion as a belonging while emphasising in his approach to religion the importance of a sense of "belonging to the ultimate-real", in other words a "cosmic belonging" that does not necessarily correspond to a sense of belonging to a particular community. Nevertheless he underlines the importance of religious institutions since they have the power to generate a sense of belonging. Although they might have a negative effect on a cosmic sense of belonging, and although there has been a decline of adherents in recent decades, religious institutions still offer a frame for a community. This is also true of "Muslims" in Germany and their affiliation to a particular mosque. See J. S. Cumpsty, *Religion as Belonging: A General Theory of Religion* (Lanham et al.: University Press of America, 1991), pp. XIV and 404ff.

12. The following thoughts are inspired by an essay by the Catholic theologist and educator Ulrich Hemel and by the voices of the interviewed adolescents. For Hemel see Ulrich Hemel, "Glaube und Religiosität: eine theologische Reflexion", in *Theo-Web*, 1 (2), 2002. [Online document: http://www.theo-web.de/zeitschrift/ausgabe-2002-02/hemel1.pdf] (Accessed 6 August 2009.)

13. J. S. Cumpsty, *Religion as Belonging*, p. XIV.

14. Hemel, "Glaube und Religiosität", p. 33.
15. See G. Davie, *Religion in Britain since 1945: Believing without belonging* (Oxford and Cambridge: Blackwell, 1994).
16. Statistisches Bundesamt 2010, microcensus 2009. More than 16 million individuals with a migration background live in Germany. They make up almost one fifth of the population (i.e. 19.6 per cent). According to estimates for the coming decades every fourth individual in Germany will have at least one parent with a migration background or a parent with another nationality other than German.
17. See, for example, R. Spielhaus, "Religion und Identität. Vom deutschen Versuch, "Ausländer" zu "Muslimen" zu machen' *Internationale Politik*, March, 2006, pp. 28–36 [Online document: http://ku-dk.academia.edu/RiemSpielhaus/Papers/260240/Religion_und_Identitat] (Accessed 28 March 2011); or J. Klausen, *Europas muslimische Eliten: Wer sie sind und was sie wollen* (Frankfurt/Main: Campus, 2006), p. 14.
18. Expert interview with Dr Nadjma Yasseri, Iranian and Austrian nationality, conducted in Hamburg, 16 April 2007.
19. See Spielhaus, *Religion und Identität*, p. 29.
20. G. Davie, "Believing without Belonging: Is this the Future of Religion in Britain?", *Social Compass*, 37 (4), 1990, pp. 455–469.
21. All names have been changed to preserve anonymity. Interview conducted 8 December 2006, Hamburg.
22. Interview conducted 6 January 2007, Hamburg.
23. Interview conducted 20 June 2008, Hamburg.
24. Interview conducted 11 December 2007, Hamburg.
25. H.-C. Koller, "Bildung als Entstehen neuen Wissens? Zur Genese des Neuen in transformatorischen. ildungsprozessen", in H.-R. Müller, W. Stravoravdis, (eds.), *Bildung im Horizont der Wissensgesellschaft* (Wiesbaden: VS Verlag, 2007), pp. 49–66, here p. 50.

Veiling and Unveiling Muslim Women: State Coercion, Islam, and the "Disciplines of the Heart"

Malika Zeghal

As emphasised in the works of Mohammed Arkoun, theological and interpretive questions surrounding Islam must be read – as in any other religious tradition – not only as textual issues but also as political stakes.[1] This is particularly true of the concept of reform (*iṣlāḥ*) in the history of Islam, a concept at the heart of the Prophet's mission: "I only came to reform" (*in urīdu illā al-iṣlāḥ*) (Qur'an 11:88). *Iṣlāḥ*, or the operation of re-ordering, correcting and transforming necessitates an interpretation of the current situation and a vision for a future one. Its object may be the individual as much as the collective entity or institution. As such, the enterprise of reform is not only the aim of individual religious reformers who write essays about the purpose and methods of reform, but is also among the interests and concerns of the modern state that crafts policies.

This paper will focus on the ways in which, in Tunisia, the postcolonial state elites, in their projects to build a cohesive nation and to reform their society, referred to Islam to mould specific domains of life, and developed, in the process, theological lines of reasoning and justifications. Among countries of the Middle East, independent Tunisia's governments are often seen as having enacted policies shaped by a strong secularist ideology and having relegated Islam to the private sphere.[2] Contrary to this common analysis, the case of Tunisia illustrates that far from being "secularist" states circumscribing religion to the private domain, authoritarian Middle Eastern states often defined themselves as "Muslim" states and produced public theological definitions that were instrumental in their enterprises of reforming their societies and defining their national identity. One privileged domain of intervention for Middle Eastern postcolonial reformist state elites is that of "the woman question". In Tunisia, the nationalist movements as well as the post-independence state elites aimed to improve women's rights. Their project defined women as full participants in the nation and helped define all Tunisians, men and women, as citizens who shared the same national values, in particular their attachment to the new state.

The "womans question" revolved around issues of gender equality in education, gender segregation, veiling, and polygamy and, as explained by Deniz Kandiyoti, "coincided with a broader agenda about 'progress' and the compatibility between Islam and modernity".[3] Kandiyoti describes two sides to the debate on women in the Middle East: on the one hand, a "secularist elite" with "progressive aspirations", and on the other hand those who "expressed in Islamic terms" a "hankering for cultural authenticity."[4] This article will show that this dichotomy, whereas used by many actors, was also highly unstable and dissimulated deep convergences between these two positions. The progressive aspirations of nationalist and state elites were framed within a repertoire of cultural authenticity that often included Islamic terms. As for the Islamist trend that emerged in the 1970s, its activists also articulated their conception of the "woman question" in the vocabulary that the nation state elites had built to speak of the "Tunisian woman" as a virtuous citizen.

The period I will concentrate on starts in the late 1920s – when Tunisian nationalism against French occupation had matured into an organised movement – and ends in 1987, the year that marked the end of Habib Bourguiba's regime. I will focus on Bourguiba's shifting position on veiling, to help us understand how the veil became a complex and multilayered political issue in Tunisia over the course of the twentieth century. I will emphasise Bourguiba's continuities with Muslim reformist thought – in particular the Tunisian al-Tahar al-Haddad's writings since the 1930s – and, perhaps more surprisingly, how the Islamist writings of the 1980s echoed the Bourguibian tropes about the Tunisian woman. In its reforming enterprise, the Tunisian independent state articulated a language and conception of religion that moulded themselves into older reformist tropes. These tropes were later re-appropriated by Islamist movements in their political opposition to the Tunisian government. If the political positions of state representatives and

Islamist opposition are conspicuously different on subjects such as the veil, they nonetheless operate under the same regime of thought regarding the relationships between nation, religion and reform. I will argue that the opposing views of the state's elite and Islamists on the subject of women's dress are in fact formulated within similar reformist vocabularies regarding female subjectivity, the place of women in the world, and the intentionality of religious norms. I will argue that state elites and Islamist activists shared similar conceptions of "religion" as circumscribed domains of interpretation and efficacy, which were in many ways comparable to the reformist ideas of the first part of the twentieth century.

1. The Controversy of 1929: Nationalism, Westernisation, and the Islamic Identity of Tunisia

On 11 January 1929, the francophone Tunisian nationalist newspaper *L'Etendard Tunisien* published an article by Habib Bourguiba, then a young nationalist activist and member of the old Destour party. The publication of the article marked one of the heated moments of the "battle of the veil". This article was Bourguiba's account of a meeting held at L'Essor, a literary socialist club, where he participated in a fiery debate with Tunisian and French socialists – among them Muhammad No'man and Joachim Durel – about the wearing of the veil by Tunisian women. In this debate, Bourguiba defended the wearing of the face veil, in particular against "a certain Miss Ourtani",[5] whom he accused of belonging to a group of "heroic apostles of dress feminism" supported by the French socialists.[6] Referring to another Tunisian young female activist, he added not without irony: "Ms. Menchari, a charming young lady, came, her face uncovered, and wanted to move us about the fate of her unfortunate sisters who are deprived of air and light and live under the triple weight of ignorance, gossip and the veil."[7] Manoubia Ouertani and Habiba Menchari were indeed young feminist activists who, as early as 1924, had defended the possibility of unveiling, and they themselves had appeared unveiled in public.[8] If Bourguiba stood against them, it was not because he was against *sufūr* (unveiling); it was because he wanted to publicly defend what he called "the Tunisian personality" (*al-shakhsiyya al-tunisiyya*) against the coloniser's intent to Westernise Tunisia, which had been under French protectorate since 1881. Indeed, for the Bourguiba of 1929, the veil could not be abandoned as French socialists proposed, because it was a signifier of the identity of a nation under occupation. Hence, to defend the veil was to perform an act of resistance against the coloniser. Bourguiba interpreted the wearing of the veil as a symbol of the nation, rather than as a religious obligation ordered by the revealed texts or a freely chosen way of dressing that resulted from voluntary and deliberate individual choices by women.

Bourguiba did not see the veil as a religious prescription. He considered it a custom (*'āda*) that had been anchored in the practices of the national community for a long time and that had become part of the mores of his society. Bourguiba's justification made the veil the symbol of a collective tradition rather than an individual preference.

> We have in front of us a custom anchored for centuries in our mores, evolving with them at the same pace, which is quite slowly. The mores of a group, be it the family, the tribe or the nation, are what is most inherent, the most irremediably subjective to this group and what distinguishes it from all others. In a word, it is what makes its proper individuality, its personality ... Is it in our interest to hasten the disappearing of our mores? ... My response, given the very special circumstances we live is without doubt: No![9]

Bourguiba defined the concept of "personality" (*shakhsiyya*) again, when addressing Mr Durel:

> The unity of territory, the community of belief, language, customs, past, the joys lived together, the failures and humiliations experienced, all of this according to Mr. Durel does not contribute to create, between the children of this country, any sentiment of solidarity, no idea of patria. ... Reality is entirely different. This is because the action of the individual on customs is extremely limited.[10]

To build a nationalist ideology, Bourguiba drew upon the concept of a "national personality", which he defined as a community of shared practices, sentiments and dispositions that crystallised through history and could be symbolised by a custom such as women's wearing of the veil. The practice was so firmly anchored that it could not be eliminated by the efforts of a few individuals. Bourguiba would later affirm – and attempt to show – that it would take the power of an independent state to uproot the custom of veil wearing.

His reaction contrasted with other opponents to unveiling, who argued that by abandoning the veil, Tunisian women would lose their respectability and fall into immorality and prostitution, subsequently leading Tunisian society into corruption. They had described the veil as a woman's "religious duty".[11] But for Bourguiba, the veil was not a device protecting women and defending the integrity of a certain moral order. He saw it as a social problem, even while defending its subsistence. In his 1929 article, he wrote, dismissing the veil's religious meaning: "I believe that it is relevant to look at the subject from a social point of view, the only point of view that presents an interest."[12]

In the words of Bourguiba, the veil was the sign of women's "unconscious atavism", but it was the veil of the colonised, and as such, it had to remain:

> The day when the Tunisian woman, going out unveiled, does not experience the strange impression that is as a scream of revolt coming from her unconscious atavism, on that day, the veil will disappear by itself without danger, because what it will be the symbol of will have disappeared. But for the moment, we are not there yet. The best proof of this is that at the end of the meeting, none of the Muslim ladies who came to listen dared to throw their veils.[13]

However, in his 1929 article he had already hinted at the necessity of unveiling in a society that had become independent, an idea that he developed later during his presidency: "Evolution must happen, otherwise, it is death. It will happen, but without a break, without a rupture. We must maintain in the perpetual evolution of our personality a unity through time that can be continually perceived by our conscience."[14] Ms Ouertani had thrown off her veil in a dramatic gesture during the debate at L'Essor. Bourguiba recognised that in principle the gesture was legitimate, and even a question of life and death, but he also warned that it was premature.

Whereas Bourguiba described the veil as an element of the Tunisian personality, another Tunisian reformer, al-Tahar al-Haddad (1899–1935), who studied at the Zaytuna between 1911 and 1923 and frequented the reformist milieus,[15] developed a notion of the veil as an obstacle to women's participation in public life, announcing Bourguiba's later shift of viewpoint. One year after the 1929 debate at L'Essor, Haddad published the controversial book *Our Woman in the Shari'a and Society*.[16] This book is relevant for my argument not only because it contains a justification for unveiling that Bourguiba would reassert after independence, but also because it deploys a line of reasoning about Islam as a potent religion (*dīn*) with a deep and positive impact on people's lives. This idea of religion as an instrument of social change and progress became instrumental for reformists who wanted to link projects of improving women's status with Islam and was redeployed by Bourguiba in the context of the postcolonial authoritarian state.

In the preface of his polemical book, Haddad wrote a long meditation on Islam and its role in social reform:

> The reform of our social condition is necessary for all aspects of our life (*wujūh al-ḥayāt*), and in particular for what touches our existence in life (*wujūdinā fī al-ḥayāt*). I see with certainty that Islam is not an obstacle against reform (*iṣlāḥ*) as the accusations proclaim. On the contrary, it is the religion relevant for reform (*dīnuhu al-qawīm*), and the inextinguishable source of reform. As for the decline of the Muslim world, it has no other cause than superstitions and customs that we have grown to like over a long time.[17]

Haddad saw Islam as an intrinsic source of vitality. Islam was "the eternal book of life and the regulating principles for useful work" (*dustūr al-ʿamal al-nāfiʿ*).[18] He made Islam a set of "regulating principles" (*dustūr*) that would prove to be "useful". The use of the word *dustūr* was not politically neutral since the old nationalist Tunisian Destour party (*al-ḥizb al-ḥurr al-dustūrī*) had been established in 1920, demanding the drafting of a constitution for Tunisia. For Haddad, who had become a member of the Central Committee of the Destour in 1923, Islam had a social and political role to play in order to provide guiding principles for social life. In addition, for Haddad and Muslim reformers of his time, Islam's meaning had to be recalibrated if it were to define the principles guiding social life. Hence, it was important for them to explain what Islam said as well as what it did not say.

On this basis, Islam's functionality in life could be established. There was a double purpose in Haddad's enterprise of reform, which could be generalised to individual and state reformers of his as well as later generations: first, a principle of delimitation of the faith's meaning, and second, a process of importing this meaning to the real world. There was therefore at the same time a limiting aspect (the circumscribing of meaning through a specific interpretive orientation) and an expanding one (the implementation of this meaning in society). Haddad, who was examining what Islam said and did not say about women, believed that in order to reform society in the light of the principles of Islam, it was necessary to sift out social practices that did not belong to the religion. Prescriptions such as polygamy or the face veil were not "inherent to the religion".[19] He distinguished between "the essence"[20] of Islam and the prescriptions that could disappear without harming Islam. For

Haddad, laws had two essential aims: "noble morality and the person's vital needs".[21] This was because Haddad saw the Qur'an as intrinsically related to life (*ḥayāt*); not only was Islam to be a constant source of life, but also "the [Qur'an's] shari'a was a result of life evolving, and not chapters formulated in advance to be imposed on life".[22] The revelation had thus been produced in response to questions emerging in everyday life and had been applied in life. Haddad felt that this dialectical relationship between religion and life – which implicitly made religion a humanly mediated set of principles – had to be reactivated.

One should note that Haddad, who had published an earlier essay on the condition of Tunisian workers and who himself came from a poor background, was deeply preoccupied with poverty, which he linked to social backwardness.[23] In *Our Women in the Shari'a and Society*, he describes at length the difficult living conditions of poor families and links this situation to the harsh treatment of women by their fathers and husbands. In these descriptions, Haddad relates misery to the "disorder" of the home.[24] He mentions domestic accidents, unattended children and the disputes between wives in polygamous families. This disorder, according to Haddad, drove the husband to lead a private life out of the home: "the wife, therefore, finds herself isolated in a world of worries and suffering."[25] A reform of family life, in which respect and love between wife and husband would prevail, was therefore seen as the basis for the reform of society. Haddad defines marriage as "a sentiment (*ātifa*) and a duty (*wājib*), the coming together of two people and reproduction (*ta'mīr*)".[26] To extend the idea of sentiment, he quotes Qur'an 30:21 (*Sūra al-Rūm*), which uses the word *mawadda* (love) and describes marriage as a relation of reciprocal trust and intimacy through the idea of "tranquility of the soul with another soul" (*sukūn al-nafs bi'l-nafs*).[27]

Haddad's adversaries fiercely rejected this evocation and public recognition of "sentiment" as a basis for marriage. They identified several reasons for their rejection of Haddad, such as his treatment of Muhammad's prophecy and his imitation of Westerners, if not his "alliance" with Christian missionaries; but one argument stood as crucial: they did not favour the public deployment of sentiments produced by the visibility of women's uncovered bodies in society. Shaykh Ibn Murad, a high-ranking scholar from the Zaytuna University, in his response to *Our Women*, addressed Haddad:

You find repugnant the education we give to the Muslim girl on the basis of the reserve (*ḥayā*) we teach her and that is one of the branches of the faith. You claim that it kills sentiment (*āṭifa*). Let this sentiment die ... Let us bury this sentiment and not raise our daughters on adornment (*tabarruj*).[28]

After independence, Bourguiba followed Haddad in his attempt to mould a new female public persona. Through his own public relations with Tunisian women, he often exemplified a public intimacy showcasing a public persona of "the Tunisian woman" and what her virtuous behaviour should be. Indeed, Bourguiba did not produce a liberal conception of the role of women. He rather envisioned a shift that the Tunisian woman had to experience – from a position of seclusion and isolation to a position from which she could communicate with the world around her. Women were expected to participate in the public arena, and this participation proceeded from the construction of family as based on reciprocal relationships and shared sentiments between husband and wife. Bourguiba later wrote in his justification for the 1956 Personal Status Code:[29]

> The family is the basis of society. It lacks all happiness and harmony if it is not founded on a man and a woman who are united by love and respect ... With our new reform, we do not only want to elevate the woman's level, but we want also to elevate the level of the Tunisian family.[30]

Hence, according to both Haddad and Bourguiba, the progress of society was irremediably linked to a reform of the family, of the woman's role and status in it, leading to her integration in a public world of reciprocal relationships.

Haddad describes the face veil (which he calls at times *ḥijab*, at others *niqab*) as the device wrongly used to protect men and women from temptation: a "material barrier",[31] the "greatest separation between man and woman that prevents them to choose one another when they want marriage"[32] and "a social protection against evil".[33] His critique takes a symbolically harsh tone when he writes: "There is not that big a difference between the *niqab* the woman uses to cover her face to prevent debauchery, and the muzzle that we put on a dog so that it does not bite the passers-by."[34] For Haddad, the veil conjures the idea of separation, closure and lack of trust, which prevents a woman from opening up to the world and in particular from having access to knowledge, be it the knowledge of her future husband, technical and scholarly knowledge or her very consciousness of the world.

Therefore, unveiling is an act by which a woman can access awareness and knowledge: rather than being imprisoned in the home, her body must be located in the world to allow contact with society. Haddad also denounces segregation between a husband and wife at home, strangely relating this issue to the wearing of the veil, which in principle was not worn at home among family members: "The use of the veil has led the husband to lead a private life (ḥayāt khāṣṣa) outside of his home, a life that women do not know."[35] This absence of a shared experience – or private life – between husband and wife could not logically be related to the wearing of the veil. The veil was in fact, in the work of Haddad, a metonymy for the broader problem of gender segregation and female seclusion, which were the themes that most preoccupied Haddad. The husband's absence produces an "abyss of death"[36] for the family and a life of "debauchery", "immoral activities, drinking, gambling and other distractions" for the husband.[37] Haddad also relates the wearing of the veil to what he sees as problematic sexual practices that occur with gender segregation: "It is well established that hiding women from men has been one of the main factors in the spread of homosexuality, lesbianism and onanism."[38] Hence, not only will unveiling integrate women into social life, but it will also provide true intimacy in the home and reinvigorate the relationships between men and women within their families.

While Haddad's project of improving the status of Tunisian women was based in part on the idea of liberty (ḥurriyya), his essay does not recommend individualism and freedom to choose any type of dress. He did not defend a Western liberal conception of women, and while he saw the movement of unveiling as "triggered by European civilisation", he was against a simple imitation of European ways.[39] He was impressed by the level of education of European women, and wanted Tunisian women to emulate them in this regard, but he also considered western influence as harmful: "our sick society ... is under the onslaught of a transformation that we do not understand and that completely assimilates us into a European trend dominating our current situation. We can only emerge alive from this ... if we cling to our inherent strength."[40] Islam, he argues, is the religion of freedom (dīn al-ḥurrīya), but Islam "accepts only the servitude towards Allah".[41] Although Haddad defends unveiling, "I will only accept emancipation in the limits of the law and morality."[42] Women will have to learn how to manage their home, which should be for them a "function" (waẓīfa) and not a "prison".[43] The goal of their emancipation is to repair the "pain and injury" (alam wa jurḥ) that is felt by women as well as men, not the realisation of a liberal type of society.[44]

2. "A Strong State Deeply Rooted in the Hearts": How Can a State Shape Individual Preferences?

While Haddad was an individual thinker and scholar of Islam, Bourguiba was a political activist who became a statesman. Early in independent Tunisia, Bourguiba took the reins of the state and authoritatively imposed reforms on Islamic institutions: he standardised the legislation related to family matters with the codification of personal status law in 1956, closed down the University of Zaytuna, and nationalised the Habous (religious endowments). In this paper I do not intend to evaluate Bourguiba's policies towards women in their effects on Tunisian social life, but rather, I attend to the subtle meanings deployed by Bourguiba when he dealt with the question of the veil, and to the personal proximity he built with Tunisian women to mobilize them in favour of the new Tunisian state. The ideas he developed with regard to the status of women were very close to Haddad's, but during these reforms, Haddad's name was not officially mentioned. Haddad had died young and politically isolated, his book having become the object of the ire of prominent 'ulama' of the Zaytuna.[45] Bourguiba imposed his reforms authoritatively, and perhaps did not want to take the risk of invoking such a contentious figure as Haddad.

Echoing the writings of Haddad, often word for word, the president of Tunisia shifted his earlier position on the veil and tried to persuade Tunisian women to unveil. His general views on the veil did not change: it was still a reproachable custom, the weight of which could not be lifted by mere individual efforts. However, the context had changed: a strong state was now presiding over the destiny of the Tunisian nation, and this state was robust enough to uproot such "atavistic" practices as the wearing of the veil. Within the larger context of state authoritarian reforms of religious institutions, Bourguiba attempted to convince Tunisians of the legitimacy of unveiling in his speeches as well as in his public performances, during which he unveiled Tunisian women in the streets.

In a speech on 5 December 1957, Bourguiba tackled a combination of issues that demonstrate the close relationship between reform, the strength of a state apparatus and the building of an emotional relationship between the state and its subjects. He developed arguments about the state's power of persuasion, the attachment of Tunisians to that state, and the question of the veil. He linked "the country's prosperity and the individuals' liberties" to the existence of "a strong state, deeply rooted in the hearts".[46] At this time, French troops were still evacuating the south of Tunisia. Bourguiba, the

Council's president since 25 July 1957, was still affirming his power: "I know that my words are listened to, that they have an effect and that my directives are followed."[47]

The metaphor of "a state deeply rooted in the hearts" expressed Bourguiba's desire for a direct and close relationship between the state and the Tunisian people. The moulding of a personality for a nation was possible only through state institutions: "There is one essential condition to safeguard a people's personality. It is necessary to have political power."[48] The highest representative of the state was also attending to the deepest emotions of Tunisians. He wanted them not only to feel emotionally attached to their nation – which they had become already – but, more deeply, to have at heart the best interests of the institution of the state. In a sense, women, more than men, were to illustrate the emotional attachment of Tunisians to the Bourguibian state, through the physical proximity Bourguiba built with them in public performances, as I will describe. This physical proximity was infused with a sense of hierarchy and emotional attachment. At the end of his speech, Bourguiba introduced the issue of women under the rubric of "social problems", as he had done in 1929, and mentioned resistances to his enterprises of persuasion regarding the veil.[49]

> We have been informed of satisfying progress in the movement that liberates the Tunisian woman from the veil. Nonetheless, it seems that there is still some resistance. I would like the public opinion to understand exactly what our aim is with this reform. Statistics reveal that sex crimes are decreasing. It is remarkable that the cases that are still occurring precisely only implicate those young women who are raised within traditional biases and in seclusion.[50]

As in Haddad's book *Our Women in the Shari'a and Society*, the veil and women's segregation were related in Bourguiba's speech to immoral and criminal behaviour, through his reference to sex crimes. In the same speech, the veil became "a horrible rag that has nothing to do with religion".[51] Unveiling was not imposed through a law by Bourguiba at that time, and nothing close to legal dress codes was put in place in Tunisia until at least 1981. Rather, the Bourguibian strategy was a subtle mix of pedagogy and legal change. However, Bourguiba also considered direct coercion. From the same 1957 speech:

> At the social level, we understand the repugnance of aged women to abandon an ancient habit but we can only regret the obstinacy of

parents who constrain young women to wear the veil to go to school. We even see civil servants go to work rigged in this horrible rag. We continuously repeat that it is abandoned in Muslim countries and that it has nothing to do with religion.[52]

He continued with implicit threats of coercion:

Parents should understand that we want the good of their children and that it is not suitable to stand against an important reform. They better not push us towards the means of constraint that we have refused to use so far.[53]

The iṣlāḥ (reform), supported and implemented by the state, assured the "protection" of the "virtue and honour" of women, and was to be "more efficient than the protection of a miserable rag".[54] These statements were repeated over the years, in continuity with the metaphors of life and death Bourguiba had used in 1929 and that were present throughout Haddad's essay.[55] In a 1959 interview in the Tunisian magazine *Faiza*, Bourguiba described the veil as "a sinister shroud that hides the face".[56] He associated state reforms with life and progress, and communicated and implemented them in rather illiberal ways that domesticated religious institutions and produced state pedagogies on the proper bodily conduct. The subtle, ambiguous mix of physical and psychological persuasion with the threat of coercion that Bourguiba used vis-à-vis Tunisian women and their families, is reflected in a documentary about the emancipation of Tunisian women aired on French television on 8 January 1968.[57] The fifty-minute black-and-white film weaves footage of Bedouin women in remote areas, working in their traditional garb, with scenes of women wearing the urban traditional veil (*safsārī*) in the city, and women from the elite wearing sleeveless dresses – "the *bourgeoisie* of Tunis," says the narrator, "who have not worn veils for a long time" – in the presidential palace in Carthage at a reception, being welcomed by President Bourguiba. Scenes of Bourguiba unveiling women on 13 August 1967, Tunisian's Woman's Day, help us to understand state reforms as a practice that deployed itself through direct, local interactions between the state's elite and ordinary Tunisians.

On the side of a road in an unknown location, where Bourguiba is probably visiting a town, Bedouin women in traditional dress are welcoming him. (Properly speaking, their dress is not a veil, since a *safsārī*, a long piece of white fabric attached at the waist and covering the whole body, would be impractical for women working in the fields.) Urban women wearing the *safsārī* are also welcoming Bourguiba, who is guarded by policemen. It is difficult to say whether the crowds have gathered spontaneously. Bourguiba was popular at that time, but these events were closely monitored and served as propaganda to appear in newspapers and on the radio.

To understand the performance of that day, it is important to comprehend the shape and use of the traditional urban veil that Tunisian women wore at that time. The *safsārī* provides some flexibility for a woman to cover and uncover because it is held on the head and shoulders by the hand or teeth rather than by pins. With a quick move of the hand, it is easy to cover and uncover one's face and shoulders.

Facing this crowd of women, Bourguiba embraces several Bedouin women and their children. The women seem spontaneously to go towards him and embrace him. He then directs his attention to a woman in a *safsārī*, and uncovers her head. This gesture seems easy and is not met with any resistance. The woman is holding the *safsārī* over her head with her hand, and the veil's fabric slides down her hair. The woman smiles, but seems slightly embarrassed, and attempts to put her veil back on her head. Bourguiba uncovers her again in the same motion. This series of successive gestures, a silent yet public exchange through physical contact between the anonymous woman in the midst of the applauding crowd and the president, concludes with the woman remaining unveiled. We do not know if she covered herself again when the camera stopped filming, but it is a fact that the wearing of the *safsārī* by Tunisian women became uncommon in Tunisia in the late 1960s and early 1970s, a sign that the changes effected by the Bourguibian elite certainly had an impact on women's dressing practices and gender relations in Tunisia. In the documentary, the atmosphere seems calm, and some policemen guarding the event are smiling and laughing with the women. The president continues to unveil some of the women before leaving with his motorcade. Revealing to the public and the camera the dresses they wear beneath their *safsārī*, the women seem happy. In this moment of public intimacy with Bourguiba, the process of unveiling does not seem to cause them pain. This atmosphere of liberation and happiness hides the enterprise of soft coercion at play in the public performance of unveiling. The unveiled women seem attracted to and entirely persuaded by – even if after slight hesitation – the path of change that Bourguiba has opened to them.

While at the first glance the film does not suggest imposition or submission, the presence of the policemen and the slight hesitation of one woman subtly indicate that the state project of liberation of women was a pedagogical endeavour disseminating new types of disciplines. A change of *habitus* – represented by the "habit" of the veil that was ingrained in body and mind – had to be brought about by the seemingly gentle physical intervention of the state's highest representative. Bourguiba's gesture was to be taken as a model to be replicated by all Tunisian women.

The desire for such a general transformation was resented in some milieus, celebrated in others, but most importantly for the argument of this paper, the desire for transformation was moulded by a state that was progressive in the sense that it aimed for progress, but was not democratic and liberal. The state did not attempt to hide its illiberal nature, and its representatives saw their function as to shape the preferences and behaviours of their population authoritatively. Important elements of patriarchy and conservatism accompanied this vision, which was not necessarily based on a conception of the nation as a collection of free individuals.[58] Family values in particular had to be preserved as well as a sense of morality, echoing Shaykh Ibn Merad's appeal to *ḥayā'* (a sense of modesty). For instance, in 1966, Bourguiba's speech to the National Union of Tunisian Women addressed women on the necessity of adhering to moral behaviour: "one has to know how to discipline her heart."[59] Bourguiba's woman, like Haddad's, was expected to shape her behaviour according to the reformers' conceptions of dignity and morality.

3. The "New" Veil: How State and Islamist Opposition Share a Reformist Stance

In the early 1970s, a new type of dress appeared in Tunisian towns and cities. Women were wearing a garment that was neither the face veil that Bourguiba was still protecting in 1929, nor the *safsārī* or any traditional type of veiling. It was the hijab we know today: a short veil covering the hair but not the face, secured with pins, and combined with a long dress or trousers. The hijab was not worn as an instrument of seclusion in the home and did not prevent women from going to school or from attending the workplace, since it was precisely in these public domains that women in this new attire made themselves visible. It showed itself publicly, exemplifying a new version of religiosity that was urban, young and educated. It was no longer the "horrible rag" that Bourguiba had associated with rural life and ignorance, but a sign that women had found the veil to be a relevant dress for the public arena. The varying interpretations of the wearing of the veil – as a way to discipline oneself into piety, an instrument for emancipation, a tool for patriarchal reproduction, a sign of female submission, an instrument of liberation – are numerous and diversified. I will not explore them in this paper,[60] but will instead underline the changes in the political elite's perceptions of the veil and the possibility for these meanings to form a multilayered, complex set of interpretations.

In the 1970s, when the new veil appeared in Tunisia, it surprised most of the intellectual and political elite, who saw it as the "symbol" of the nascent Islamist political opposition who wanted to signal its new power, and not as a way to public piety and virtue on the part of veiled women. The ways in which different segments of society viewed the hijab were in fact linked with the state of relations between government and the Islamist opposition. In 1981, an administrative decree (no. 108)[61] that forbade the wearing of the hijab in schools, described it as "confessional and sectarian".[62] This was two years after the Iranian revolution, when Tunisia was witnessing the influence of foreign Islamist movements within its borders, as well as the emergence, since the end of the 1970s, of a potent domestic oppositional Islamist movement. This decree was not applied in any systematic way, but was used at random by the authorities when dealing with the Islamist opposition, in particular in secondary schools and on college campuses.

To understand how the Islamist opposition dealt with the question of veiling and related to Bourguiba's interpretation, I will refer to Rashid al-Ghannushi's writings on the Tunisian woman. In his book *The Muslim Woman in Tunisia*,[63] he develops a critique of the submission of women to men. Echoing Haddad and Bourguiba, he is critical of the conception of a woman as a person lacking strength and autonomy. However, his focus on the definition of the "ideal Muslim woman" differs in the sense that it is formulated in an anti-imperialist tone. For Ghannushi, the market economy and Westernisation had weakened women; they now submitted to a culture of consumption that gave physical appearance too much significance in their lives. For Ghannushi, Western colonisation as well as neo-colonialism had destroyed traditional life, and with it the sense of honour in women – a value that should be recovered. Against this new culture, he insisted on the primacy of "traditional values". The Islamist discourse hence inverted Bourguiba's dichotomy between the "modern" (associated with progress) and the "traditional" (related to ignorance). Indeed, Bourguiba criticised practices that he saw as "traditional" – that is, values and practices that merely imitated past customs (*taqlīd*).

It is rarely noted that both the Bourguibian and Islamist visions rely on the desire to define and mould a national personality. Ghannushi recognised the decline of religion and its institutions before independence, and the necessity to reform them. In his view, Bourguiba dissolved (*tamyīʿ*) Islam,[64] especially in his policies of reform toward the Zaytuna, the shariʿa, the religious endowments and the status of women. While both agreed that a shared community of sentiments was necessary to build a nation, the Islamist conception did not accept the Bourguibian state's claims to shaping these "disciplines of the heart".

Ghannushi was in agreement with Bourguiba, however, about the condition of women in the twentieth century. According to Ghannushi, the twentieth-century woman "had been deprived of her personality (*shakhsiyya*) as a person entirely responsible".[65] "She had been deprived of the light (*nūr*) of knowledge and Gnosticism (*irfān*)."[66] "Decline (*inhiṭāṭ*) had touched her like it touched man, but worse."[67] In the same vein, Haddad and Bourguiba had diagnosed Tunisian women as twice subjugated. Bourguiba declared before and after independence that women were living under the yoke of both colonialism and patriarchy.[68] Echoing Haddad's *Our Women*, Ghannushi wrote in the 1970s: "She was not allowed to even choose her husband. She was deprived even of her part of inheritance and to decide what to do with her own property."[69] And, he added, "this was not, at that time and in that place, because of the values of Islam."[70] Here again, Islamist activist Ghannushi was in agreement with statesman Bourguiba's diagnosis: Islam was not the culprit. But, he said, the fact that the Tunisian woman had progressed so far in education could not be attributed to the Personal Status Code or to Bourguiba himself. Such progress would have happened no matter what. "Nowadays women are educated and work in all Arab countries," he wrote. "This is thanks to the movement of religious reform of the nineteenth century."[71]

For Ghannushi, it seemed, reform could not be conceived or implemented by the state, but came from the historical influence of new ideas. In this way, Ghannushi erased Bourguiba from the history of religious and social reform, whereas Bourguiba had tried to place himself in this historical line of Muslim reformers, whom, except for Haddad, he often quoted. The contention around the Personal Status Code, and more broadly Bourguiba's understanding of the role of women, was not so much a struggle between two different visions of women's role in the public arena as a competition – and an unequal one at that – between two political actors struggling to be part of the "reformist" legacy. Indeed, recognising the positive elements in the new 1956 code, Ghannushi wrote a discreet footnote to his *al-Marʾa al-muslima fī tunis*: "All is not bad in the Code of Personal Status. The great majority of its texts are a copy and sometimes a distortion of Shaykh Dj'ayyit's codification, after it was purged from its Islamic values and principles."[72] His reference to Shaykh Muhammad al-'Aziz al-Dj'ayyit's 1948 codification of Tunisian law showed Ghannushi's interest and desire to connect his own ideas to those of earlier reformers. He also quoted, in reference to the reform of the status of women, Jamal al-Din al-Afghani, Muhammad 'Abduh, Hassan al-Banna and the two Tunisian shaykhs, al-Tahar and al-Fadhel Ben Achour. These names formed an eclectic group. The reference to al-Fadhel Ben Achour – then in the service of the postcolonial Bourguibian regime – may seem strange, but perhaps Ghannushi's point was to refer to the legacy of reformist 'ulama' that Bourguiba had submitted to the modern state, rather than build a rigorous intellectual chain of legacy and influence. For Ghannushi, the Personal Status Code went beyond the Bourguibian policies and was part of a strategy to "de-Islamise" the country on the part of the West: "It is indirect colonisation," he wrote.[73]

Ghannushi believed that it was a mistake to "think that we only need little changes such as longer dresses and the abandoning of lipstick to become an Islamic society".[74] Islam, he wrote:

> does not interact with women by talking to them about their dresses' length or width, but rather, it is interested in the woman's vision of life and what this vision leads her towards. The aim is for her ... to look at life as ... an opportunity to elevate the persons from the level of the animal to the human level.[75]

Bourguiba and Ghannushi had different understandings of the veil, but they shared a repertoire for talking about the Tunisian woman's place in society. What mattered for both of them, as well as for Haddad, was the vision women had of the world that surrounded them. They were both interested in women's subjectivity and awareness: they were particularly intent on linking female subjectivity with access to knowledge, morality and responsibility, all in the name of "progress". Women also had to be integrated into the public arena. For Bourguiba, this path had to be taken without the veil; for Ghannushi, the path could only be taken with the veil. But for both of them, the destination was the same, especially in terms of women's education. Ghannushi wrote:

> We have to differentiate between the question of the education of women and the question of dress. To insist that the young woman (al-fatāt) must show modesty (ḥishma) and virtue ('iffa) in her dress does

not mean depriving her of her legal right to learn all the sciences she wants. Or has it been written that the Muslim young woman, unlike all the other women, should not have access to knowledge without letting go of the principles that make her national personality? Was this imposed to the young Japanese and Chinese women? They have reached the highest scientific level and retained at the same time their national personalities. Why is it only the young Muslim woman who should accept to erase her personality in exchange for obtaining some knowledge?[76]

In this particular writing, the defence of the veil by Ghannushi does not come as a "legal prescription" but as a defence of the national personality in opposition to the West, exactly as in Bourguiba's words in the 1929 "battle of the veil". One can recognise in this quotation the influence of Bourguibian postcolonial vocabulary, interweaving "the discipline of the heart", morality and virtue with the primacy of a people's personality. However, Ghannushi also reproached Bourguiba for his Western influences and the erasing of Islam that, in his view, the Personal Status Code caused.[77] Knowing that Islamic theological justifications were given by Bourguiba for the Personal Status Code, he added: "If Islam was evoked, this was to prepare some of its texts and modify them in order to use them to feed the masses so that they swallow the bitter pill of the Western solutions."[78]

Conclusion

What can we infer from the continuities between the postcolonial state's conception of veiling and that of the Islamist opposition? Both conceptions sprang from the desire to form a new and in the end similar "habitus" for Tunisians. Bourguiba's intent was to mould the Tunisian woman's personality and behaviour into the image he had of the Tunisian nation: a Muslim and Mediterranean entity anchored in European culture. Bourguiba wanted to regulate the physical behaviour and body of Tunisian women in combination with circumscribing the prerogatives of Islamic law. This combination did not reflect a "liberal" conception of the body but an authoritarian vision of the nation and of the subjectivity of its citizens as "enlightened", "reasonable" and "virtuous". In addition, Islam had to play a substantial part in the definition of this specific type of subjectivity. For Islamists such as Ghannushi, Bourguiba's conception imposed a deplorable rupture in history. However, their evaluation of the postcolonial state's policies was the product of their oppositional standing, rather than of an entirely different conception of society. In fact, in Ghannushi's idea of the Muslim veiled Tunisian woman, the body was disciplined within a representation of the nation that one could find in Zaytuna-educated Haddad's, as well as in President Bourguiba's unveiled woman.

Veiling and unveiling were in fact two contrasting disciplines given to women to fulfil the same end: that of an educated woman taking care of her family, as well as integrated in the public arena. These political postures opposing and in favour of the veil perhaps also defined each other in a competition that reified the two positions as "Islamic" and "secularist", and in which women were seldom authorised to intervene. The first difference between Ghannushi and Bourguiba was not their view on Islam, for both referenced it as a "religion of life", but their will or refusal to refer to the West. Second – and as a direct consequence of their political roles – Bourguiba made Islam a province of the state, whereas Ghannushi did not accept the construction of such a monopoly, which made the state define and administer the conduct of individual and collective piety. Ghannushi's refusal to accept this illiberal set of constraints on Islam could not prevent him from speaking the language of the state itself on normative conduct, a direct product of reformist thought and of the postcolonial state's legal and ideological new constructs.

These continuities between reformist thought, postcolonial conceptions of Islam and Islamist oppositional discourses help underline the role played by the modern postcolonial state (prior to the emergence of Islamist movements) in developing and disseminating normative prescriptions and body disciplines that also helped the state appropriate Islamic narratives and domesticate religious institutions. These normative prescriptions were in turn used by Islamist movements for their own political purposes. Whereas states and Islamists are today in a relationship of political opposition and competition, I argue that in order to explain the religious language of Islamist movements, and more generally the mobilising power of Islam on the political scene, one must turn to the shaping and use of the tradition of Islam by the postcolonial state's elite. This elite institutionalised Islam as a political resource, thereby providing a foundation on which Islamists could formulate their ideologies.

Acknowledgements

I wish to acknowledge the financial support of the Carnegie Corporation for the research and writing of this article. I also thank Mohammed Arkoun, Akeel Bilgrami, Abdou Filali-Ansary, Silvia Marsans-Sakly and Mark Sedgwick for their comments, as well as Lauren Osborne for her research assistance.

Notes

1. For instance, M. Arkoun, "Actualité du problème de la personne dans la pensée islamique", *Die Welt des Islams*, News Series, Bd. 29, Nr. 1/4 , 1989, p. 1–29.

2. To cite only a few examples, J. Entelis writes: "The Tunisian experience has shown that there can be such a thing as a liberal secularist authoritarian regime", in *Islam, Democracy, and the State in North Africa* (Bloomington, IN: Indiana University Press, 1997), p. 4. O. Roy provides a similar description for Algeria, Turkey and Tunisia, in *Globalized Islam: The Search for a New Ummah* (New York: Columbia University Press, 2004), in particular on pp. 5, 82 and 96–7.

3. D. Kandiyoti, "Introduction," in D. Kandiyoti ed., *Women, Islam and the State*. (Philadelphia, Temple University Press), p. 3.

4. D. Kandiyoti, p. 3. For a similar formulation, see also M. Charrad, *States and Women's Rights: The Making of Postcolonial Tunisia, Algeria and Morocco*. (Berkeley: University of California Press, 2001).

5. For a more detailed account of the meeting and those involved, see I. Marzouki, "Le voile des colonisées, Tunisie, 1924–1936", *Revue de l'Institut des Belles Lettres Arabes*, 51 (61), pp. 59–89.

6. H. Bourguiba, "Le voile", *L'Etendard Tunisien*, 11 January 1929. The article is reproduced in H. Bourguiba, *Articles de Presse, 1929–1934* (Tunis: Centre de Documentation Nationale, 1967), pp. 1–6.

7. Ibid. p. 1.

8. I. Marzouki, *Mouvement des femmes en Tunisie au XXème siècle* (Paris: Maisonneuve et Larose, 1993), Chapter 2.

9. Bourguiba, *Articles de Presse* (Tunis: Centre de Documentation Nationale, 1967), pp. 2–3. Translation by the author.

10. Ibid. p. 4. Translation by the author.

11. The reactions against *sufūr* are described by I. Marzouki, "Le voile des colonisées, Tunisie, 1924–1936", *Revue de l'Institut des Belles Lettres Arabes* 51 (61), pp. 59–89.

12. Bourguiba, *Articles de Presse* (Tunis: Centre de Documentation Nationale, 1967), p. 2. Author's translation.

13. Ibid. p. 5.

14. Ibid. p. 5.

15. A. Khalid, "Al-taʿrif bi'l-tahir al-ḥaddad", in T. al-Haddad (ed.), *al-Aʿmal al-kamila* (Tunis: al-Dar al-ʿarabiyya li'l-kitab, 1999), p. 14.

16. T. al-Haddad, "Imra'atuna fi'l-shariʿa wa al-mujtamaʿ", in *al-Aʿmal al-kamila*, vol. 3 (Tunis: al-Dar al-ʿarabiyya li'l-kitab, 1999).

17. Ibid. p. 20.

18. Ibid. p. 24.

19. Ibid. p. 25. When discussing the issue of the veil (*ḥijab* and *niqab* are the two terms Haddad uses), Haddad refers to the face veil.

20. Ibid. p. 25. This essence consisted in "*unicity*, the highest morality, justice and equality between people".

21. Ibid. p. 26.

22. Ibid. p. 24.

23. T. al-Haddad, *al-ʿUmmal al-tunisiyyun wa zuhur al-ḥaraka al-niqabiyya* (Tunis: Maktabat al-ʿarab, 1927).

24. T. al-Haddad, *al-Aʿmal al-kamila* (Tunis: al-Dar al-ʿarabiyya li'l-kitab, 1999), p. 201.

25. Ibid. p. 203.

26. Ibid. p. 58.

27. Ibid. p. 59.

28. M. S. Ibn Murad, *al-Ḥidad 'ala imra'at al-ḥaddad* (Tunis: al-Maṭba'a al-tunisiya, 1931), p. 18.

29. Proclaimed in 1956, the Personal Status Code consisted of legislation that regulated family matters. It was meant to improve women's rights, and in particular, it made polygamy and divorce by repudiation illegal. It took pains to justify these measures through Islamic references.

30. H. Bourguiba, Speech given at the promulgation of the Personal Status Code, 10 August 1956, in T. al-Haddad, "Imra'atuna", *al-A'mal al-kamila*, vol. 3 (Tunis: al-Dar al-'arabiyya li'l-kitab, 1999), p. 8.

31. Ibid. p. 209.

32. Ibid. p. 210.

33. Ibid. p. 209.

34. Ibid. p. 208.

35. Ibid. p. 211.

36. Ibid. p. 211.

37. Ibid. p. 211.

38. Ibid. p. 212. Note that Haddad uses "al-luwat, al-musaḥaqa wa'l-'ada al-sirriya".

39. Ibid. p. 215.

40. Ibid. p. 215.

41. Ibid. p. 46.

42. Ibid. p. 218.

43. Ibid. p. 237.

44. Ibid. pp. 218–220. Note that the word *alam* (pain) is repeated several times.

45. M. S. Ibn Murad, *al-Ḥidad 'ala imra'at al-ḥaddad* (Tunis: al-Maṭba'a al-tūnisīya, 1931).

46. H. Bourguiba, "Coordination des services, respect des individus et libération de la femme", Speech given on 5 December 1957, *Discours*, 4, 1975, p. 17.

47. Ibid. p. 18.

48. H. Bourguiba, "Discours du 18 mars 1974", *Discours*, 23, 1973–4, p. 194.

49. H. Bourguiba, "Coordination des services", Speech given on 5 December 1957, *Discours*, 4, 1975, p. 21.

50. Ibid. p. 21.

51. Ibid. p. 21.

52. Ibid. p. 21.

53. Ibid. p. 21.

54. Ibid. p. 21.

55. Note 13: "Evolution must happen, otherwise, it is death."

56. Quoted in C. Debbash, *La République Tunisienne* (Paris: Librairie Générale de Droit et de Jurisprudence, 1962), p. 150.

57. Ina.fr, "Bourguiba Femmes". Available at: http://www.ina.fr/recherche/recherche/search/Bourguiba+femmes (Accessed 8 February, 2011).

58. L. B. Youssef-Zayzafun, *The Production of the Muslim Woman: Negotiating Text, History, and Ideology* (Boulder: Lexington Books, 2005), Chapter 4.

59. Quoted in "Chroniques", *Revue de l'Institut des Belles Lettres Arabes*, 30ème année, no. 118–119, 2ème-3ème trimestres 1967, p. 292.

60. See N. Göle, *The Forbidden Modern: Civilisation and Veiling* (Ann Arbor: University of Michigan Press, 1996) and S. Mahmood, The Politics of Piety: The Islamic Revival and The Feminist Subject (Princeton: Princeton University Press, 2005).

61. A *manshur* is a decision made authoritatively within the administration of the state to regulate its day to day functioning. Manshur 108 of the Prime Ministry, 1981, deals

with students' dress. Manshur 102, 1986, deals with the teachers and workers' dress in public education. The dress should not exhibit "fanatism (*tatarruf*) or anything out of the ordinary".

62. Quoted by L. Chouikha, in "La question du hijab en Tunisie", in F. Lorcerie (ed.), *La politisation du voile* (Paris: L'Harmattan, 2005), p. 162.

63. R. al-Ghannushi, *al-Mar'a al-muslima fi tunis: Bayna Tawjihat al-qur'an wa'l-mujtama' al-tunisi* (Kuwait: Dar al-Qalam, 1988), pp. 87–149.

64. Ibid. p. 91.

65. Ibid. p. 136.

66. Ibid. p. 136.

67. Ibid. p. 136.

68. In his speech of 25 November 1958, Bourguiba said: "Half of Tunisia's population lived in seclusion ... This true hemiplegia that afflicted the country originated from an old mentality that it is necessary to uproot." Quoted in C. Debbash, *La République Tunisienne* (Paris: Librairie Générale de Droit et de Jurisprudence, 1962), p. 150. We find the same idea in al-Haddad's "Imra'atuna fi'l-shari'a wa al-mujtama'", *al-A'mal al-kamila*, vol. 3, p. 213: "A people cannot reach the greatness it desires as long as half of it lives in the shadows".

69. R. al-Ghannushi, *al-Mar'a al-muslima fi tunis* (Kuwait: Dar al-Qalam, 1988), p. 136.

70. Ibid. p. 136.

71. Ibid. pp. 137–138.

72. Ibid. p. 141.

73. Ibid. p 148.

74. Ibid. p. 124.

75. Ibid. p. 125.

76. Ibid. pp. 125–126.

77. Ibid. p. 138.

78. Ibid. pp. 138–139.

Coming to Believe:
the (Elusive) Time of Conversion

Souleymane Bachir Diagne

William James in *The Varieties of Religious Experience* establishes a distinction between two types or archetypes of conversion.[1] Conversion being defined "in general terms" as "the process, gradual or sudden, by which a self hitherto divided, and consciously wrong, inferior and unhappy, becomes unified and consciously right, superior and happy, in consequence of its firmer hold upon religious realities",[2] two modalities of it are distinguished: on the one hand, the "striking instantaneous" conversion "of which Saint Paul's is the most eminent" and the effect of which is that "a complete division is established in the twinkling of an eye between the old life and the new";[3] and on the other hand, the gradual conversion which is conscious and voluntary. Apparently, then, the crisis conversion, unlike the gradual conversion, has its *moment*. Thus, James gives the example of an Oxford graduate who converted "at precisely three o'clock in the afternoon of a hot July day (July 13, 1886),"[4] experiencing that in that instant "his poor divided mind became unified for good."[5] In the same way, there is *the* moment when Saint Augustine heard *"tolle lege"* ("pick up and read!"); the moment when Saint Paul experienced rapture on the road to Damascus; and the moment of Blaise Pascal's *nuit de feu* (night of fire) in 1654.

It would be natural to think that authenticity is on the side of that type of conversion, while it would be assumed that there is too much preparation, hesitation and even calculation in the gradual type of conversion; that there is always in it something which sounds like Henri IV's famous exclamation

"Paris vaut bien une messe!" ("Paris is worth a mass!") when he announced his intention to convert to Catholicism in order to be accepted as the King of France. Conversions that aim to solve problems of intermarriages, to take a more banal example, would fall under the same category. As a psychologist, James examined how sudden conversions could be understood as "uprushes into the ordinary consciousness" of processes taking place in the subliminal region of the mind, so that "what makes the difference between a sudden and a gradual convert is not necessarily the presence of divine miracle in the case of one and something less divine in that of the other, but rather a simple psychological peculiarity, the fact, namely, that in the recipient of the more instantaneous grace we have one of those Subjects who are in possession of a large region in which mental work can go on subliminally ..."[6]

I would like to push that statement further and examine, with regard to conversion, the Sufi understanding that the experience of conversion is all about the "ruse of God" (*makr Allah*) which transforms even the "wrong" or unauthentic reasons for conversion – self-interested calculation, for example – into the divine favour of faith. Such a notion of a "ruse" implies that the distinction between gradual and critical conversion is to be relativised as irrelevant, any critical transformation being always prepared by a gradual process, while the gradual (maybe subliminal) development itself unfolds through critical moments. As this chapter examines different cases or figures of conversion, it raises the following interconnected questions: what is the time of conversion? At what moment can we say that a person has now entered a new belief system? What does conversion tell us about time?[7]

Allow me first to recall a story of conversion which impressed me when I was a little boy of about six. My parents had been sent by the administration of the Senegalese postal services, for which they both worked, to the Casamance region of Senegal. At that time, just a few years after the country's independence, Casamance had an important population of recent converts to Islam and Christianity, as well as followers of traditional African religions (improperly called "animists"). The people who had a long ancient Islamic tradition were generally civil servants from the North, like my parents. My father, in particular, was born into a family of Islamic scholars. Like many middle-class families, we had hired local people to help run the house, and there was one young man, Alexis, whose main task was to take me to and from school. On Thursdays and Saturdays he would also take me to the Qur'anic school and wait for me to finish my classes and recite my verses for the day so that he could walk me back home. Alexis had a Christian first name because the church was trying to convert his group, but in fact his religion was an African endogenous belief system.

One day, people from his village saw Alexis waiting for me at the Qur'anic school and reported to his parents that he had become a Muslim. His father immediately sent a messenger with a letter written in red ink (my mother still recalls that ominous detail) threatening him with all sorts of calamities if the news of his conversion turned out to be true. Alexis was totally terrified and asked my parents for permission to return to his village and clarify that he was just my *pedagogue* in the Greek sense and not a student at the school. He explained that he had to do this, because in his anger his father could in fact make him fall ill or even die through mystical means. But then, before he left, he told my parents that there was actually some truth to the story – that he was attracted to the Islamic religion, especially, he added, since all the bosses (*les patrons*) in the city of Ziguinchor, most of them northerners, were Muslims: he wanted to become a "patron" too, one day. My parents paid him his wages plus some extra money and explained, without insisting, that in Islam, one does not believe that any power other than God's could actually kill you using magical forces as punishment for becoming a Muslim convert. Many years later, when we were living in Dakar, Alexis came to see my father and told him that since his parents had passed away, he could now freely embrace Islam. My father had him proclaim the *shahada*. Let me add here that this story is an individual and personal expression of a larger sociological phenomenon, which is that of the rapid Islamisation of the southern regions of Senegal, under the influence of northern populations, whose Islamisation is many centuries more ancient. Obviously, Alexis's case of conversion was not only gradual but calculated.

I will now consider the early days of Islam in Mecca, before the hijra to Medina. This was, of course, the time of the famous, historic conversions of those who are known as the companions of the Prophet: Khadija, who believed in her husband, the Prophet, even as he did not believe in himself; Ali, who entered Islam as a child; Umar, who was convinced by reading the Surah Ta Ha, and so on. But the narrative of conversion I will evoke is that of Hamzah, the Prophet's uncle. The story is famous. The tradition is that Abu Jahl, one of those who showed the most hatred toward the Prophet, one day abused him with the worst possible insults, while the Prophet simply looked at him and said nothing. When Hamzah heard what happened and the way in which his nephew had been treated, he is reported to have felt an anger he had never experienced before; to have gone straight to Abu Jahl and struck him hard with his bow (he had been out hunting), shouting:

"Will you insult him now that I am of his religion, and now that I profess what he professes?" That was quite a singular profession of faith, on the spur of the moment, bursting out of anger and sounding like a dare.

Let me now compare Alexis's long-delayed conversion to Hamzah's instantaneous conversion by asking the questions: what happened and when did it happen? How did they come to believe? Considering the time frame, one could say that Alexis gradually constructed his Islamic "belief" as he came to reflect on a religion he'd discovered to be the secret of the "bosses", and on the very atmosphere of the Qur'anic school. One might even think that the miracle of the Qur'anic verses he was hearing, even though of course he did not understand them, gradually operated on him in the way Islamic traditions report: that they can lead many to think that there is something magical in them. But then the idea that Alexis's attraction to Islam was not disinterested, that there was some calculation about the best way of becoming a "boss", could also mean that there was something flawed and inauthentic in what drove him to "conversion". Especially if we add that the main reason for delaying the formal profession of faith was the most anti-Islamic reason possible: conformity to the religion of the forefathers and belief that what they worship could be in any way useful or harmful. Many Qur'anic verses could be quoted. Suffice it to recall that what defines the Abrahamic faith is precisely the break from the fathers' tradition: "But when they are told, 'Follow what God has bestowed from on high,' some answer, 'Nay! We shall follow [only] that which we found our forefathers believing in and doing.' Why, even if their forefathers did not use their reason at all, and were devoid of guidance?"[8] and also: "(Abraham) said: 'Do you then worship, besides God, things that can neither be of any good to you nor do you harm?'"[9]

Shall we then say that to have waited until the time when there could be no objection from the family altered the nature of his conversion by showing that in fact he did not understand at all what he was converting to? But isn't it natural that the meaning of Islam as a radical break from the ways of the fathers could only be clear to him after he actually converted from those ways and began to learn the belief system he was adopting? Are we saying then that (true) conversion comes only after conversion? One could perfectly imagine Alexis, many years later, thinking that he was lucky, or, in religious terms, blessed, not to have died before formally converting, having postponed his admission to the community of Muslims for so long. But if indeed in retrospect he were to understand that "luck" as a "blessing" or a "grace", would he also think that God had already converted him before he had even thought of conversion? "I convert" is indeed a strange performative, as in order for me to be able to say it, it means "I have already converted."

Hamzah's conversion could then be understood not as something that happened instantaneously out of a burst of extreme anger, but as an expression of an already present but deeply buried belief in the new message and its promise of a new social and ethical order.[10] What anger did then was tear down the barriers that repressed the belief inside his unconscious. It is the paradox of conversion that it cannot be assigned, as it seems to take place at some uncertain moment situated at once before and after the actual declaration of faith, or maybe at a time outside serial time, for which "before" and "after" make no sense.

There is, I believe, no better account than Saint Augustine's narrative of the paradox of conversion as a spiritual event that seems to have always already taken place before it actually happens, signalling therefore what seems to be a time outside the serial time which constitutes one's life.[11] In Jean-Francois Lyotard's *Le Différend* (1983), we read an important passage in paragraph 125, about Augustine and time: "The God of Augustine or the Living Present of Husserl is presented as the name of the instance which synthesizes the nows. But it is such by means of the sentences in which it is presented, and the now of each of those sentences remains to be synthesized with the others, in a new sentence. God is for later, 'in a moment'; the Living Present is to come. They only happen by not arriving. That is what Beckett means. Time does not fail consciousness, it makes it fail itself."[12]

"God is for later, 'in a moment'." That describes perfectly the *Confessions* as a narrative of the deferral or the continuous postponement of a conversion which, nevertheless, has somehow already happened. Augustine himself explains that his life had been just such a continuous postponement, comparing it to the state of the sleeper who always pleads for "just a minute", "one more minute", "let me have a little longer": "No one wants to be asleep all the time," he writes in Book VIII of *Confessions*, "and it is generally agreed among sensible people that being awake is a better state, yet it often happens that a person puts off the moment when he must shake himself out of sleep because his limbs are heavy with a lassitude that pulls him toward the more attractive alternative, even though he is already trying to resist it and the hour for rising has come ..."[13] First there is the deferral of his baptism. When he fell suddenly ill in his boyhood, baptism became a matter of extreme urgency, and it is "with distress and faith" that he "earnestly begged", he recounts, "to be baptized into (...) Christ".[14] And, of course, his mother, Saint Monica, "would have hastened to ensure that [he] was initiated into the saving sacraments".[15] But then he recovered and therefore, as he explains, "[his] cleansing was deferred on the pretext that if [he] lived [he] would inevitably soil himself again..."[16] And as we know, soil himself he did! But during all that time of deferral, his mother never ceased to see things as going to an already accomplished divine plan. For example, while Augustine's father wanted him to study for vain worldly reasons, his mother saw academic pursuits as "a considerable help toward [his] gaining [God] eventually".[17] And for that reason she did not want him to be encumbered with a wife, even though marriage could have been a way of securing a more Christian life. Her words, as when she cautioned him against fornication, especially against "adultery with any man's wife", were in fact the words of God that never ceased to be sung "into his ears",[18] although he did not recognise them as such at that stage. And when his mother felt desperate because of the kind of life her son was living, God sent a vision to console her and reassure her that where she was, her son would be too.[19]

Finally, when the time comes, Augustine is able to hear the Word of God, even though it is not as direct and clear as when he heard it through his mother or in his own readings. (He confesses that he preferred Cicero to the Bible.) What distinguishes that moment? What makes it, in the words of Saint Augustine, "the hour for rising"? Nothing, compared to more dramatic moments in his life. Except that this time he is able to recognise it, *as if he had already lived it before and knew exactly what response was expected from him.* When a voice from a house (that of a boy or a girl, Augustine says) is heard saying, "Pick it up and read," he knows that he is the addressee and then he knows exactly what to read and what that means. The only change that now makes him able to convert – that is, to turn around who he is and what his life is going to be – is that the time has come; that time which has always been present or *a presence* in his life: even if he deferred acknowledging the encounter with God's Word addressed to him, that encounter is what was leading him all along. One can say, in the language of the quotation from Lyotard's *Le Différend*, that the *Confessions* are the succession of "nows" towards the Living Present that would synthesize them. But that Living Present belongs to another order, and is not embarked on in the succession of serial time. Hence the paradoxical formula of Saint Augustine: to search for God is already to have found him. As he writes: "You were within me but I was outside and it was there that I searched for you." Blaise Pascal will repeat the same fundamental truth of conversion in his *Mystère de Jésus*: "*console-toi tu ne me chercherais pas si tu ne m'avais trouvé.*" To search for God outside, while he is inside, is still to search. In that search there is no opposite or wrong direction. What is said in the language of space is in fact meant to be understood in the language of time: I looked in serial time, in the time of succession, while what I was looking for remained in a living – that is eternal – Present.

Following the story of Augustine's conversion and reflections on memory, Book XI of the *Confessions* is devoted to the notions of "time" and "eternity", sometimes put into meaningless questions such as, "What was God doing before he made heaven and earth?" His general response to this kind of paradox about "time before time" is to acknowledge that "you have precedence over the past by the loftiness of your ever-present eternity, and you live beyond all the future, because future times are future, but as soon as they have arrived they will be past, whereas you are ever the same, and your years fail not";[20] trying to think of time in itself, without spatialising it as the "movement of a body"[21] or considering it as measurable while it has no extension.[22] The Book ends with the opposition between "our time" and God's eternity. The *Confessions* is a meditation on time and on that opposition between the outside of postponement and the inside of Presence. The time of conversion is eternity.

About the archetypal nature of Augustine's conversion, Ann H. Hawkins writes:

> In the *Confessions*, as in many spiritual autobiographies that will pattern themselves after it, life before conversion is perceived as a kind of labyrinthine maze with numerous false passages and wrong turnings, but one that eventually and inevitably culminates in conversion. Accordingly the first nine books are the story of Augustine's personal life, of his spiritual wandering in the 'distant country' that is the Earthly City. But in the last four books the quest of pagan epic and Old Testament Scripture turns into the metaphor of the Christian pilgrimage, the *peregrinatio* where the 'true haven' or 'final resting-place' is the City of God [...] a reality not attainable in this life. It is against this one eternal city that we are to see the many secular cities – Thagaste, Carthage, Rome, even Milan – in the story of Augustine's spiritual quest.[23]

The *Confessions* does allow many different narratives of conversion to "pattern themselves after it". That is especially true, maybe unexpectedly, of *The Autobiography of Malcolm X*. It is indeed full of "false passages and wrong turnings", especially the ones that "culminate in conversion"; the pilgrimage, the *peregrinatio* to the "true haven", is just such a culmination: in this case the City of God is Mecca, where Malcolm X found the peace that eluded him all his life, peace with others beyond the division of humanity into races, peace with himself beyond anger and hatred, and consequently peace with his newly found God. That peace is the very meaning of Islam.

Again, the question here is *when* did Malcolm's conversion take place? When is the moment corresponding to his affirmation that "[he] found Allah and the religion of Islam and it completely transformed [his] life"?[24] Is it the first time he declared "I don't eat pork", having just received the message from his brother Philbert that by giving up pork and cigarettes, he would be shown how to get out of prison? He explains that later, after he had "read and studied Islam a good deal" he came to realise that the decision he thus made had been, without his being conscious of it, his "first pre-Islamic submission".[25] That is, he adds, the meaning of the Muslim teaching about conversion, that "if you take one step toward Allah – Allah will take two steps toward you."[26] But which of the many steps that he took in his life was the first step on the path to conversion? Was it when his brother Reginald visited him in prison and told him about what he considered "the natural religion for the black man" which he called the "Nation of Islam"? When he felt the urge to study, to read, to write and to debate? When he prayed to Allah for his brother Reginald when he was suspended from the Nation of Islam? When he met Elijah Muhammad? When he lost faith in him? When he said to his sister Ella who had become what he himself calls in his autobiography "orthodox Muslims": "I want to make the pilgrimage to Mecca", thus "converting" again to mainstream Islam? When he started chanting the words that all pilgrims repeat again and again during the pilgrimage: "Here I come, O Lord! Here I come"? Or was it when, through the pilgrimage and in particular at the station of Arafat, he discovered the simple truth that had eluded him all his life, that "We are truly all the same"?[27]

When he explains that the pilgrimage to Mecca had "forced him to *re-arrange* much of [his] thought-patterns previously held" (and that is the meaning of conversion) he seems to indicate that the true moment of conversion happened then, but he also acknowledges that his "whole life had been a chronology of – *changes*".[28] So again, we can see in Malcolm X's narrative of conversion the paradox of a life reconstructed after the fact as getting closer, by deferral, to a presence that never ceased to be active in one's life.

From these stories of conversion, I would like to draw two general conclusions.

1.   Conversion appears as an experience of non-serial time that may be called the "living present" (Lyotard) or "duration" (Bergson). To say it in the language of Blaise Pascal, beyond the order of the flesh and beyond the order of the intellect, both under the domination of serial time, it takes place in a third order, incommensurable to those two: that of "charity". As Pascal's experience shows, in the move from one order to another there exist both gradualness and crisis. His "night of fire" was possible only when the path of the intellect met a dead end, which is similar to what Ghazali describes in his own *Confession*. In fact, if gradualism were not always part of conversion, there would be no sense in Pascal's enterprise of converting the "Libertines".

2.   It follows, then, that conversion is an act of God and not of the subject, or that in and through every act of the subject God himself acts. This defines the "ruse of God" of which the Islamic tradition quoted by Malcolm X is an expression: "If you take one step toward God – God will take two steps toward you." In fact, even that first step cannot be consciously taken as a voluntary step toward God. Actually, anything could count as a first step; the paradox of conversion being that its authenticity cannot be questioned. There are no bad reasons for it, only good ones, but in retrospect: wanting to become a boss, like Alexis; seeing it as a way of avenging an offence (Hamzah); or accepting the pressure to declare one's faith in a given religion in order to marry the person you love. The Qur'anic word *taūbah* (conversion) captures the notion that although conversion is voluntary, its ultimate agent is God alone. "Accept our repentance, You are the Acceptor of repentance, the Dispenser of Grace" is a canonical translation of a prayer expressing conversion.[29] Jacques Berque, whose rendition of the Qur'an always keeps the original meaning of words, translates the prayer as follows: "Repent in our favour, You are prone to repent."[30] That when his creature converts, it is God who converts (or repents) may be a strange translation. It is, nevertheless, a true account of the paradox of conversion.

Notes

1. *Archetypes of Conversion: The Autobiographies of Augustine, Bunyan, and Merton* is a study of conversion, reflecting on James's account of it, by A. H. Hawkins (Lewisburg, PA: Bucknell University Press, 1985).

2. W. James, *The Varieties of Religious Experience: A Study in Human Nature* (New York: Longmans, Green, and Co., 1902), p. 186.

3. Ibid. p. 213.

4. Ibid. p. 217.

5. Ibid. p. 213.

6. Ibid. p. 232.

7. An undergraduate research project of a former student of mine, Caitlin Buysse at Northwestern University, on conversions to Islam in the Chicago area, shows that quite often, subjects who convert did consider the move for some time but also insist on presenting it as the result of a decisive moment, like a dream.

8. Qur'an 2:170. All references to the Qur'an are taken from the Muhammad Asad translation (Gibraltar: Dar Al-Andalus, 1980).

9. Qur'an 21:66.

10. It is reported by traditions that many at that time, especially the young, were dissatisfied with the prevailing social order, founded on the Arab tribal law that it would be the purpose of Islam to destroy.

11. The exemplarity of the narrative explains why, when Derrida felt like turning towards the past ("turning around" is the meaning of "conversion") and revisiting the faith of his mother (who was dying in Nice), he wrote his *Circonfession* as a conversation with Augustine's *Confessions* (New York: Vintage, 1997).

12. J. F. Lyotard, *Le Différend* (Paris: Minuit, 1983), p. 118.

13. Saint Augustine, *The Confessions* (New York: Vintage, 1997), p. 154.

14. Ibid. p. 14.

15. Ibid. p. 14.

16. Ibid. p. 14.

17. Ibid. p. 29.

18. Ibid. p. 28.

19. Ibid. p. 51.

20. Ibid. p. 255.

21. Ibid. p. 265.

22. Ibid. p. 267.

23. A. H. Hawkins, *Archetypes of Conversion* (Lewisburg, PA: Bucknell University Press, 1985), pp. 30–1.

24. A. Haley, *The Autobiography of Malcolm X* (New York: Grove Press, 1965), p. 151.

25. Ibid. p. 157.

26. Ibid. p. 157.

27. Ibid. p. 345.

28. Ibid. p. 344.

29. Qur'an 2:128.

30. I am translating Berque's rendition in French here literally. See J. Berque, *Le Coran: Essai de traduction* (Paris: Albin Michel, 2002).

The Shadow of Terror on Distant Muslims

Akeel Bilgrami

Everybody is obsessively talking and writing about religion these days. Foundations fund its study more, perhaps, than any other subject in the study of human society. In drawing rooms and dining rooms all over the world people speak about religion as if they were all pundits. That in itself is hardly surprising since religious practice of one kind or another, orthodox and heterodox, established as well as populist, has shown no real decline, despite the spread of modern science and technology to most of the distant parts of the world. In fact, some of the most ardent practitioners of religion live in the most technologically developed and modern societies in the world. If Europe is something of an exception, the explanation that comes most readily to mind reveals a lot about the recent history of the West.

But first, it should be said that some of the writing on religion (by Richard Dawkins and Daniel Dennett, to name just two recent authors) that is most widely read and considered the most controversial is in fact utterly irrelevant to the deep issues at stake. The prolific authors who scorn the irrationality of such beliefs as those that the world was created in six days a few thousand years ago have revived tired Victorian debates for our time, without understanding that what religion means for most people has very little to do with arcane beliefs of that kind. This is not to deny that large numbers of people hold those beliefs. But what religion means for the very people who might believe in such events goes much deeper than is often countenanced by the authors of these books. If they were to study the social and psychological issues at stake, they might deserve to be taken more seriously. Until then, their books are a waste of our time and a waste of their great intelligence.

It is a plain fact that religion today (and perhaps at all times in history) has been much more a matter of practice than of belief. It is true that religious people have always claimed the importance of their beliefs, and we know very well that they have persecuted those who did not share them. But for the most part, the beliefs mattered because practices of various kinds, which flowed from them or were tied to them, also mattered. What is more, often beliefs were dogmatically pronounced even as practices substantially changed without any corresponding articulation in revised beliefs. As a result, considerable de facto secularity has been achieved in many parts of the world, including within Islamic practice, without any formulated acknowledgement of the secular at the level of doctrine.

In this respect, polls which report widespread religious rigidity are misleading. If you were to wave a microphone at someone in Teheran and ask, "Do you believe in the shari'a?" he is very unlikely to say "No." But if you cast a studious glance at his life and see how his practices square with the strict demands of the shari'a, you will often find it quite distant from what he has avowed when polled. The same is true if you wave a microphone at someone in Nebraska and ask, "Do you believe in creationism?" The point is not that the polls that ask these questions and get these answers record nothing. The point is rather that they can't always be taken at face value; what they track is much more complicated than the conclusion registered by polls: "X percentage of the population of such-and-such a place believes that society should subscribe to the shari'a (or believes that creationism is a fact)." To put it differently, assent to such questions are "performatives" rather than strict avowals of one's doctrinal beliefs. Like all performatives, they should be interpreted and diagnosed as expressing and revealing something deeply felt, often inarticulate; something that is often at the level of practice and personal aspiration and yearning rather than at the level of surface propositional statement and assertion.

This descriptive distinction between religion as *practice* or way of life (which is essentially fluid and malleable) and religion as *belief* or doctrine (that, by contrast, can be susceptible to more rigidly codified and explicitly pronounced subscription) is well worth exploring as it applies to many regions of the world. Let me explore it briefly for the religion of my own background, Islam, and for the part of the world from where I grew up, before returning to more global political issues regarding religion.

Islam had travelled to India via trade from West Asia long before the emergence of the Sultanates, who are usually described as forming the "Islamic period" of Indian history. Even when Islam arrived in the form of conquest and Sultanate and then Mughal rule, it came via Persia, Central Asia and Afghanistan. Through all this it acquired so many accretions of local customs and culture that it bears little resemblance to the scriptural and normative demands of the doctrine that is believed to mark the original Islam of the Arabian lands. Historians and anthropologists have compared the great continuity of Muslim practice and life with that of local Hindu religious culture when it settled into its Indian surroundings.

In the midst of this livelier, slowly accreted and accumulated homegrown religious culture, for centuries the formal, bookish elements of Islam were often unknown to ordinary Muslims. These elements had to be recalled in self-conscious ways and unusual circumstances. For the most part, everyday life reflected the common syncretic culture that Muslims shared with Hindus, and it flowered vividly in such aesthetic forms as the great "gharanas" of Hindusthani music as well as in the distinctly twentieth-century culture around Bombay cinema. In the balance between these two contrasting elements – of form and root – the latter dominated the former through the centuries and continues to do so today. However, it is made increasingly precarious by developments of recent decades, and by some striking recent events – of which 9/11 and its aftermath are the most momentous.

There is to begin with the relative poverty of Muslims in India ever since the more landed and educated Muslims, fearing loss of estate and discrimination in career opportunities in India, left for Pakistan during Partition. For those who stayed, those fears have largely been realised. There was also another major loss: that of their language, Urdu, indeed the language of many Hindus in north India as well, which was given away as an exclusive gift to Pakistan.

The Indian leaders, for all their avowed pluralism and secularism, were unable to withstand the nationalistic pique of Hindu ideologues in their own Indian National Congress party, who applied great pressure to have Urdu dropped as a medium of instruction in the national and regional school curricula. And in general, ever since the passing of Nehru, the Congress party has tended to adopt the most debased and cynical strategy that democracy allows – that of trying to win elections by appealing to the majoritarian sentiment as opposed to minorities such as Muslims and Sikhs. This strategy culminated in three hideous events: the pogrom against the Sikhs after Indira Gandhi's assassination, the destruction of the mosque at Ayodhya by Hindu political activists, and the slaughter of roughly two thousand Muslims in Gujarat in 2002. Ironically, the strategy had led (until recently) to the repeated defeat of the Congress party at the hands of a Hindu nationalist party which can play the majoritarian game much more openly and brazenly than the Congress, with its hypocritical avowals of secularism. Even when in power, as it has been in the last few years, the Congress has not reasserted the secularism towards which Nehru had tried (not always successfully) to steer it.

The Muslim "minority" in India, therefore, has had the ideological potential to vex this growing Hindu majoritarian outlook in at least two ways. First, it is open to perception as a minority descended from the Muslim conquerors who ruled for centuries over a predominantly Hindu people, and thus a good target for "historical" revenge. Second, it is open to the perception of being a "residual" population, one that had the choice of leaving for the newly created Muslim nation of Pakistan in 1947, but which chose to stay, so it must now adapt in accordance with the culture of the Hindu nation it opted for.

This ideological perception was once merely the vision of a fringe labelled the "Hindu Right", which was opposed to the secular tendencies of the central leadership of the freedom movement and of post-Independent India, most particularly of Gandhi and Nehru. It is now very much the vision of the majoritarian Hindu ideology that pervaded the national government at the centre for a substantial period until very recently, as well as in some (but by no means all) of the states and regions in the country.

Even putting aside the dubious conceptual elements in these perceptions (that is, the very idea of "historical" revenge, and the restriction of choice to the options "Either go to a Muslim nation or stay in a Hindu one") there are plain historical facts that expose their falsity.

With regard to the first perception, there is the fact that most Muslims today are not descendants of a conquering people, but Hindu converts; and there is the fact that a number of the Muslim rulers of India showed remarkable religious tolerance, comparable at least to the Muslim rule in medieval Spain. With regard to the second, there is the fact of the helplessly sedentary nature of the poor and labouring classes, which meant that immigration over thousands of miles was not a serious option. There is also the fact of the idealism of both this class and the much smaller – but admittedly more mobile – educated middle class of Muslims, who believed that a secular India was preferable to a nation created on the basis of religion. But these are mere contemptible facts; and ideological perceptions, as we know, are the products of a free social imagination.

This ideological situation has made Indian Muslims deeply resentful and defensive in their mentality. And this mentality is adversely affecting the double movement I have mentioned of rooted quotidian syncretic diversity and invocation of scriptural form and fundamentals. This mentality threatens to tilt the balance in favour of the latter over the former. In a situation where material life as well as self-respect is increasingly threatened by alarming majoritarian tendencies in the polity, the absolutist doctrinal side of the double movement is holding out promise of dignity and autonomy in the name of Islam, especially among the young. The attractions are illusory, of course: they are manifestly undemocratic; they are deeply reactionary on issues of gender; and they are phobic of modernity in the extreme – phobic even to a homegrown, non-Western path to modernity. They are "reactionary" in every sense of the term, including that of reacting to feelings of helplessness and defeat, and the seeming lack of viable alternatives to cope with these feelings.

An example of reaction-formation is one response to the combination of poverty, lack of career opportunities and loss of Urdu, which has been the rise of the *madrasa*, which are religious schools peppered all over the country, especially in northern India. Often financed by Saudi Arabian largesse, these schools offer free education in Urdu and a place for boys from poverty-stricken families to live for free while they are trained according to strict scriptural doctrine. To some extent, these schools provide a recruitment ground for future careers in fundamentalist movements. (I say "some" extent and mean it. The extent may well be highly exaggerated by a careless journalistic class.) This is just one example, and all of it predictably leads to a backlash from Hindu ideologues, and in turn defensiveness, surfacing in aggressive reactions among Muslims.

I would like to say something about this defensive and reactive Muslim mentality. What is most striking is that precisely this mentality is found all over the Muslim world, even where Muslims are an overwhelming majority – the only difference being that the reaction is of course not to Hindus, but to American presence and dominance. I will not catalogue the familiar (and dreary if it weren't so palpable) litany of the wrongs of American foreign policy in the Middle East, not to mention in Vietnam, East Timor, Chile and various other parts of Latin America. From the overthrow of a decent and humane leader like Mossadegh in Iran; to the support of corrupt, elitist, and tyrannical leaders in Saudi Arabia, Iraq, Iran, and so on; to the cynical arming and training of Muslim extremists in Afghanistan; to the longstanding support for occupation by expansionist settlement in

Palestinian territories; America – driven as always by corporate interests – has bred resentment among non-elite sections of the population all over Muslim lands.

That all of this follows a long history of colonial subjugation and condescension by European powers, even after decolonisation, involves the West as the target of such reaction. For some years now, this resentment has taken on an explicitly religious, Islamist rhetoric – again because Islam seems to provide an ideological peg of dignity and resistance upon which to hang these resentments.

All this is familiar. Though perhaps what is less so is that initially, and even until a very few years ago, specifically "anti-American" (or what are sometimes called "anti-imperialist") versions of Islamism were much more prevalent in Iran than in client states such as Saudi Arabia; but as a result of Al-Jazeera and other forms of communication made possible by new technologies, Muslims even in Saudi Arabia who had hitherto been uncritically "pro-American" in their sympathies have been exposed to some of the political and economic realities in Arab nations, and have been able to detach themselves from the cognitive clutch of the royal family and elites. And some of the most volatile and restless among them have (again as a result of the new communications technologies) been able to join with similar anti-American groups in both neighbouring and far-flung lands, from the caves of Afghanistan to cells in Hamburg, London and New Jersey.

The point of importance, however, is this: that this Islamist rhetoric is a dangerous, brittle source of self-respect is obvious to most Muslims in these countries, but there does not seem to be, even to them, any viable alternative. This conflicted position of many Muslims should be crucial to any analysis of our present time.

I think it can safely be said that as a matter of ubiquitous empirical fact – whether in Mumbai or Cairo, Karachi or Tehran, Afghanistan or Saudi Arabia, New Jersey or Bradford – most Muslims are not absolutists, and are in fact deeply opposed to the absolutists in their midst. This is evident in the fact that before 9/11, during elections, the "fundamentalist" parties failed to gain power, whether in Iran or in Pakistan. Even those who did not oppose the fundamentalists were too busy with their own affairs to be seduced by absolutist fantasies about an Islamic revival.

Yet these ordinary Muslims, who form the overwhelming majority in Muslim nations, have not had the confidence and courage to openly criticise the absolutists, and this is because they, too, are affected by the defensive mentality that pervades these regions. To them, to openly criticise seems to capitulate to Western habits and attitudes of arrogant domination, in colonial history and even today. What would give them the confidence and courage to criticise the absolutists in their midst? This question is of utmost urgency in our time, and it should be on the mind of every humane and sensitive American and European today.

What is perfectly obvious is that destroying impoverished nations such as Afghanistan and Iraq is not going to help, nor is the constant portrayal of the problem as Islam versus freedom and modernity. It is not freedom that ordinary non-fundamentalist Muslims are against and it is not modernity they want to shun; it is the naked, corporate-driven, geo-politically motivated wrongs of American and Western dominance of their regions which they oppose. If they stand by, silent and confused, as Islam is invoked in grotesque distortions by the most detestable elements in their society as the ultimate source of resistance against this domination, it behoves those of us who have escaped these resentments and their causes to give them the confidence to see their way out of this confusion.

To do so, we will have to call things as they are, evident to everyone except some insular American and European citizens who are unaware of the effects of their governments' actions in the world, and much more culpably, the journalists who speak and write in the mainstream media as well as mandarin intellectuals in universities. We will have to say that what happened on 9/11 was an act of atrocious, senseless and unpardonable cruelty. No effort to understand Muslim mentality, as my effort is, should or could muffle this criticism. But we will also have to say that the bombing of a parched and hungry nation like Afghanistan, of creating what seems like almost permanent insurgent mayhem in Iraq – which was already devastated by years of a cruel and immoral embargo – and then allowing the destruction of Lebanon and now Gaza, are merely the last and among the worst in a century filled with such immoral interventions. All of this can be only the first step in addressing the deep historical and contemporary sources of this defensive mentality.

We cannot forget that the confused Islamist rhetorical veneer, by which this defensive mentality presents itself to the world, is a reactionary rhetoric of the supposed pieties and glories of an Islamic *past*. But the hopes and aspirations of ordinary Muslims who have succumbed to their rhetoric are the existential hopes and aspirations for a *future* in which a radically politicised Islam has no particular place or point. If we clearly see this dialectical point, our own efforts need not fall into the confusion that the rhetoric encourages, as some writers (Christopher Hitchens, Martin Amis, Hirst

Ali, Irshad Manji, Michael Ignatieff, Niall Fergusson, Thomas Friedman, and Andrew Sullivan, to name just a few) clearly have done when they write widely read articles and books with titles such as "This is a Religious War"[1] and *The Trouble with Islam*.[2] With their shrill rhetoric, these writers, much lauded in the mainstream Western press that shapes a great deal of public opinion, are buying into the very confusion of those whom they oppose. In so doing, they are letting down the millions of ordinary Muslims all over the world who, in the end, are the only weapons America and Europe have against their terrorist enemies.

Notes

1. Andrew Sullivan, "This is a Religious War", *The New York Times*, 7 October 2001.
2. Irshad Manji, *The Trouble with Islam: A Muslim's Call for Reform in her Faith* (United States: St. Martin's Press, 2004).

Citational Exegesis of the Qur'an:
Towards a Theoretical Framework for the Construction of Meaning in Classical Islamic Thought.
The Case of the *Epistles of the Pure Brethren*
(*Rasā'il Ikhwān al-Ṣafā'*)*

Omar Alí-de-Unzaga

> ... the example of the Qur'an has been especially neglected, both by Muslim scholarship and Orientalist erudition. Very few attempts have been made to apply modern linguistic tools and conceptualization to Qur'anic Discourse without any concession to the theological vocabulary.
>
> As for the literary approach, there is nothing equivalent to N. Frye (The great code).
>
> **Mohammed Arkoun**[1]

* This paper was commissioned especially for this Festschrift; it was not presented at the workshop held at AKU-ISMC in October 2009. It was written as a tribute to Professor Arkoun by a former student of his, highlighting a particular aspect of Professor Arkoun's work. Although it is not in the same vein as the other papers, we felt it appropriate to include it in the Festschrift.

Nobody would attempt to study Islamic culture without starting with the Koran, or Hindu culture without starting with the Vedas and Upanishads.

Northrop Frye[2]

The Bible has been called the Great Code of Christian culture [...]; this is true in at least a similar measure of the Qur'an's role in Islamic culture. Therefore it is not surprising that the study of the Qur'an is not merely one particular field of study besides others, but that at the same time it fulfils the role of encyclopaedic knowledge for the devout Muslim. To us it becomes a source for the Muslim self-image.

Claude Gilliot[3]

I was Mohammed Arkoun's student between 1994–6 at the newly established Graduate Programme in Islamic Studies and Humanities at the Institute of Ismaili Studies. Professor Arkoun opened up his students' eyes to the possibility of exploring the subjects traditionally covered by Islamic Studies in a new way and continuously invited us to apply the tools developed by various disciplines to the study of the history, religion and thought of predominantly Muslim societies (a long circumlocution to avoid using the term "Islam" as an essentialised construct). This article is a contribution to honour his memory by applying concepts from linguistics, literary criticism, and philosophy of language to classical Arabic texts. It is part of a larger project on the citations of the Qur'an and their philosophical exegesis in the *Epistles of the Pure Brethren (Rasā'il Ikhwān al-ṣafā')*.

I. The Great Code

The two remarks used as heading quotes in the present chapter were both made in connection with *The Great Code*, a book by the Canadian literary critic Northrop Frye (d. 1991) on the influence of the Bible on Western literature, art and creative imagination (the equivalent to Arkoun's French *imaginaire*) in general.[4] Frye, an authority on the English Romantic poet William Blake (d. 1827), both borrowed from, and was inspired by, Blake's memorable aphorism: 'The Old & New Testaments are the Great Code of Art.'[5]

Mohammed Arkoun lamented that neither traditional Muslim scholarship nor those engaged in critical Islamic Studies have produced anything comparable to Frye's understanding of how a text or discourse turned into seminal text (in his case, the Bible, in our case the Qur'an) has become an overwhelming referent, intrinsically woven into the intellectual and literary output of a culture (in his case Anglo-Saxon literature, in our case literature in Arabic but also Persian, Turkish, and so on). Frye himself hinted to this (as seen in the heading quote).

Here I will take as a given premise that a culture or cultural network is best seen in the intertextual relations that occur between the texts produced in a socio-linguistic setting, an intertextuality that to a large extent revolves around an axial text which is both the main source of intellectual and creative inspiration, and the point to which all else relates in some way or the other. Intertextuality, however, does not merely refer to formal literary borrowings between texts but explains the dynamics of a whole socio-religio-intellectual cultural sphere (classical Islamic thought) and its relation with the texts that –with time – come to be seen as "foundational".[6] The culture, then, perceives the text as its *foundational* text, although in reality the text is shaped and reshaped by virtue of being read and re-created, so to speak, by succeeding generations and in various contexts. In this regard, we can speak of the re-creation of meaning, which is the result of a long history of reception. This is also true of the Qur'an and Islamic culture. In this chapter, I will explore how we can approach the intertextuality of Islamic literature and thought vis-à-vis the Qur'an and the reshaping of its meanings, by looking at the phenomenon of citational exegesis. Arkoun, naturally, also expressed his dismay at the paucity of the application of the findings of the social sciences (linguistics, semiotics and literary criticism in particular) to the critical scholarship on Islamic thought. This chapter builds on two of the most central ideas if Mohamed Arkoun's thought: applied *islamology*, on the one hand; and *logocentricism* on the other.

The work of the virtuoso poet Abū'l-ʿAlā' al-Maʿarrī contains many traces of an intimate thematic and structural intertextuality with the Qur'an. This is especially true of his work *al-Fuṣūl wa'l-ghayāt*, a book now only partially extant.[7] Some accused him of attempting to imitate the Qur'an or to surpass it;[8] others, however, did not see such intention.[9] Regardless of the poet's intention, what is interesting for our present purpose is that, due to religious scruples and the theological dogma of *iʿjāz* or inimitability of the Qur'an,[10] Maʿarrī's critics failed to analyse this intertextuality from a literary point of view as well as from a stance of intellectual neutrality. Indeed, the poet is reported to have said about his book, when confronted about the similarities of his work and the Qur'an:

لم تصقله المحاريب أربعمائة سنة

lam taṣqulhu'l-maḥārīb arba'a-mi'a sana
The miḥrabs have not polished it for four hundred years[11]

As we can see from this quote, attributed to Ma'arrī, he was allegedly commenting on the authority gained by the Qur'an over the centuries. This was partially due to the Qur'an's exposure to, and acceptance by, generations and generations of minds for whom it was the ultimate source of authority and truth.

It is desirable to undertake a project that allows us to enhance our understanding of the construction of meaning in classical Islamic thought. The present study is part of a project that intends to analyse the engagement of authors in various fields of knowledge with the text of the Qur'an, with regards to their citational borrowings in particular and with a view to understand the exegesis implied in the citation processes. This must be done in a manner that is free from the constraints of religious affiliation and ideological persuasion that has dominated Islamic thought, traditionally concerned about what is "orthodox" or "correct", and also without the Orientalist obsession with superficial origins of ideas, or what has been termed "parallelomania", although it could easily be termed "origin-mania".[12] The desideratum here is not to see how the Qur'an has influenced or coloured later literature and thought, but to understand the processes through which Muslim authors, in their attempt to understand the Qur'an, have actually *recreated* its meanings (and continue to do so) generation after generation and century after century, across all schools, approaches and disciplines by citing from the Qur'an in their works.

II. Citational Exegesis

This chapter is an attempt to contribute to the construction of a theoretical framework that aspires to facilitate the analysis of what can be termed *citational exegesis*, a terms that refers to the insertion or "quotational borrowing" of Qur'anic elements – verses, idioms, words, concepts, images and figures – verbatim or by way of reminiscence or echoing of the Qur'an, in works of classical Islamic thought. This citational process implies an interpretation, a particular reading, of the text which is the result of the process of transportation and adaptation that a textual element from the Qur'an undergoes from its original setting to its new interpretive *locus*. It is important to remark that here I am not referring to formal Qur'anic exegesis (*tafsīr*), nor even to explicit interpretations of particular Qur'anic motifs in intellectual or literary works. By exegesis I mean the intellectual process that allows authors to confer, attach or impose meaning onto a Qur'anic element in the process of its quotation. The quotation, then, is a transposition of the Qur'anic element into a new setting (which we will call the recipient text) that inevitably results in the semantic transformation of both the recipient text and in the interpretive reading of the Qur'an. Once a Qur'anic element or textual unit is cited in another work with an implied meaning, this immediately indicates that the way that element is understood when reading it in the text of the Qur'an itself is coloured and limited by the meaning implied in the citation.

Our case study here will be the *Epistles of the Pure Brethren* (*Rasā'il Ikhwān al-ṣafā'*), a fourth/tenth-century work produced in Iraq.[13] The *Epistles* are an anonymous work, though presumably composed by a group of thinkers based in Basra whose names are identified by Abū Ḥayyān al-Tawḥīdī (d. 414/1023).[14] They comprise fifty-two treatises organised in four parts: mathematics-logics, natural sciences, soul-related disciplines and treatises on religion and divine law.[15]

To illustrate the point I wish to make about citational exegesis, we may refer to the following cryptic expression of the Qur'an:[16] *wa 'alayhā tisʿata 'ashara* – over it are nineteen and the way it is interpreted in the *Epistles*. The Qur'anic text is part of Sūrat al-Muddaththir, one of the very earliest suras to be communicated by Muhammad to his fellow Meccans. In this sura, through a powerful string of short verses mostly in rhyme (for the first part of the verse) the voice of the communicator (presumably God) addresses a second person singular (presumably Muhammad) who is described as shrouded in a mantle and is exhorted to arise and preach. It then goes on to refer to those who are successful but haughtily reject the revelation as "nothing but mortal speech". The verse then describes the terrible destiny of such people: they will be roasted in "Saqar", a mysterious word and place of which we are only told two things: *lā tubqī wa lā tadharu, lawwāḥatun li'l-bashari, wa 'alayhā tisʿata 'ashara* – it spares not, neither leaves alone scorching the flesh; over it are nineteen. After this obscure numerical reference, the text continues into what seems to be a gloss verse,[17] which contains a totally different internal structure and feel. It is a self-referential commentary on the allusive and metaphorical language of the Qur'an. The image (*mathal*) is explained: the Fire (*al-nār*) is guarded by angels, whose number is a "trial" (*fitna*) for all, believers and unbelievers alike. Due to this gloss verse, most commentators interpreted the *over it are nineteen* verse as containing an ellipsis which should be understood as "nineteen angels". However, when we read how this phrase has been cited by the Ikhwān al-ṣafāʾ we find a different interpretation. In Epistle 30, "On the Specificity of Pleasures and the Wisdom and Quiddity of Life and Death", the Ikhwān al-ṣafāʾ define Hell (*jahannam*) as "the world of generation and decay" (*ʿālam al-kawn waʾl-fasād*) which corresponds to the sublunar world, and Paradise (*janna*) as "the world of spirits and the extent of heavens" (*ʿālam al-arwāḥ wa saʿat al-samāwāt*).[18] As a result, the inhabitants of the former are the souls that are attached to animal bodies that are affected by pain and aching; those of the latter are the angelic souls that inhabit the world of the spheres. For the Ikhwān al-ṣafāʾ it is possible to exit the lower world, given that *jahannam* (and they quote from a verse of Qurʾan which refers to the followers of Iblīs[19]) *has seven gates* (*lahā sabʿatu abwābin*). They identify the *seven gates* with the seven planets (*al-sabʿa al-sayyāra*, literally, the seven wandering [stars], the expression used to refer to the visibly travelling heavenly bodies – Moon, Sun, Mercury, Venus, Mars, Jupiter and Saturn, as opposed to the fixed stars). The influence of the seven planets on the affairs and beings of this world, in the astral philosophy of the Ikhwan al-ṣafāʾ manifests itself through their passing by the twelve zodiacal signs, thus making in total nineteen.[20] The point here is that it is only after the Qurʾanic verse on the "nineteen" is cited in this astral context, that it is possible to read the Qurʾan again in a new light: *lā tubqī wa lā tadharu, lawwāḥatun liʾl-bashari, wa ʿalayhā tisʿata ʿashara* – it spares not, neither leaves alone scorching the flesh; over it are nineteen, would mean that the earth is the place of suffering for the souls trapped into bodies and which are under the influence of the seven planets and the twelve signs. The implied exegesis of a citation has had an effect on the received meaning of the Qurʾan text and many readers would have understood the Qurʾan differently after reading the citation in the *Epistles of the Ikhwān al-ṣafāʾ*.

I will limit myself here to suggesting some lines of enquiry based on a number of tools developed in recent decades in the fields of philosophy of language, literary criticism and theories of meaning and pragmatics. It is not possible here to provide material from a practical text analysis to contrast such a theory.[21] Neither is this the place to elaborate on the philological and literary theory concepts elaborated in classical Arabic sources with regards to the phenomenon of citation. I am referring to the classifications of "quotational borrowings", or unmarked, non-explicit citations – quotations in poetry and prose literature and in intellectual production in general, of poetic lines and later also of Qurʾanic verses, hadiths, proverbs and aphorisms. The main technical terms used were *taḍmīn* (embedded quotation) and *iqtibās* (umarked quotation), but also other terms whose positive or negative connotations change according to the critics – *tamaththul* and *tamthīl* ("citation"), *ijtilāb* and *istilḥāq* ("injection" and annexation of familiar verses in new compositions), *istizāda* ("supplementation"), *ḥusn al-taḍmīn* ("good quotation"), *intiḥāl* ("plagiarism"), *diʿāma* ("propping up"), and *iṣṭirāf* ("expropriation" which implies claiming authorship), *ihtidām* ("cannibalisation", a substantial borrowing with only a few changes from the original), *iḥāla* ("insinuation"), *ishāra* and *talmīḥ* ("allusion"), *irād al-mathal* (borrowing of part of a proverb), *tasmīṭ, tawshīḥ, talmīḥ, talwīḥ* (later terms equivalent to *taḍmīn*), *istiʿāna* (borrowing a whole verse or more), *idāʿ/rafw* ("padding", borrowing less than a line), *istishhād* ("illustrative citation" of poetry in prose), *ḥall* ("prosification").[22]

It is worth nothing in this regard that classical Arabic literary theory, sophisticated as it is, is insufficient and even inadequate to tackle the issue at hand, the implicit citational exegesis of the Qurʾan. By way of illustration we can refer to Gustav E. Grunebaum's mention of the 4–5th/10–11th century Ashʿarī *mutakallim* and Mālikī jurisprudent Abū Bakr Muḥammad b. al-Ṭayyib al-Baqillānī,[23] "who disposes of a rich terminology with respect to poetical figures and tropes" and yet "has no terms to designate the different types of literary dependency with which he is constantly concerned in his discussion of the uniqueness of the Koran".[24]

III. Citing the Qurʾan: Quotation Formulas and their Exegetical Rile. The Case of the Epistles of the Pure Brethren (*Rasāʾil Ikhwān al-Ṣafāʾ*)

The Qurʾanic material present in the *Epistles* may be divided into three types: *echoes*, *mentions* and *quotations*. The *echoes* are Qurʾanic words or phrases used in their original form or slightly modified in the text of the *Epistles* without an explicit reference to their Qurʾanic origin (for example, "those firmly grounded in its knowledge" *al-rāsikhūna fī ʿilmihā*, an echo of a Qurʾanic verse;[25] the Encompassing Pedestal *al-kursiyy al-wāsiʿ* another Qurʾanic echo[26]). The most common example of Qurʾanic echo in the *Epistles* is the oft-repeated formula "Know, oh brother, may God support you and us with a spirit [sent] from Him (...) *Iʿlam, yā akhī, ayyadakaʾllāhu wa iyyānā bi-rūḥin minhu*" which is used as a header for the introduction of new topics. This phrase derives from a Qurʾanic verse[27] in which the authors of the *Epistles* could find the basis of their spiritual brotherhood as opposed to blood or tribal kinship or partisanship.

The *mentions* are references to particular subjects that are explicitly indicated as part of the Qur'an (or any of the other revealed Books). These mentions may be *specified*, followed by one or more Qur'anic verses, for example, "(...) the pleasure of the drinks of paradise (*ladhdhat sharāb al-jinān*), [which is] mentioned in the Qur'an", is followed by a Qur'anic verse[28], or *unspecified*, in which no particular verse is given, for example "(...) the scent and breath *al-rawḥ wa'l-rayḥān*, [which are] mentioned in the Qur'an"[29]. *Mentions* can be quantified in three ways:

a) in a *general way*, in which the subject is identified as being mentioned numerous times for example, "(...) and there are many verses in the Qur'an with that meaning"[30]; b) in a *particular way*, with reference to particular sūras of the Qur'an, for example, "(...) and He also mentioned the features of the hypocrites (...) in many verses, especially in Sūrat al-Anfāl , Sūrat al-Tawba, and Sūrat al-Aḥzāb"[31] and c) in a *numerical way*, giving the number of verses in which the subject appears for example, "(...) and God has mentioned His promise to the believers in the Qur'an in about one thousand verses"[32].

The *quotations* are the literal citations of whole verses or part of them that are usually found following an idea or concept developed in the *Epistles*. Whether they appear individually or as a series of verses joined together, quotations are introduced, expanded, commented on, or even interpreted by words or phrases placed both before and after the verses that will be termed *prefixed* and *suffixed* formulas, as the following sections explain.

1. Prefixed Introductory Formulas

More than one fifth of quotations (319 or 22.8 per cent) are *unmarked*, that is, they are introduced in the text with no textual indication that they are citations from the Qur'an. The rest, that is, more than three quarters of all quotations (1080 or 77.2 per cent) have prefixed introductory formulas, which can be divided into five categories: simple citation formulas, allusion, corroboration, deictic and direct speech formulas.

1.1 Simple Citation Formulas[33]

The quotations introduced by simple formulas are among the most common in the *Epistles*. They consist of expressions of the type '*kamā qāla* [*Allāh*]', or *kamā dhakara Allāh bi-qawlihi*. Other variants include: *wa qad qāla Allāh*; *wa qāla; thumma qāla; wa kadhālika qāla; wa innamā qāla; wa qawluhu; wa bi-qawlihi; wa ka-qawlihi; fa-hakadhā qawluhu; thumma yaqūlu'llāh*;

wa Allāh yaqūl; wa huwa yuqāl. Some are in the impersonal passive: *wa qīla;* according to the type of verb used, they may imply mention (*kamā / wa dhakara Allāh* [+/- *bi-qawlihi / fa-qāla*]; *kamā dhakarahu Allāh; kamā dhakara fa-qāla; wa qad dhakara Allāh dhālika fī'l-Qur'an al-Karīm idh yaqūl*); command (*kamā amara Allāh bi-qawlihi; lammā amara Allāh bi'l-taʿāwun ḥaythu qāl; wa amarahu bi'l-malāṭifa fa-qāla t.; ... amara bi-jihādihi fa-qāla Allāh*); explanation (*kamā bayyana Allāh*); description (*kamā waṣafa Allāh*) or promise (*kamā waʿada Allāh* [+/- *bi-qawlihi*]). Other less frequent verbs are: warn (*mā qad nabbahaka Allāh lahu wa dhakaraka iyyāhu bi-qawlihi; wa kamā nabbahanā Allāh wa qāl*); summarise (*wa'khtaṣara bi-qawlihi*); stamp, finish (*mā khatamahā bihi qawluhu*).

The role of the particle *kamā* is often exegetical, though not in a straight-forward manner, as can be seen in the following example: the *Epistles* argue that every human being partakes from the "universal human soul" (*al-nafs al-kulliyya al-insāniyya*), and conclude "as [God] mentions in his statement (*kamā dhakara bi-qawlihi*) 'your creation and your uprising are as but as a single soul *(wa mā khalqukum wa-lā baʿthukum illā ka-nafsin wāḥida)*'."[34] The particle *kamā* (and indeed other equivalent particles such as *wa qad, thumma, wa kadhālika, wa innamā,* and so forth) has a double function: it acts both as a link with the previous co-text and as introduction of the Qur'anic verse, in such a way that the Qur'anic individual is equated to the universal soul of Neoplatonist thought. The particularity of the *Epistles* is that these formulas are not textually transparent (as one would expect with the use of *kamā*), since they usually imply an interpretation of the text. Another example of this can be found when the *Epistles* discuss the universal force that gives life to all creatures.[35] This force is said to have penetrated all the upper spheres down to the centre of the earth and is expected to return to the outer sphere (*al-muḥīṭ*), causing "the raising, the ascension and the resurrection (*baʿth, nushūr, miʿrāj, qiyāma*) *as God mentions:* 'To Him the angels and the Spirit mount up in a day whereof the measure is fifty thousand years *(yaʿruju'l-malāʾikatu wa'l-rūḥu ilayhi fī yawmin kāna miqdāruhu khamsīna alfa sana)*'."[36] Here, not only is this obscure eschatological reference identified with the resurrection (which in itself is already interpretative) but the angels and spirit are also equated with a universal physical force.

Occasionally, the simple citation formula includes additional, appended information which refers to the characters involved in the Qur'anic narration. Thus, we find: a) references to the addressee, following a formula of the type '*wa qāla li-nabiyyihi.*' This addressee is usually Muḥammad, but it can also be other prophets like Moses, or other characters like Iblīs and the angels; b) the speech of a Qur'anic character other than God, introduced by formulas of the type "*kamā qāla/ dhakara Allāh ḥikāyatan 'an ...*"[37] in which the main speaker, God, "cites" or "relates" from *(ḥikāyatan 'an)* the speech of different characters such as the angels, the prophets, Iblīs, the jinn, Pharaoh, other characters involved in Pharaoh's story, and so on; c) the identification (exegetical in character) of some of the Qur'anic speakers. For instance, while discussing the spiritual force *(quwwa rūḥāniyya)* that upholds the existence of the "inhabitants of the heavens and the earth", the authors say: "and [God] relates from them *(wa qāla ḥikāyatan 'anhum)*: 'None of us is there, but has a known station ...*(wa mā minnā illā lahu maqāmun ma'lūm)*'."[38]

1.2 Allusion Formulas

Allusion formulas follow the type "*wa ilayhi ashāra bi-qawlihi*" and are highly representative of the exegesis practised in the *Epistles*, one based on allusion, word-association and contextual interpretation. An example of this is the discussion of the status of souls after death. Evil souls are potential devils which become actual devils when they separate from the body and begin to "whisper" *(waswasa)* and incite those souls still embodied to evil acts. The authors add: "and it is to these souls that [God] alludes when He says 'from the evil of the sneaking whisperer who whispers in the hearts of mankind [etc.] *(min sharri'l-waswāsi'l-khannās, alladhī yuwaswisu fī ṣudūri'l-nās)*'."[39] Allusion formulas are also used to introduce an interpretation not of a particular person or a name, but of a concept, with the formula "*wa ilā hādhā'l-ma'nā ashāra bi-qawlihi*". For instance, the *Epistles* compare the relation between the number one and the other numbers (units, tens, hundreds and so forth) to the relation between the bringer of the religious path *(ṣāḥib al-sharī'a)* and the successive generations of people, who are divided in a series of ranks till the day of resurrection, when "all of them will become a single group *(jumla wāḥida)* as [God] mentioned with his statement alluding to this concept: 'Upon the day when the Spirit and the angels stand in ranks they shall speak not *(yawma yaqūmu'l-rūḥu wa'l-malā'ikatu ṣaffan lā yatakallamūn)*'"[40] and "'We muster them so that We leave not so much as one of them behind; and they shall be presented before their Lord in ranks *(wa ḥasharnāhum fa-lam nughādir minhum aḥad; wa 'uriḍū 'alā rabbika ṣaffā)*'."[41] The basis for the allusion is the term *ṣaffan* (in ranks), which the *Epistles* seem to interpret as meaning not only "ranks" but also "one group." The term *rūḥ* is also interpreted as referring to the totality of human souls, which, as was explained before, will return to their origin as one single soul.

1.3 Corroboration Formulas

Corroboration formulas are those used by the authors of the *Epistles* to present the verse as a proof of authority for what they have just said. These formulas follow the types *wa taṣdīq dhālika qawl Allāh, wa al-dalīl ʿalā dhālika qawluhu, al-dalīl ʿalā ṣiḥḥat mā qulnā wa ḥaqīqat mā waṣafnā qawluʾllāh*, among others.[42] For instance, the *Epistles* identify the Hell of the revealed scriptures with the philosophical world of generation and corruption (*ʿālam al-kawn waʾl-fasād*). In order to substantiate that belief, they say: "and the proof (*dalīl*) of this is [God's] statement: 'depart unto the triple-massing shadow![43] (*ẓillin dhī thalāthi shuʿab*)'."[44] This verse has been interpreted as referring to three columns of smoke rising from the fires of Hell.[45] However, the Pure Brethren see it as "an allusion (*ishāra*) to the souls confined in bodies with length, breadth and depth, which are under in sub-lunar sphere." This is an indication of how the *Epistles* bridge the obscurities of revealed lexicon and philosophical concepts.

1.4 Deictic Formulas

Through these formulas, particular elements from the text of the *Epistles* are related to Qurʾanic words and verses in a process of identification. They may contain relative pronouns (following the types *fa-hiya al-lātī dhakarahā Allāhu bi-qawlihī*; *al-ladhīna dhammahum bi-qawlihī*), personal pronouns (*kamā madaḥahum Allāh*) or regular nouns (*wa akhbara ʿan ahl al-jahāla fa-qāla*). The words used in these formulas vary from meanings of praise (*al-ladhīna madaḥahum Allāh t. bi-qawlihī*) to reproval (*al-ladhīna dhammahum rabb al-ʿālamīn bi-qawlihī*), promise (*kamā waʿada Allāh dhālika bi-qawlihī*), description (*kamā waṣafahā Allāh; wa qāla fī ṣifat ahl al-janna; kamā dhakara Allāh a.j. fī waṣf al-malāʾika*) and so on. Although this type of formula is the most likely to provide the ground for interpretation and semantic expansion, only two examples are mentioned here. In both cases, the *Epistles* easily identify Qurʾanic elements by applying a verse to a particular kind of person, concept or situation. For instance, the authors exhort their reader: "be not of those who walk on [the earth] and forsake and are neglectful of its signs (*āyāt*),"[46] and proceed:

"they are those about whom God says: 'I made them not witnesses of the creation of the heavens and earth, neither of the creation of themselves; I would never take those who lead others astray to be My supporters' (*mā ashhattuhum khalqa'l-samāwāti wa'l-arḍi wa-lā khalqa anfusihim wa mā kuntu muttakhidha'l-muḍillīn 'aduḍā).*"[47] On another occasion, we are told that if humans nurture their soul, they can reach the highest human level, which borders on the angelical condition, and come close to their Creator, a reward for which there can be no description; the authors add: "as God describes (*waṣafa*) when He says: 'No soul knows what comfort is laid up for them secretly, as a recompense for what they were doing' (*fa-lā ta'lamu nafsun mā ukhfiya lahum min qurrati a'yunin jazā'a bi-mā kānū ya'lamūn).* "[48] In this latter case the *Epistles* interpret the soul's ignorance of the reward as the impossibility of describing it, since they themselves have identified the reward as the ascension of a human being to the angelical level and proximity to God.

1.5 Direct Speech Formulas

Finally, other quotations cite the words of different Qur'anic personae and are introduced with formulas of direct speech, such as: *alladhīna yaqūlūna; ḥaythu qālū; wa qālū; wa min dhālika qawl al-mu'minīn; qawl al-rabbāniyyīn; ḥīna qālū li-Qārūn; wa Iblīs (...) qāla; wa qāla Yūsuf; kamā sa'ala Yūsuf al-ṣiddīq; wa kadhālika Ibrāhīm*, and so on.

2. Suffixed Formulas

Some quotations are followed by *suffixed* formulas, which are mostly exegetical as they consist of a single word or phrase such as *ya'nī, ay* or *wa huwa*, devices typical of paraphrastic *tafsīr*.[49] To cite just one example of the use of *ya'nī*, let us consider the citation of the verse '*ilayhi yaṣ'adu'l-kalimu'l-ṭayyibu wa'l-'amalu'l-ṣāliḥu yarfa'uhu*' (Unto Him good words ascend, and the pious deed does He exalt).[50] Five out of the six times this verse is quoted the authors add: *ya'nī rūḥ al-mu'min* ("that is, the spirit of the believer").[51] Thus, the *Epistles* interpret the ascension of good words to God as the ascension of the soul to the world of the spirits ('*ālam al-arwāḥ*) after its separation from the body.[52]

IV. The Art of Ignoring Qur'anic Citations

The *Epistles* were criticised by Abū Sulaymān al-Manṭiqī al-Sijistānī (d. c. 375/985) and a certain Jarīrī for supposedly having attempted to mix philosophy and revealed religion.[53] My contention is that this is because of the high number of Qur'anic citations in a work whose thought is engrained in a Neoplatonic framework. There are more than 1,600 citations of the Qur'an in the *Epistles*, not counting the many echoes and reminiscences which do not count as actual citations. It is also my contention that while some classical sources condemned the *Epistles'* use and interpretation of the Qur'an as unacceptable, most contemporary scholars have ignored their use of the Qur'an as irrelevant and superfluous.[54]

One such scholar is Ian Netton, whose book *Muslim Neoplatonists* (henceforth *MN*) was the only English monograph on the *Epistles* for a long time since its first publication in 1982.[55] Netton's book has become an important reference for students and scholars who approach the subject. Until recently it remained "the standard short introduction in English to the Brethren of Purity".[56] *MN* is commendable for its comprehensiveness and clarity, for having redirected attention to the text itself, away from discussions on the authorship, and for having identified and critically analysed the main sources of the *Epistles*.[57]

However, *MN* presents a number of important limitations. By considering that "the *Rasā'il* contain not only Greek, Judaeo-Christian, and Qur'anic influences but also a variety of Persian, Indian, Buddhist, Zoroastrian, and Manichean elements as well"[58] Netton downgrades the importance that the Qur'an has for the authors to a mere influence among many. In fact, the section on "The Cloak of the Qur'an"[59] occupies less than two thirds of chapter 5 "Uses of Literature", which also contains a section on "Indian literature." In addition, Netton's approach to the use of the Qur'an in the *Epistles* leads him to some questionable conclusions in two regards: the "disguise" of "heterodox" positions with a Qur'anic "garb" or "cloak," and the issue of the authors' "heterodoxy". Netton's approach may be summarised as follows:

1. The Qur'an as a "Smoke-Screen"

Netton states that there is "nothing unusual" about using the Qur'an "to document particular doctrines and concepts", since "numerous Arab [sic] authors have done likewise."[60] In the *Epistles* both "Qur'anic revelation and pagan dogma and philosophy have a place," and therefore the Qur'an should be seen as a "fertile source of inspiration and backing" for the authors mainly Neoplatonic doctrine.[61] According to Netton, however, the authors' "relationship with Islam" was "uneasy to say the least."[62] As a result, in his view, the "thoroughly Qur'anic substrate", which Netton admits the *Epistles* have,[63] prevent them from being called "*un-Islamic* with no qualification."[64]. Next, Netton asserts that the authors accepted the Qur'an, but adds that "they went far beyond" it. In Netton's understanding, the authors used the Qur'an as "an excellent smoke-screen for doctrines which were entirely un-Qur'anic."[65] They attempted to "cloak" their "wilder Neoplatonic heresies" from "hostile eyes" with "the Islamic orthodoxy of the [Qur'an]" or, in other words, with a "liberal sprinkling of Qur'anic quotations."[66] In order to disguise ("or at least, make less obvious to unfriendly eyes") their "Neoplatonism and eclectic toleration" the authors used an "external cloak" "woven from the Qur'an."[67] Netton's explanation as to why it was "necessary" for the authors to cloak their doctrines "in an orthodox Islamic garb" is that "their teaching may provoke unrest" and their safety would be at risk.[68] Finally, Netton says that the authors were successful in disguising "some of the unorthodox implications of their philosophy." To support this claim, Netton presents the circulation of the *Epistles* "among orthodox Muslims" as a proof.[69]

2. Orthodoxy[70]

Netton's approach to what "orthodoxy" is, is clear: the Qur'an, he says, is "the basic scriptural text of orthodox Islam."[71] He sees the *Epistles* operating "basically from a framework of Qur'anic orthodoxy"[72] but he asks the question, "how Islamically orthodox are the *Rasā'il?*" Netton argues that the *Epistles* "contain much that would have been unacceptable to Sunnī Islam",[73] and that the authors' tolerance and acceptance go "beyond the limited standards of early Islam; if argued to their logical conclusion they would result in heresy [sic] (*bid'a*)";[74] similarly, "many of their beliefs were entirely outside the pale of Islam" and, for instance, their concept of God "differed radically from that of orthodox Islam".[75] The "single focus" that inspired the authors' acceptance of diverse sources, Netton believes, was "the universal concept of purity, and not Islam."[76] He concludes that the authors are "reluctant Muslims"[77] but that they are "eager to maintain" an "impression of orthodoxy", as when they declare that their thought is "the creed of our father Abraham".[78]

Netton's arguments have remained unchallenged for several years,[79] with a notable exception:[80] Salim Kemal has questioned Netton's idea that the authors included many Qur'anic quotations so that a superficial reading would "fail to identify" non-Islamic elements. Instead, Kemal highlights the importance of paying attention to the authors' self-perception. As "doctors of the soul" they started from the acceptance of the Qur'anic injunctions and then attempted to show "the comprehensiveness of Islamic thought and doctrine" by examining critically and incorporating "much of the apparently non-Islamic cultural and philosophical alternatives".[81]

To depict the tenth century, as Netton's conclusions would suggest, in terms of a static distinction between orthodoxy and heterodoxy misses the complex realities of the time. The same view is held by other scholars, such as Bosworth, who holds that the "religious or philosophical orthodoxy" of the *ikhwān al-ṣafāʾ* were "dubious in the eyes of the official spokesmen for Islam,"[82] a vague and misleading denomination that is left unidentified. An important question is left unexplored: What happens when two or more competing groups claim to be orthodox at the same time and the same place with different dogmas?[83]

Netton's approach can be visualised in the following diagram:

Diagram 1

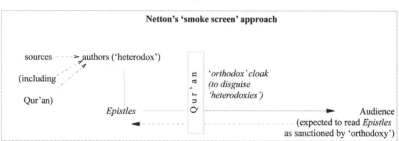

V. Theoretical Framework

In order to study the use of the Qur'an in the *Epistles of the Pure Brethren*, I draw from a theoretical framework propounded by Arkoun in his study of *al-Iʿlām bi-Manāqib al-Islām*[84] by Abūʾl-Ḥasan al-ʿĀmirī.[85] In Arkoun's words, in order to "exploit a document related to the history of thought, we must restore the relationship writing-text-reading in all its complexity. [...] The relationship is further complicated by the fact that every author has been a reader before, while the reader has not always been an author."

Arkoun's approach to classical texts aims at a research that is "extended to include analysis of the implicit information contained in any discourse," and strives to "become simultaneously aware of the content of a given discourse as an act of knowing and of our situation, as readers, in relation to that discourse."[86] With this in mind, our exegetical approach can be differentiated from Netton's with the following diagram.

Diagram 2

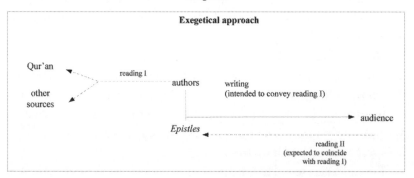

Netton's *MN* considers the authors of the *Epistles* fundamentally as Neoplatonist syncretists and only secondarily as "reluctant Muslims". In this scheme, the Qur'an represents orthodoxy and Neoplatonism heterodoxy. The combination of the two in the *Epistles* leads Netton to suggest that the authors consciously concealed and embellished the "heterodox" character of their work with a façade of Qur'anic quotations. However, this view disregards the exegetical character of the *Epistles*, both as a *writing* and as a *reading*, that is, as an exercise in which the authors are as much writers as they are readers (of their sources). The *Epistles*-as-writing are a result of the *Epistles*-as-reading. Similarly, the use of Qur'anic quotations are the result of the way the authors interpreted them. Our approach is therefore fundamentally exegetical and contends that the Qur'anic quotations are best analysed when attention is paid to the implicit exegetical value of each use or quote.

Four concepts originating in the field of philosophy of language as well as the disciplines of semantic linguistics and pragmatics can be applied for our purposes.[87] These concepts are (1) the importance of usage for the meaning, and the role of the context and the co-text in the determination of meaning; (2) the principle of cooperation and implicature; (3) the principle of relevance; and (4) intertextuality and intratextuality.[88]

1. Determining Meaning: Use and Context

In his *Philosophical Investigations*, Ludwig Wittgenstein highlighted the importance of analysing the use of words to understand their meaning. Wittgenstein set himself to examine the "language-game," an expression used to refer to the whole consisting of language and the context into which it is woven. He advised: "Let the use of the words teach you their meaning."[89] In addition, he stated that "for a large class of cases – though not for all – in which we employ the word "meaning" it can be defined thus: the meaning of a word is its use in the language,"[90] and that "meaning is the use of the word."[91]

This study retains Wittgenstein's meaning-as-use theory as well as the idea that language fulfils a multiplicity of communicative functions, and that those functions can be studied by paying attention to the actual uses of language and by retracing the steps by which those uses are reached. In Wittgenstein's words: "one cannot guess the way a word functions. One must *look* at its use and learn from that."[92]

These ideas are tested here in order to analyse the use (or rather, uses) of Qur'anic quotations in the *Epistles*. My contention is that the *meaning* that each quote from the scriptures (in this case the Qur'an, though the same is true of the Torah or the Gospels) has for the authors of the *Epistles* can be determined if we examine the *uses* of that quote in the text as a whole. Each quotation, each use of a Qur'anic verse in the *Epistles*, is embedded in a co-text, an immediate and surrounding textual context. The extended textual context or co-text are the *Epistles* as a whole, and the context of situation is the intellectual and political moment in history in which they were produced.[93] The difficulties surrounding the exact historical contextualisation of the *Epistles* oblige us to look closely at the co-texts in which Qur'anic quotations are inserted. This perspective allows the researcher to focus on the disambiguation role – that is the role played by the co-text (in this case the *Epistles*) in the selection of one interpretation among many possible ones.

2. The Principle of Cooperation; the Concept of Implicature

Another crucial concept is the "principle of cooperation" as defined by philosopher Paul Grice. The participants in a conversation "cooperate" in order to communicate, and expect the others to make the required contributions in their exchange. For a speaking subject to mean something by a certain utterance, according to Grice, is for him to intend that such an utterance has an effect on the audience "by means of the recognition of this intention."[94]

Moreover, the meaning of an utterance is said to include the proposition expressed and what the proposition implies or "implicature," in Grace's terminology.[95] Therefore, in extrapolating these concepts to apply them to textual analysis – such as that performed here on the *Epistles* – the reader must assume that the authors are cooperative and therefore must make implicatures about the text, especially about exegetical ones. Furthermore, the reader must *recognise* the *intention* of the authors – in our case, in the way and manner in which they quote from the Qur'an.

3. The Principle of Relevance

The pragmatic principle of relevance[96] says that to communicate is to claim an individual's attention, which implies that the information communicated is relevant. In order to "perceive" the relevance of an utterance, the hearer must be able to supply some premises and derive contextual implications.[97] When the hearer fails to do so, he is unable to see the intended relevance.

4. Intertextuality and Intratextuality

Intertextuality, a concept coined by linguist and psychoanalyst Julia Kristeva,[98] refers to the participation of both author and reader in a variety of overlapping meanings with regard to the relationships between a given text and other texts. A more recent term, intratextuality, refers to the relationships that exist between parts of a text (or between the parts and the whole)[99] that contribute to the understanding of the text.

VI. How Context Determines Meaning

In the relationship between meaning and context, three levels must be considered: text (for example a verse), co-text (the surrounding text, which may include other verses too), and context (which may be textual, for example, the *Epistles*, or situational, for example, the intellectual and socio-political conditions in which the work appeared).

A text is marked by connectedness, that is, cohesion in form (through certain devices) and coherence in content, and by relevance to the participants in the communicative process (authors-readers). Taking Netton's smoke screen theory to its logical consequences, the *Epistles* would appear to be a non-cohesive text, a text that can be read without the Qur'anic quotations without much modification (as in Bausani's summary). In these readings, the quotations are regarded as not more than intrusions, or as a seal used to authenticate and sanctify certain ideas. In this way, the relevance of the quotations is considered to be minimal.

However, the *intertextual* character of the work is clear, since the reader of the *Epistles* is repeatedly referred to the Qur'an. Similarly, an *intratextual* approach is essential when one considers that a vast number of verses are quoted several times in different places in the *Epistles*. Each use is determined by the different contexts and the surrounding co-text. Paraphrasing Wittgenstein, in order to understand the total meaning given to a particular verse by the authors we must look for the sum of its uses, which will be found in how and where they are quoted.

The contention of this study is that the Qur'anic quotations provide cohesion to the *Epistles*. Each Qur'anic verse quoted is, in linguistic terms, a text-unit and each quotation represents a transfer of context, as can be seen in the following diagram.

Diagram 3

The citational process

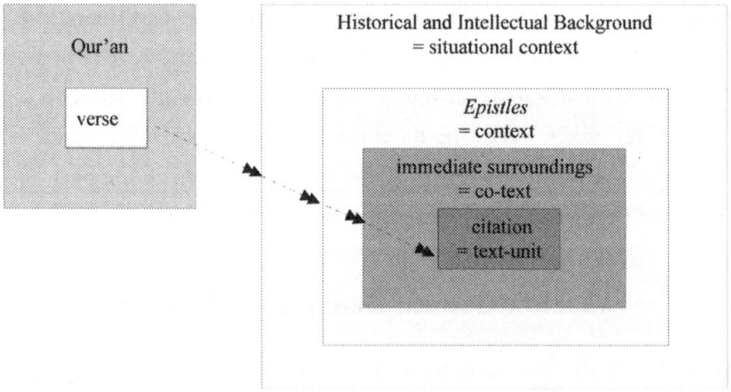

In the *Epistles*, Qur'anic quotations are normally introduced after an idea is developed. An introductory formula usually precedes the verses, though this is not always the case. The meaning given to the verse by the authors is intimately linked to the surrounding (mainly preceding) co-text. Often, it is possible to read the text backwards (the quotations first and then the preceding paragraph) in such a way that the text seems to be an explanation, that is a *tafsīr*, of the verses quoted.[100] Thus, the quotation of a verse in a particular context (or rather co-text) often implies an interpretation of the verse. In other words, the meaning of the verse and that of the context that surrounds it are intimately linked. They cannot be separated because they were conceived as different expressions of the same truths.

Therefore, in order to "uncover" this contextual interpretation, we must:

1. Identify the text-units that have undergone a transfer of context, the Qur'anic verses quoted in the Epistles.
2. Classify the co-textual relationship with each verse and determine: whether there is a) an explicit expansion of its meaning (by way of prefixed or suffixed formulas or other exegetical comments), or b) an implicit expansion (this happens in most cases).
3. Detect the role of the context in order to understand the meaning assigned to the verses by the authors (contextual exegesis).

In addition, it would be useful to carry out a comparative study with other exegetical works (such as formal, traditionalist commentaries of the Qur'an, or Sufi commentaries) to check the uniqueness or similarities of the use and interpretation of the Qur'anic material in the *Epistles*. However, this is outside the scope of this study.

To address the issue of the combination of philosophy and scripture we may ask whether the Qur'an is in fact the authors' doctrinal starting point and whether consequently they embrace philosophical ideas that agree with their Qur'anic interpretation, or rather (and this would be Netton's position) whether their main purpose is to establish philosophical concepts and then to find solace in discovering coincidences in the Qur'an. This study has proposed that the answer lies in neither one nor the other approach. Instead, we find the answer in what can be described as the hermeneutics of correspondence or harmonising exegesis.

Notes

1. Mohammed Arkoun, *The Unthought in Contemporary Islamic Thought* (London: Saqi Books in association with The Institute of Ismaili Studies, 2002), p. 80 and p. 58, respectively.

2. Northrop Frye, *Words with Power, being a second study of "The Bible and Literature"*, ed. Michael Dolzani, Toronto, University of Toronto Press, 2008, p. 14.

3. Claude Gilliot, 'Kontinuität und Wandel in der "klassichen" islamischen Koranuslegung (II.VII.-XII./XIX. Jh.), *Der Islam*, 85 (2010), p. 3. I would like to thank Gwendolin Goldbllom for the translation from the original German.

4. Northrop Frye, *The Great Code. The Bible and Literature* (New York: Harcourt Brace Jovanovich, 1981).

5. This sentence was written by Blake in his last illuminated work, an annotated print including maxims that surrounded the image of a classical statue of Laocoön. See William Blake, *The Complete Poetry and Prose of William Blake*, ed. David V. Erdman, commentary by Harold Bloom (Garden City, NY: Doubleday, 1965), p. 271.

6. On the concept of intertextuality see below, p. 185.

7. Abū'l-'Alā' al-Ma'arrī, *Al-Fuṣūl wa'l-ghāyāt fī tamjīd Allāh wa'l-mawā'iẓ*, ed. Maḥmūd Ḥasan Zanātī (Cairo, Maṭba'at Ḥijāzī, 1356/1938); ed. al-Sa'īd al-Sayyid 'Ibāda as *al-Fahāris al-mufaṣṣala li'l-fuṣūl wa'l-ghayāt* (Ma'had al-Makhṭūṭāt al-'Arabiyya, 1999); on this work see August Fischer, *Der Koran des Abu 'l-'Alā' al-Ma'arri*, Verhandlungen der Sächsischen Akademie der Wissenschaft, Philologisch-Historische Klasse, 94 (Leipzig, 1942), no. 2, and Richard Hartmann, *Zu dem Kitāb al-Fuṣūl wa l-ghāyāt des Abu 'l-'Alā' al-Ma'arri*, Abhandlungen der Preussischen Akademie der Wissenschaften, Philosophisch-historische Klasse (Berlin, 1944).

8. See for example, Kamāl al-Dīn Ibn al-'Adīm, *Bughyat al-ṭalab fī ta'rīkh Ḥalab*, ed. Suhayl Zakkār (Beirut, Dār al-Fikr, 1988-9), vol. 2, p. 879-880; Shams al-Dīn al-Dhahabī, *Ta'rīkh al-islām*, ed. Bashshār 'Awwād Ma'rūf (Beirut, Dār al-Gharb al-Islāmī, 1424/2003), vol. 9, p. 726; Dhahabī, *Siyar a'lām al-nubalā'*, ed. Muṣṭafā 'Abd al-Qādir 'Aṭā (Beirut, Dār al-Kutub al-'Ilmiyya, 14252003/), vol. 11, p. 388; Ibn Ḥajar al-'Asqalānī, *Lisān al-mīzān*, ed. 'Alī Aḥmad 'Abd al-Mawjūd and 'Alī Muḥammad Mu'awwaḍ (Beirut: Dār al-Kutub al-'Ilmiyya, 1996), vol. 1, p. 302; and Yāqūt al-Ḥamawī, *Mu'jam al-Udabā' Irshād al-arīb ilā ma'rifat al-adīb*, ed. Iḥsān 'Abbās (Beirut: Dār al-Gharb al-Islāmī, 1993), vol. 1, p. 418); see also Jār Allāh al-Zamakhsharī, *al-Kashshāf 'an ḥaqā'iq al-tanzīl wa 'uyūn al-aqāwīl fī wujūh al-ta'wīl* (Beirut, Dār al-Ma'rifa, 139-/197-), vol. 4, p. 204, who claims that a verse by Ma'arrī which has a Qur'anic echo was composed in imitation of the Qur'anic verse on hell-fire *"innahā tarmī bi-shararin ka'l-qaṣr- that throws out sparks like castles"* (Qur'an 77:32). The verse in question is *"ḥamrā'a sāti'ata'l-dhawā'ibi fī'l-dujā/ tarmī bi-kulli sharāratin ka-ṭirāf"* (red, with hairs shining in the darkness, that throws out every spark like a tent). As was pointed out by Ignaz Goldziher, *Mohammedanische Studien* (Halle: Max Niemeyer, 1888–90, repr. Hildesheim: Georg Olms, 1961) vol. 2, pp. 403–4; English tr. Christa R. Barber and Samuel M. Stern (Chicago: Aldine, 1966), vol. 2, pp. 364–5, this verse describes the fires in the houses that shelter travellers, and is part of a consolation *qaṣīda* that Ma'arrī composed at the death of the renowned 'Alid Abū Aḥmad al-Sharīf al-Ṭāhir al-Mūsawī (d. 400/1009), the father of the famous al-Sharīf al-Raḍī and al-Sharīf al-Murtaḍā; see Ma'arrī, *Diwān Saqṭ al-Zand*, ed. N. Riḍā (Beirut: Manshūrāt Dār Maktabat al-Ḥayāt), poem no. 50, p. 152.

For the Ikhwān al-Ṣafā''s interpretation of Qur'an 77:30-33, see below, p. 172 and notes 43-45.

9. See, for example, Ibn al-'Adīm, *Kitāb al-inṣāf wa'l-taḥarrī fī daf' al-ẓulm wa'l-tajarrī 'an Abī'l-'Alā' al-Ma'arrī*, ed. Ṭāhā Ḥusayn, in *Ta'rīf al-qudamā' bi-Abī'l-'Alā'* (Cairo: Dār al-Kutub al-Miṣriyya, 1363/1944), p. 527, who says that "the book has absolutely nothing to do with imitating [the Qur'an]"; Fakhr al-Dīn al-Rāzī, *al-Tafsīr al-kabīr* (Tehran, Dār al-Kutub al-'Ilmiyya, 139-/197-), vol. 30, p. 277, who disagrees with Zamakhsharī's suggestions that Ma'arrī tried to imitate the Qur'an (although he does believe that Qur'an's imagery is rhetorically superior to Ma'arrī's); Nāṣir-i Khusraw, *Safarnāma*, ed. and tr. Wheeler M. Thackston as *Nāṣer-e Khosraw's Book of Travels* (Albany, NY, Bibliotheca Persica, 1986), p. 15, who describes it as a book "in which he speaks in enigmatic parables. Although eloquent and amazing, the book can be understood only by a very few and by those who have read it with him"; 'Alī b. al-Ḥasan al-Bākharzī (d. 467/1074) also mentions it in his *Dumyat al-qaṣr wa 'uṣrat ahl al-'aṣr*, ed. 'Abd al-Fattāḥ Muḥammad al-Ḥuluww (Cairo: Dār al-Fikr al-'Arabī, 1971), vol. 1, p. 202.

10. The defenders of *i'jāz* were against anything that could resemble the Qur'an for fear of seeing its uniqueness compromised. On this concept see Gustav E. von Grunebaum, 'I'djāz', *EI2*, vol. 3, pp. 1018-1020, and Richard C. Martin, 'Inimitability', *EQ*, vol. 2, p. 526-536.

11. Ibn al-'Adīm, *Bughyat al-ṭalab*, vol. 2, p. 879, reports that this was the poets' answer to the question "where is this in the Qur'an?" (*ayna hādhā min al-Qur'ān?*). Another report given by Ibn al-'Adīm (*ibid*, p. 880) gives an alterative account where someone is supposed to have said "This [book] is only just good (*malīḥ*), but it does not have the elegant beauty (*ṭalāwa*) of the Qur'an!" to which Ma'arrī reportedly said: "[wait] until the tongues polish it for four hundred years, and then you will see how it becomes!"

12. On this concept, see Samuel Sandmel, 'Parallelomania', *Journal of Biblical Literature* 81 (1962), pp. 1-13. I would like to thank Stephen Burge for bringing this article to my attention.

13. *Rasā'il Ikhwān al-ṣafā' wa khullān al-wafā'* , ed. Buṭrus al-Bustānī (Beirut: Dār al-Ṣādir, 1957), repr. (Beirut, Dār Bayrūt, 1983). The first ever critical edition is being published with English transaltions by Oxford University Press in association with the Institute of Ismaili Studies.

14. Abū Ḥayyān al-Tawḥīdī, *Kitāb al-Imtā' wa'l-mu'ānasa*, ed. Aḥmad Amīn and Aḥmad al-Zayn (Cairo: Maṭba'at Lajnat al-Ta'līf wa'l-Tarjama wa'l-Nashr), 1939–1944, vol. 2, pp. 4–5.

15. On the *Epistles*, see generally two recent introductions: Godefroid de Callataÿ, *Ikhwan al-Safa': A Brotherhood of Idealists on the Fringe of Orthodox Islam* (Oxford: Oneworld, 2005) and Nader El-Bizri (ed.), *Epistles of the Brethren of Purity: the Ikhwan al-Ṣafā' and their Rasā'il: An Introduction* (Oxford: Oxford University Press in association with the Institute of Ismaili Studies, 2008); for a more detailed analysis of its contents, see Yves Marquet, *La philosophie des Ihwān al-Ṣafā'*, 2nd rev. edn (Paris and Milan, S.É.H.A. and Archè, 1999).

16. Qur'an, 74:30. Qur'anic citations are referred to by the *sūra* and *āya* number. Translations from the Qur'an are my own modified versions of Arthur. J. Arberry, *The Koran Interpreted* (London: Allen and Unwin, 1955).

17. Qur'an 74:31.

18. *Rasā'il*, vol. 3, p. 63.

19. Qur'an 15:4344-.

20. *Rasā'il*, vol. 3, p. 64.

21. This article is part of my larger research project on *A Philosophical Reading of the Qur'an*, based mainly on the *Epistles of the Ikhwān al-ṣafā'*.
22. For a study on quotational borrowings, from where the translations of these technical terms are taken, see Amidu Sanni, "again on *taḍmīn* in Arabic theoretical discourse", *Bulletin of the School of Oriental and African Studies* 61i (1998), pp. 1–19. See also the most extended study by Amidu Sanni, *The Arabic Theory of Prosification and Versification: On Ḥall and Naẓm in Arabic Theoretical Discourse* (Beirut, 1998).
23. Baqillānī died in d. 403-1013.
24. Gustave E. von Grunebaum, "The Concept of Plagiarism in Arabic Theory", *Journal of Near Eastern Studies*, 3iv (1944), p. 236, repr. in Gustave E. von Grunebaum, *Themes in Medieval Arabic Literature*, ed. Dunning S. Wilson (London: Variorum reprints, 1981), referring to Abū Bakr Muḥammad b. al-Ṭayyib al-Baqillānī's *I'jāz al-Qur'ān* (Cairo, 1930-1349), *passim*, esp. pp. 69ff, 129ff and 172ff.
25. Qur'an 3:7. See *Rasā'il*, vol. 1, p. 357.
26. Qur'an 2:255. See *Rasā'il*, vol. 2, p. 82.
27. Qur'an 58:22. Note the use of the word "brothers" (*ikhwān*) in this verse.
28. Qur'an 7:50. See *Rasā'il*, vol. 1, p. 138.
29. *Rasā'il*, vol. 2, p. 23.
30. *Rasā'il*, vol. 1, p. 331.
31. These are sūras 8, 9 and 33 of the Qur'an, respectively. See *Rasā'il*, vol. 3, p. 346.
32. *Rasā'il*, vol. 1, p. 338.
33. Mention of laudatory expressions such as *ta'āla, jalla thanā'uhu, 'alayhi'l-salām*, etc. are omitted.
34. Qur'an 31:28. See *Rasā'il*, vol. 1, p. 306 and vol. 2, p. 140.
35. *Rasā'il*, vol. 2, p. 135.
36. Qur'an 70:4.
37. Other variants include: *wa min dhālika qawluhu ḥikāyatan 'an ... ; kamā dhakara t. bi-qawlihi ḥikāyatan 'an ...; wa qawluhu ḥikāyatan 'an ... qawlihim/-hu [+/- li...]; wa qāla fī ḥikāyatin 'an ...;*
38. Qur'an 37:164. See *Rasā'il*, vol. 2, p. 148.
39. Qur'an 144:4–5. See *Rasā'il*, vol. 3, p. 81.
40. Qur'an 78:38. See *Rasā'il*, vol. 1, pp. 321–2.
41. Qur'an 18:47–48.
42. *wa taṣdīquhu/ dhālika/ hadhā'l-ra'y qawl Allāh; wa qāla Allāh t. taṣdīqan li-qawli rasūli'llāh; wa dhālika ma'nā qawlihi; wa dhālika qawluhu.*
43. This is Arberry's translation. Alternative translations are "unto the shadow falling threefold" (Pickthall); "to a shadow (of smoke ascending) in three columns" (Yusuf Ali).
44. Qur'an 77:30. See *Rasā'il*, vol. 2, p. 21; vol. 3, pp. 63, 362.
45. See, for example, Abū Ja'far al-Ṭabarī, *Jāmi' al-bayān fī tafsīr al-Qur'ān*, ed. Muḥammad al-Zuhrī al-Ghumrawī *et al.* (Cairo, al-Maṭba'a al-Maymaniyya, 1903–1321), vol. 29, p. 128.
46. *Rasā'il*, vol. 2, p. 86.
47. Qur'an 18:51.
48. Qur'an 32:17. See *Rasā'il*, vol. 1, p. 448.
49. Examples of paraphrastic *tafsīr* are the commentaries by Mujāhid b. Jabr (103 /722), Muḥammad al-Kalbī (145-763), Muqātil b. Sulaymān (150 /767) and Sufyān al-Thawrī (161-778).
50. Qur'an 35:10.
51. *Rasā'il*, vol. 1, p. 336, 360; vol. 2, p. 83; vol. 3, p. 15; vol. 4, p. 23.
52. See *Rasā'il*, vol 1, p. 360.

53. For Sijistānī's critique see Tawḥīdī, *K. Al-Imtā'*, vol. 2, pp. 6, 20-21; for Jarīrī's critique, see ibid., pp. 11-18. For a summary of the debate, see Mohammed Arkoun, *Contribution a l'étude de l'humanisme arabe au Ive/Xe siècle: Miskawayh (320/325-421)=(932/936-1030) philosophe et historien* (Paris: J. Vrin, 1970), pp. 180-183. For more on philosophical and doctrinal condemnations of the *Epistles* see Omar Alí-de-Unzaga, "The Use of the Qur'ān in the *Epistles of the Pure Brethren (Rasā'il Ikhwān al-Ṣafā')*", Unpublished PhD dissertation (University of Cambridge, 2004), ch. 2 (pp. 75-119). I am currently preparing the work in book format.

54. Apart from Ian Netton, discussed below, mention must be made of the summary of the *Epistles* published by Alessandro Bausani, *L'enciclopedia dei fratelli della purità: riassunto, con introduzione e breve commento, dei 52 trattati o epistole degli Ikhwān aṣ-Ṣafā'* (Naples: Istituto Universitario Orientale, 1978), which, in the most, does not seem to consider the Qur'anic citations relevant at all for the thought of the Ikhwān al-ṣafā'.

55. Ian Richard Netton, *Muslim Neoplatonists: an Introduction to the Thought of the Brethren of Purity (Ikhwān al-Ṣafā')* (London and Boston: G. Allen & Unwin, 1982). It has been reprinted twice (Edinburgh: Edinburgh University Press, 1991; London: Routledge; Curzon, 2002) with some corrections of misprints, but no alteration of content.

56. As stated on the back of the latest reprint. Netton's ascendancy, however, is clearly seen in the fact that many recent reference entries on the *Epistles* have been written by him: Ian Richard Netton, "The Brethren of Purity (Ikhwân al-Safâ')", in Seyyed Hossein Nasr and Oliver Leaman (eds), *History of Islamic Philosophy* (London: Routledge, 1996), pp. 222-230; "The Brethren of Purity (Ikhwān al-Ṣafā')," in the *Routledge Encyclopaedia of Philosophy*, general ed. Edward Craig (London and New York: Routledge, 1998), vol. 4, pp. 685-688; and "Ikhwān al-Ṣafā'," in Julie Scott Meisami and Paul Starkey (eds) *Encyclopedia of Arabic Literature* (London: Routledge, 1998), pp. 391-392.

57. As Madelung has pointed out in his review of the book, published in *New Blackfriars* 65, no. 764 (February, 1984), pp. 86-87, Netton "is primarily concerned with the ultimate sources and only secondarily with the channels and immediate sources through which their ideas may have reached the authors." This leaves a gap in the contextualisation of the work.

58. Netton, *Muslim Neoplatonists*, p. 88.

59. Ibid., p. 78-89. In fact this section consists of little more than a catalogue of Qur'ānic references to prophets.

60. Ibid, p. 82. As Netton adds, the *Epistles* differ from other works in their conception of the Torah and the Gospel as on a par with the Qur'ān.

61. Ibid, p. 41.

62. Ibid, p. 107.

63. Ibid, p. 108.

64. Ibid, p. 107. The emphasis is from the original.

65. Ibid, p. 79.

66. Ibid, p. 89.

67. Ibid, p. 79.

68. Ibid, p. 78.

69. Ibid, p. 78. Netton is probably thinking of Tawḥīdī's and Sijistānī's access to the work, but forgets their (and later) condemnations.

70. It is not clear what exactly is meant by "orthodoxy" in *MN*, since the term is left undefined. It is beyond the scope of this paper to engage with the problems surrounding the use of this term. Suffice it to mention three notable contributions

on this subject: Alexander Knysh, "'Orthodoxy' and 'Heresy' in Medieval Islam: An Essay in Reassessment", *The Muslim World* 83i (1993), pp. 48–67, Norman Calder, "The Limits of Islamic Orthodoxy," in Farhad Daftary (ed.), *Intellectual Traditions in Islam* (London: I.B. Tauris, 2000), and M. Brett Wilson, "The Failure of Nomenclature. The Concept of 'Orthodoxy' in the Study of Islam", *Comparative Islamic Studies* 3ii (2007), 167-194. I would like to thank Brett Wilson for having sent me a copy of his paper even before it was published.

71. Ibid, p. 79.

72. Ibid, p. 81.

73. Ibid, p. 78.

74. Ibid, p. 7.

75. Ibid, p. 106.

76. Ibid, p. 106.

77. Ibid,

78. Ibid, p. 85. See Epistle 47 "On the Divine *Nomos*", *Rasā'il*, vol. 4, p. 126.

79. Both in the field of Ikhwānian studies and in most reviews; see, for instance, the reviews by Alessandro Bausani, *Rivista degli Studi Orientali* 56 (1982), pp. 205–206; Jorge E. Gracia, *Choice: Current Reviews for Academic Libraries* 20 x (June 1983), p. 1469; John N. Mattock, *Journal of the Royal Asiatic Society* (1984), pp. 127–128; Charles Burnett, *Bulletin of the School of Oriental and African Studies* 56ii (1993), p. 431; Bernd Radtke, *Der Islam* 72i (1995), p. 169; and Raif G. Khoury, *Bibliotheca Orientalis* 54iii-iv (1997), pp. 504–505.

80. The other exception is the review by Jules L. Janssens, *Tijdschrift voor Filosofie* 55 I (1993), pp. 157-8, who has pointed at the danger of bypassing the "uniqueness," contribution and subsequent influence of the *Epistles* if they are judged only on the basis of a study of their sources: "The crucial question seems to us whether an all-encompassing system of thought as that of the Ikhwān may be judged only on the basis of the study of sources, however full of meaning it might be. Isn't the danger, whether conscious or unconscious, to pass by the deepest uniqueness of the system? That is: isn't Netton underestimating the Ikhwān's own contribution, whose system had an important influence on subsequent Islamic thought?" I thank Dr Christine van Ruymbeke for helping me with the Dutch text.

81. Salim Kemal, Review of Ian Netton's *Muslim Neoplatonists, Journal of Islamic Studies* 6ii (1995), pp. 262-265.

82. Clifford Edmund Bosworth, "The Persian Impact on Arabic Literature," ch. 23 in Alfred F.L. Beeston et al. (eds) *The Cambridge History of Arabic Literature (I): Arabic Literature to the End of the Umayyad Period* (Cambridge, Cambridge University Press, 1983), pp. 487-488.

83. Other questions that may be raised are, what is orthodox when a creed is followed by the majority in one region and another by the majority in another region? (for example, the Sunnīs and the Shī'īs)?; or when the majority belief is not the creed of the rulers, who may impose their own (the Caliph al-Ma'mūn and his *miḥna*; the Shī'ī Safavids in Sunni Irān) or not (the Fatimids in North Africa, the current Sunnī sultans of Shī'ī Bahrein)?

84. Mohammed Arkoun, "Logocentrisme et vérité religieuse dans la pensée islamique," *Studia Islamica* 35 (1972), pp. 5-51; repr. in Mohammed Arkoun, *Essais sur la pensée islamique* (Paris: Maisonneuve et Larose, 1984), pp. 185-231; English tr. in Mohammed Arkoun, *The Unthought in Contemporary Islamic Thought* (London: Saqi Books, 2002), pp. 170–203.

85. 'Āmirī died in 381/992. The potential similarities between 'Āmirī and the Ikhwān al-ṣafā' are worth exploring. Incidentally, Jarīrī, in his critique of the *Epistles* refers to

'Āmirī as one of the "people of old and new" who had "attempted this trick", by which he means combining religion and philosophy, but ultimately "gave up their purpose disappointedly and fell flat on their faces unsuccessfully"; see Tawḥīdī, *Kitāb al-Imtā'*, vol. 2, p. 15. Jarīrī also mentions among such people Abū Zayd al-Balkhī and Abū Tammām al-Nīsābūrī (4th/10th c.).

86. Arkoun, *Logocentrisme*, Studia Islamica 35 (1972), p. 6; reproduced in Arkoun, *Essais*, p. 86; English tr. in Arkoun, *The Unthought in Contemporary Islamic Thought*, p. 170.

87. The relatively recently discipline of Pragmatics is the study of the relation between the structure of a semiotic system (notably language) and its usage in context. Along with semantics, it forms part of the general theory of meaning. See Stephen Levinson, *Pragmatics* (Cambridge: Cambridge University Press, 1983), and Steven Davis (ed.), *Pragmatics. A Reader* (Oxford: Oxford University Press, 1991).

88. See Ludwig Wittgenstein, *Philosophical Investigations. Philosophische Untersuchungen* (Parallel German and English Texts), tr. Gertrude E.M. Anscombe; ed. Rush Rhees (Oxford: Blackwell, 1953); John Langshaw Austin, *How to do Things with Words* (Oxford: OUP, 1962); H. Paul Grice, *Studies in the Way of Words* (Cambridge, Mass.: Harvard University Press, 1989); John Searle, *Speech Acts: An Essay in the Philosophy of Language* (London: Cambridge University Press, 1969); Dan Sperber and Deirdre Wilson, *Relevance, Communication and Cognition* (Oxford: Blackwell, 1986, 2nd ed. 1995).

89. Wittgenstein, *Philosophical Investigations*, p. 220 (sec. II xi): "Lass dich die Bedeutung der Worte von ihren Verwerdungen lehren!"

90. Ibid, p. 20 (sec. 43).

91. Ibid, p. 215 (sec. IIxi): "Bedeutung der Gebrauch des Wortes ist".

92. Ibid, p. 109 (sec. 340).

93. The role of the contexts of situation on the different purposes of one same sentence has been one of the major contributions of the discipline of pragmatics. A common example is the sentence "do you know what time it is?" which can be used as a question, or as a polite request, or even as a reprimand to somebody who arrives late.

94. H. Paul Grice, "Meaning," *Philosophical Review* 66 (1957), p. 384; repr. in Grice, *Studies in the Way of Words*, p. 219.

95. H. Paul Grice, "Logic and Conversation," in Peter Cole and Jerry L. Morgan (eds), *Syntax and Semantics 3: Speech Acts* (New York: Academic Press, 1975), p. 43 ff.; repr. in Grice, *Studies in the Way of Words*, p. 24ff.

96. As developed by Sperber and Wilson, *Relevance, Communication and Cognition*, esp. chapter 3 "Relevance", pp. 118–171.

97. As in the case of a dialogue of the type "– Are you coming to the lecture on Saturday? – There is a match on television." The reply makes sense for both the speaker and the hearer because of its relevance in the context and because both share the implicatures (such as that the match is on the same day and at the same time as the lecture, that the second person might prefer football to the topic of the lecture, that he/she intends to watch the match and that the reply might be a "no"). On the principle of relevance see Mary M. Talbot, "Relevance," in Jacob L. Mey (ed.), *Concise Encyclopedia of Pragmatics* (Amsterdam and Oxford: Elsevier, 1998), pp. 775–778.

98. Julia Kristeva, *La rèvolution du language poetique* (Paris: Seouil, 1974), English tr. by Margaret Waller as *Revolution in Poetic Language* (New York: Columbia University Press, 1984).

99. In Alison Sharrock's words, "how parts relate to parts, wholes, and holes": Alison Sharrock and Helen Morales, *Intratextuality: Greek and Roman Textual Relations* (Oxford: Oxford University Press, 2000), p. 5.

100. See, for example. Epistle 43 "On the Way to God", *Rasā'il*, vol. 3, pp. 5–9.

Afterword

Mohammed Arkoun Replies and Comments

It is always a rich experience to listen to Professor van Ess. Whenever I read or hear him I am reminded of the wonderful expression, *bihâr al-anwâr* ("oceans of light"). However, I missed one strand of enlightenment in those which he presented to us today. This is the idea of legitimacy. Legitimacy is the basis for power as well as authority. Discourses in the spheres of politics, philosophy or theology are instances of a regime for truth. As I heard Professor van Ess speak, I kept asking myself whether he came across an explicit or implicit presence of claims to legitimacy in the materials he has researched. Even more importantly, I am curious about the Arabic word that might express the idea. This is important because of the danger of anachronism to which I am always opposed.

Take for example the famous formula, *La Hukma illa li-Allah* (there is no power but God's). There is in this at least the pretence, if not more, of legitimacy. It is linked to the notion of the true religion which, as we know, is an ancient concept. St Augustine is one of the earliest voices on this topic for Catholics, constructing the idea of true religion employing a philosophical (Platonic) basis, and a basis for what was later to become theology. Again, there is the Dutch thinker, Grotius. He also had an enormous influence, through the idea of a true religion, in the development of a notion of legitimacy. True religion, in turn, enabled political legitimacy. For political legitimacy fails to exist if it is not founded on a regime of truth which is accepted, by agreement, to be a truth.

The Qur'an employs the concept, *din-al-haq*, precisely in this way. The disputes mentioned in Professor van Ess's paper would appear in a new light if they were to be seen as part of a search for legitimacy, which I missed in the paper.

My interest in this all-important topic has its basis in what we find today. As we know, none of the states in the Muslim world today, which I call party states (a single party state) which emerged after the Second World War, can pretend to any legitimacy whatever. The absence of legitimacy is the most serious factor in the Muslim world today, because where there is no legitimacy there is no legality. People are conscious of its absence, and they see how the states cynically manipulate the show of political legitimacy, let alone the regime of truth. This is the reason why I am interested to see how the notion worked, or was manipulated, in the whole history of Islam and religion.

In Stephen Humphrey's paper the concept in need of clarification is that of authenticity. Today we are obliged to distinguish between two kinds of authenticity, reflecting two kinds of history. There is the history practised in the tradition of the nineteenth century which took the form of philological criticism of texts. And there is the other branch of history, historical psychology, which still remains neglected.

What counts as authentic in historical psychology is very different from what authenticity represents in traditional academic history. In the latter, anachronisms have no place. But believers in a faith typically indulge in anachronisms. When critical history insists on its own criteria of truth or authenticity as the face of what believers take to be authentic, when historians challenge the anachronisms which religious belief is constructed from, the result is a total failure of communication. The believer will not understand the critique of anachronism. Where there is no mutual understanding there can be no conversation.

Belief belongs to the sphere of psychology. A believer's speech is determined by emotion. He does not employ the tools of criticism that we do when we study history or take care to report something with accuracy.

A personal example is in order here. When, at an early age, I was a secondary school teacher, in a lycée near Algiers, I used to assume the idea of divine authenticity of the Qur'an. Afterwards I wrote an article on this concept which I presented in a *festschrift* to my teacher in philosophy when I was in Oran. My teacher challenged this idea, asking: how can God, who defines himself as invisible, eternal and mysterious, be considered to speak? That was when I first recognised the problematic character of the idea. I had simply assumed, like all Muslims, that God speaks. I recognised this belief as a mental obstacle in myself. It is still a prevalent belief.

That is why historical psychology is extremely important. There is the problem, of course, that we do not have access now to the people whose traditions have been reported in the texts we study as historians. All these texts, and the oral traditions quoted in them are, as Humphreys indicates, unreliable. But then there is this other kind of history, where we may use these texts to reconstruct the psychology of the societies concerned. Although the texts may not be taken as authentic representations of history, they are also authentic in that they express the spontaneous experience of the people.

This text is of continued relevance today. Nowadays all Muslim discourses are a tissue of contradictions. It is no use simply opposing scientific history to these. It is more important to relate to Muslims today at the level of psychology. The Muslim world reflects a *fait accompli* at the end of a whole history of Islamic thought. From the earliest time Islamic discourse, represented in texts like those which Humphreys has discussed, was mythical rather than historical. Today, Islam is totally cut off from any kind of historical reasoning whatsoever. That is why it is impossible to engage in the kind of discussion we are having today in Cairo or Algiers or Pakistan. If you attempt to do so you will find people reacting very emotionally, making it impossible for you to continue.

Your only option therefore is to converse at the level of the psychology of your interlocutors. This way you may hope to bring people pedagogically to a realisation that when you read the *sira* (the biography of the Prophet Muhammad) for example, you have before you a text which has a linguistically mythical structure, rather than historical inquiry. When Muslims read the *sira* they are throughout in the mode of devotion. It is nothing else but devotion. In this mode there is no place for thinking, analysing or discussing anything with reference to our modern understanding of authenticity. This is very clear when you consider, as I constantly find, that in Arabic there is no word for anachronism up to now. This shows that the people do not have an idea or need of this reality, this methodology of an open mind.

Still, it may happen that by starting in terms of psychology, which is the foundation of all belief, you may be able to bring them ultimately to appreciate critical history, which is what we exclusively do in schools or universities. This is the approach I practise with my students. I start out by introducing them to this distinction between two levels of authenticity. I try to apply this to the Qur'an and the other texts which have been a basis for the construction of belief over so many centuries. In general I find that the students are very uncomfortable with this new idea at first. But after a year or so, they become receptive and enthusiastic.

What I have just said about the idea of history is also true of the idea of reason. It seems to me that the paper by Stefan Wild is based on the postulate that all the social actors he refers to, from Muhammad Abduh to Pope Benedict, are using reason. It is a common assumption that all discourses, whether religious, historical, political or theological, are founded on reason. But this assumption does not hold.

What is neglected when we appeal to reason is *imaginaire*: *l'imaginaire social*, and *l'imaginaire religieux*. The psychological reality of social life and of religious life is not reason. It is emotion. We make a big mistake when we take religious postulates to be postulates of reason. But religious discourse is built out of *l'imaginaire*, and *l'imaginaire* is always aligned to emotion rather than rational thought.

This was true of many discourses in the past. It is also true of the ideological discourses of today. The majority of discourses in the West today are dominated by emotion. I am reminded at this point of a recent book by Dominique Moisi called *The Geopolitics of Emotion*. This is a great idea, because it helps to free us from the assumption that we always argue rationally, that reason is free and autonomous. We tend, in the name of reason, to want to dominate and silence *l'imaginaire*. Reason in this sense has a dominating role, alienated from emotions. The attempt to ignore *l'imaginaire* never works, not even in learned conferences such as now.

This dialectic is linked to another one I have been insisting on for a long time now. This is the "thought of" and the "unthought". In the first instance there are sociological concepts rather than philosophical or intellectual ones (these are secondary). There is a strong dialectic between these. Moreover, it keeps varying. Reason is full of vicissitudes. What we take to be a single, unproblematic reason is in fact an ever-changing reason, governed by changing *epistemes*. Every epistemic framework contains the un-thinkable, and together dictates the shape and operation of reason in every phase of history.

The eighteenth century in Europe saw the breakdown of all traditional *epistemes*. The sequel to this is a new, emerging reason. But even in Europe the ancient *epistemes* have by no means disappeared.

The type of reason prevailing in the first century of the Muslim era has nothing in comparison with our *episteme* today. Similarly, classical Islamic reason, what we find in the debate between al-Ghazzali and Averroes, has nothing in common with what is invoked in Muslim discourse today.

In fact, the *episteme* of contemporary Muslim societies lies outside any kind of possible reference whatsoever and I find it impossible to define it, to distinguish any criteria governing it. If you look at Muhammad Shahrur's pronouncements, for example, you will see that they are simply assertions, and have nothing to do with either emotion or critical reason. When contemporary Muslims invoke the *dawla* ("state"), this does not refer to anything. Still, we report in our scholarly writings what Muslims "think" of *dawla*. In fact it is more correct to say that contemporary Muslims "talk" rather than "think". They deliver discourses, but are not aware that this is really all that they do. This, as a fact, remains unthought.

In Bachir Diagne we have a philosopher, with a philosophical presentation. This is fact to rejoice in, having a philosopher among us. Now, like mystics, philosophers enjoy a privilege, which consists of a certain freedom with words. We could apply to philosophy what Lévi-Strauss said about myth, that it is an ideological palace built out of the rubble of a people's social discourse. This freedom is a privilege of philosophers – the freedom to make beautiful constructions.

However, the topic on which Professor Diagne has spoken is conversion. This has aspects which make it necessary for us to think beyond philosophy. I always think that conversion, which occurs out of a subjective decision, carries risks. The person who converts is unable to see these risks because he acts out of an inner impulse to change the frame of his sense of belonging – to change his identity. This entails risks which are out of reach of the subject's mind.

When you convert, you do so on the basis of an idea of truth. But, as a convert, you do not have a mastery or control over this idea. We all know how dangerous the concept of the true religion is. That is why, no matter what reasons you invoke in personal conversion, they remain subjective, and are linked to very specific, personal circumstances. Conversion is inevitably a personal adventure whose implications are not under the convert's conscious mastery.

I appreciate the fact that Professor Diagne discussed four specific individuals. This is a way of focussing on the aspect of personality, and giving a clearer idea about the actual processes involved in conversion. Even more pleasing to me is his reference to St Augustine. About St Augustine I must say that I have a deeply personal relation to him – I don't know how else to put it. I read Augustine's *Confessions* when I was at the lycée, learning Latin from my Jesuit teachers. The process of converting to something which feels to be more full of truth than in your current state is described wonderfully in this book.

Even more exciting was my discovery, through my teachers, that

Augustine was an Algerian! This is, of course, to talk anachronistically, but I hope the sense behind it will be clear. I emphasise this because I find it most intolerable that a mind like Augustine's has been obliterated from the record in the very place in which he lived and taught. He belongs to the same territory which I call mine, so I have a right, in a certain sense, to demand his presence in this region of ours. If only the period of the achievements of Roman culture and civilisation and of the church had been preserved and made present in the history of what we call the Maghreb! We can only imagine what a rich presence this would be. It has been obliterated, however. All this is because of the concept of the true religion.

There is an example in this of how history is constructed. Because of this, we have been deprived, in what we today call "Algeria", of an intellectually very rich part of its heritage. This is why I prefer to call the whole region North Africa rather than the Maghreb. For, in using the latter term, we reinforce the exclusion of this part of the history, so as to give it an exclusively Arabic and Muslim identity.

Finally, with regard to Professor Diagne's paper, I would plead with him to listen to the voice of history while he exercises the freedom which philosophy gives. Professor Diagne talked about *tawbah*. Of course, the word does have the religious meaning he mentions. But we must not forget that the same word occurs in Sura 9 in the Qur'an, in the so-called *ayâtu-s-saif* (the "verse of the sword"). There, *tawbah* signifies unconditional surrender. Read in context and, in linguistic terms, synchronically, it means just this: surrender without conditions, because this is the long-awaited true religion.

The lesson to be learned is that philosophy should not ignore history. It is a wonderful subject, but if in the process, one ignores history one ends up putting up ideological palaces. The decoration on these palaces becomes illusory. It disguises the truth – the historical, linguistic truth; the truth in the context in which words are used.

The context which Malika Zeghal's paper presents is of Bourguiba. Bourguiba is a case study in its own right. It illustrates the situation of party states in the whole Muslim world in modern times. Bourguiba exemplifies the model of the third French republic, a model in which education was provided free, by the state, and was founded on the principle of laicism. Laicism is more extreme than secularism. Bourguiba was completely under the influence of this model. However, his decisions reflected political strategy rather than his convictions as an intellectual in the image of the third French republic. This is true of the entire North Africa where, even though the French ruled for more than a century, there was no legacy of statecraft. This is what accounts for the condition of these states. Contrary to what many assume, it has nothing to do with Islam.

We must not assume, to start with, that Islam was the single or all-determining force in the traditions of the North African zone. My own background is a case in point. I come from the Kabyle tribe in Algeria. Where I grew up we never heard what we nowadays call the *shahada*. We did not have Islamic law or courts. We had none of the components of so-called "Islam". We were truly a part of the African continent, with animist beliefs and practices. Where, in such a society, can one find a general "Islam"? Of course, the situation was different in Morocco or Tunisia, where there was the existence of the Universities of Qarawiyyin and Zaytuna. But, again, what kind of "Islam" shall we say existed there?

The lived Islam, the living Islam on the ground at the start of the Muslim period, was totally cut off from whatever we know of the Islamic tradition of the classical age, the formative period. From this Islam there was no link to the modern age. Consider Ibn Abd al-Wahhab, for instance, whose life was contemporaneous with that of Immanuel Kant. Kant was a major figure (among others of course) who radically changed the idea of human reason but was ignorant of this kind of thinking. Not only that, he did not even have the horizons of mind of someone like Ibn Hanbal in the eighth century. Men like him were, in a sense, religious humanists who were open to all the knowledge available at the time.

Clearly, there was no way to build a sound system of modernity on the basis of the Islam of the early moments or out of the existing traditions. Today, people call for a revival of Islam. But what Islam is there to the revived? There is no intellectual Islam that can serve us in today's world by being revived.

The problem is not to do with Islam alone. It is also to do with modernity, which bears the aspect of its historical alliance with colonialism. Modernity has not risen as yet to a universal level of thought. Modernity has produced intellectual tools which have still a contribution to make. What is regrettable about it is its hegemonic aspect. This we must combat.

The dual problem of Islam and modernity is well illustrated in the history of modern Turkey. Mustapha Kemal was a courageous leader who dared to make a leap, but his lacked foundation in a culture that could support a new beginning. The two traditions available were, on one hand, an Islam which had no means for the construction of a modern state, and on the other hand, a modernity which was based in solidarity with colonial systems.

The historical situation has affected the entire Muslim world. However, it has never been properly analysed and understood. The generation at the time when the countries concerned became independent needed to understand this, but there were no teachers or scholars who could fulfil this task. The case remains exactly the same today. There are no educated teachers in our schools who can explain what I call the inverse temporalities in the history of Islam on one hand and of Europe on the other. Islam completely lost the theology, philosophy and aspects of humanism which had contributed to its glorious classical past, whereas Europe embarked on the Renaissance without discontinuity, and with cultural energy and enthusiasm at its hand.

The result of all this is a total split in the Mediterranean region between the North and the South. This in itself is not properly understood in the so-called Muslim countries of the region, which continued to exist in a state of what I call "institutionalised ignorance" of the historical processes affecting them.

In Ursula Günter's paper what pleases me most is that it brings out the problems inherent in the word "Islam". This word is used loosely and everywhere. It is a portmanteau word that I have wanted to be rid of. Yet it is impossible, even in scholarship, to do without it. It becomes a real obstacle to thinking and to realising the complexity it hides.

There is a real need for a more conceptualised language for such complexities, including in Western societies where the idea of secularisation is more complex than it appears. The concept of religion is similarly complex, hiding the difference between a religious expression of the self and religion as ideology.

Lack of a sophisticated conceptualisation of these words and ideas has huge effects – for example, in the classroom where the teacher who has not been made aware in his training to their complexity refers to Islam, Christianity, and so on, in straightforward terms.

I would like to preface my final remarks to this symposium by expressing my joy and my gratitude to everyone who is united, in a shared intellectual solidarity, in the search for a common intellectual and conceptual ground for scholars, visitors and artists in the face of the issues germane to Islam as a religion, Islam as a culture and, lately, Islam as a historical force which has today upset an established equilibrium, whatever its rights and wrongs, to generate a challenge based on violence. This is not a violence issuing from within Islamic history, or Islamic doctrines. It is in part a violence arising from rivalry between Islam as a religion and Christianity as a religion. But there is also a lot more to it than this.

We cannot begin to understand this unless we get used to the idea of the geo-historical space of the Mediterranean, an idea that has concerned me for many years now. I say "geo-historical" rather than "geo-political", because the latter limits us to a short-term perspective, dating from the Second World War – a period in which there has been one war after another, recapitulating all the problems that we have been discussing, with no resolution in sight.

On the other side there is modernity which replaces earlier forms of authority, justified by political theologies (as opposed to political philosophies). In this, furthermore, there is a double axis, one going back to the origin of the monotheistic religions, the other to the Greeks. This double heritage still determines our struggle.

The Mediterranean space is the area where these two historical, doctrinal axis have unfolded and given rise to a violence which, to be sure, we cannot simply blame on either religion or modernity. But they have played their part in this violence. Both monotheistic religion at one time and modernity held up a promise for us – a promise to elevate the human mind, to liberate it from ignorance and violence, and to produce culture.

I am not one of those who say that modernity has entirely failed in its promise. Undoubtedly, it brought new possibilities and new visions of the human condition. We cannot think or progress today, or develop a culture of peace without making use of the tools of modernity. But as historians we have to face up to its failures as well as achievements. Having done this, we must look forward to the future.

In doing so, we have to realise that we cannot continue thinking of this space by dividing it, as we once did, in separate theological streams. Each community built its theological vision of revelation and of the human condition in mutual exclusion of each other, each claiming to be the true religion. Even now, as is the case in divinity schools or departments of theology, we continue to think in terms of separate theological systems, with its implicit mutual exclusions. Political theology continues to influence us. Its historical effects are still with us, and neither the religions nor the democratic political regimes of today are able to break free from this history.

The Mediterranean space saw the two religions of Christianity and Islam spread from there to all over the world, crossing cultural, ethnic and political frontiers. With their expansion came the spread of Greek thought and the Roman concepts of law and the republic. In every society influenced by Islam or Christianity there is at least some consciousness of this legacy, though more so in Christianity because there has been a more continuous interface there, while in Islam the contact with Greek thought was more tenuous, because Muslim jurists and theologians rejected it as alien (*al-Ulum al-Dakhila*) representing the intrusion of a foreign mentality. It was in this belief that Ibn Qutayba wrote his main work attacking Aristotle, whom the Arab philosophers called the First Teacher (*al-mu'allim al-awwal*).

This old controversy refers us back to the remarks of Pope Benedict mentioned earlier in this conference. Although he spoke rhetorically, quoting a text which he ought not to have quoted, there is a partial truth in what he said because of this denunciation of philosophy in classical Islam.

The upshot of this is a complex and problematic situation, an incomplete modernity and a so-called Islam of which it is hard to make sense. That is why, in my view, we have to make a clean break with all this talk about Islam and about religion and develop a new vocabulary for a new conceptualisation of the situation in which we are today.

Failure to do this is what is keeping us back today. The way the Qur'an is taken as an absolute authority, is the way any inquiry is stopped well before it can produce results. You are forbidden from taking the Qur'an as anything but sacred. But, what one forgets is that this text or discourse that we call the Qur'an was *made* sacred, and *is* made sacred, through a historical and social process. If you truly understand this, you would stop using the Qur'an as a constant reference as is done today. You would go beyond what I call the official closed corpus. Only then will we have the chance to initiate a new conceptualisation.

This will not be a religious conceptualisation, referring to Islam or Christianity, and so on. What I have in mind is an anthropological vision in which all sacralised scriptures of every religion are opened up to a common inquiry. To close the texts to inquiry, to sacralise them, has enormous consequences. This is true of history, but it is equally true today. That is why I was disappointed by President Obama's citations from the Qur'an in his speech at Cairo. To speak as he did is to reproduce the Muslim discourse of today, which is a demagogic way of talking about issues, where the issues get hidden rather than openly confronted. Today there is an urgent need to speak about the Qur'an in real terms. The Qur'an cannot function productively as a text of constant reference unless its status as knowledge is properly established.

This is why I have called one of my studies, "the cognitive status of revelation". My aim is to use a method of analysis that may apply equally to all works which are sanctified through historical, social, political processes and turned into texts with a holy or divine attribution.

In the current controversies which surround Muslim beliefs and practices in the West today we find the Qur'an cited on all sides to justify this or that position. I am constantly asked by certain government ministers in France to clarify what the verses say, exactly, on these controversial positions. My response is always the same. I say to them "My dear sir, in asking this question, in this way, you are only reinforcing the dogmatic discourse of Muslim ideologies. Like them, you are treating the text as an obligatory source of reference before examining the basis of its authority. Let us first clarify this status, and only then see what it says."

In other words, we need to put aside all theological discourse about the Qur'an, all exegeses of the text, so as to start with the question of the linguistic and epistemological status of the discourse. This is not to disregard belief, but to understand it in a new context, beyond the frontiers of theology.

Failure to carry out this task is responsible for the situation in Muslim societies which I describe as living on fictions. In fact, this is a wider problem, from which even democratic societies in Europe and America are not exempt. Even there we find manipulations leading to crises of legitimacy. In support of this point I only have to refer to the misinformation spread by George Bush and Tony Blair, in the very democratic societies they led, to wage the war in Iraq which had no legitimacy whatsoever.

Legitimacy, or the lack of it, is an attribute of knowledge as well. The kind of beliefs propagated in Muslim societies since the rise of the modern states are purely ideological. The discourse in the ever-increasing numbers of mosques built in these countries is, without exception, ideological. There is a whole spate of books nowadays by sociologists or political scientists in the West talking about fundamentalism. But this present-minded approach sheds no light on the real issue, which requires long-term, historical analysis with the right tools. There is a difference between fundamental and foundational. This also needs to be explained. The fiction that the very "voice of God" speaks in the Qur'an and the Hadith, and that these are to be the basis of the Sharia, which is to be seen as divine law, was constructed long ago, and was maintained by special mechanisms over a long period leading to today.

It was in history that what we call "belief" and the "word of God" was created. Today, this belief is propagated, without any change, in *madrasas* (religious schools). To be sure, in the West as well the vocabulary of "transcendence", "God", "revelation" and so on, has an on-going existence.

I do not say that this vocabulary should be forgotten. It is what has formed our history. But this vocabulary, as it remains, will not help us tackle the serious problems of today – like how we might handle the phenomenon of religion in French schools, which is a big, serious, politically urgent issue in France today.

In the Muslim world, what I call the fiction of Islam, which is disconnected from the realities of history or today, has been aggravated by the failure of modernity. In speaking of Algeria during the period I was growing up – for example, in the 1950s – I mentioned that "Islam" was a label which did not correspond to any reality – linguistic, ethnographic or cultural. But scholars, who should know better, continue to speak of the Islamic or Muslim world as if "Islam", never properly defined, is a reality of this world. At the time of independence the people of this region hoped to benefit from the culture and products of modernity. But the party-states that came into being betrayed their hopes, and now, in the interests of identity and legitimacy, what is offered is the fiction of a return of an imaginary Medina promoted by the ulama, in alliance with party-states. This fiction has no connection whatsoever with history or with the needed modernity.

What role does a scholar have in this situation? I reject the stance of Orientalists who do their research on texts, working in Western universities, with no interest or involvement, through their scholarship, with the problems of knowledge and education in the relevant societies. It is as a means to this involvement that I have proposed the concept of applied Islamology, on the model of what is called applied anthropology. I believe that a scholar who studies a people must give them something in return for his privilege. This is the principle, combining scholarship with engagement, which has guided all my work.

Mohammed Arkoun
Lecture delivered at Aga Khan University Institute
for the Study of Muslim Civilisations,
London, October 2009

Mohammed Arkoun:
A Passionate Critic

Mohammed Arkoun (1928–2010) was an outstanding scholar of Islamic history. A Berber by birth, he grew up in Algeria, witnessing both French rule and its nationalist aftermath. This experience led him to a radical and critical revaluation of the role that religious and Islamic concepts as well as ideas of modernity have played in ideological struggles between and within so-called "Islamic" and "Western" societies in historical and contemporary times.

He pursued these investigations by drawing on the theoretical resources of modern social sciences, especially linguistics, anthropology and semiology applying these to materials of Islamic traditions in novel and telling ways. He developed these methods during a long career in research and teaching at the University of Sorbonne in Paris. A series of publications on varied topics reflected his developing thinking on these issues. They ranged from the "humanist" thinker during the fourth century of Islam, al-Miskawayhi, to the Qur'an, on which he published a set of semiological readings, reflecting a highly original approach to this fundamental text for Muslims. The way this text has been understood and deployed in Muslim history excited his lifelong critical acumen, and he returned to it, time and again in his lecturing and publishing career.

Despite the academic and theoretical basis of his career, Arkoun was never content to work solely within academic confines. He longed to make a difference to Muslim cultures at large. This led him to a passionate engagement with Muslim institutions of learning and the arts with creative ambitions and possibilities. He contributed energetically, in an intellectual capacity, to the Aga Khan Award for Architecture, and to the Institute of Ismaili Studies in London, of whose Board of Governors (headed by His

Highness the Aga Khan) he was a member until his death. Arkoun valued the opportunities he had for these and other such contributions beyond the academia as part of what he called "Applied Islamology", an endeavour in which he aimed at uniting his theoretical and practical concerns and interests.

Equally dissenting from traditionalism in Islamic theology as well as Orientalist scholarship and modernist trends in contemporary Islam, his was a highly original and individual voice in a field which is of undeniably increasing importance today.

About the Contributors

Abdou Filali-Ansary

Professor Filali-Ansary has been Director of the Aga Khan University Institute for the Study of Muslim Civilisations (AKU-ISMC) in London since 2002. Previously he served as the founding Director of the King Abdul-Aziz Foundation for Islamic Studies and Human Sciences in Casablanca, Morocco and as Secretary-General of the Mohammed V University in Rabat, having also taught modern philosophy there. He has contributed widely to the academic discourse on Islam and modernity, and democratisation and civil society in the Middle East. His most recent work, *Le sens de l'histoire* ("The Meaning and End of History"), published jointly by the Roi Abdul Aziz Foundation, Casablanca and the Konrad Adenauer Foundation in 2008, is the result of a symposium held in Casablanca by the Roi Abdul Aziz Foundation for the Etudes Islamiques et les Sciences Humaines. Professor Filali-Ansary is the author of numerous books and articles on Islam's reformist traditions, including *Is Islam Hostile to Secularism?* (1996, 1999), *Reforming Islam: an Introduction to Contemporary Debates* (2003), and a French translation of 'Ali 'Abd al-Raziq's landmark work *Islam and the Foundations of Political Power* (1994). In 1993, he co-founded the bilingual Arabic-French journal *Prologues: revue maghrébine du livre.*

Akeel Bilgrami

Akeel Bilgrami studied English literature in Bombay, then went to Oxford as a Rhodes Scholar to study philosophy, politics and economics. He was awarded a PhD from the University of Chicago and has taught at Columbia University since the mid-1980s, where he is now the Johnsonian Professor of Philosophy. He is a member of the Committee on Global Thought and Director of the Humanities Institute at Columbia. Bilgrami's works include *Belief and Meaning* (Blackwell, 1992), *Self-knowledge and Resentment* (Harvard University Press, 2006), *What is a Muslim? The Moral Psychology of Political Identity* (Princeton University Press, 2012), and *Gandhi's Integrity* (Columbia University Press, 2010). He has also published many articles on philosophy of language and philosophy of psychology.

Aziz Esmail

Aziz Esmail is the former Dean of The Institute of Ismaili Studies, London (1988–98) and since 1998 has served as one of its Governors. Schooled in philosophy, literature and religion, Dr Esmail has held lecturing and research positions at various American universities as well as the University of Nairobi, Kenya. He has been associated with the Committee on Social Thought at the University of Chicago as well as Harvard University's Center for the Study of World Religions and Graduate School of Education. Dr Esmail has been consultant to, among other institutions, the Humanities division of the Rockefeller Foundation. In addition to his journal articles, his writings include *The Poetics of Religious Experience: The Islamic Context* (I. B. Tauris in association with The Institute of Ismaili Studies, 1996) and *A Scent of Sandalwood: Indo-Ismaili Religious Lyrics* (I. B. Tauris in association with The Institute of Ismaili Studies, 2002).

Josef van Ess

Professor Josef van Ess is Emeritus Professor of Islamic Studies and Semitic Languages, University of Tübingen, Germany, where he took up a full professorship in 1968. He is a leading scholar in the history of the Islamic world and Islamic theology and philosophy, especially the formative period (eighth to tenth centuries) and the age of the Mongol conquest (thirteenth to fourteenth centuries), and Islamic mysticism, and has published extensively in these areas. Professor van Ess has been a visiting Professor at the University of California, Los Angeles, the American University of Beirut, Princeton and Paris (Collège de France and Ecole Pratique des Hautes Etudes). His major work is *Theology and Society in the 2nd and 3rd Century Hijrah: A history of religious thought in early Islam*. He has received honorary degrees from the Ecole Pratique des Hautes Etudes (Sorbonne, Paris), Georgetown University and the Union of Arab Historians. Among other honours, in

2009 he became a member of the Orden Pour le Mérite für Wissenschaften und Künste (the Order Pour le Mérite for Sciences and Arts) in Germany.

Malika Zeghal

Malika Zeghal is a political scientist who studies religion through the perspective of Islam and power. She is particularly interested in Islamist movements and in the institutionalisation of Islam in the Muslim world, with focus on the Middle East and North Africa in the postcolonial period and on Muslim diasporas in North America and Western Europe. She has published a study of central religious institutions in Egypt, *Gardiens de l'Islam: Les oulémas d'al-Azhar dans l'Egypte contemporaine* (Presses de Sciences Po, 1996), and a volume on Islam and politics in Morocco, *Islamism in Morocco: Religion, Authoritarianism, and Electoral Politics* (Markus Wiener, 2008), which won the French Voices–Pen American Center Award. She was editor of a special issue of the *Revue des Mondes Musulmans et de la Méditerranée, Intellectuels de l'islam contemporain: Nouvelles générations, nouveaux débats* (123, 2008), on intellectual debates in contemporary Islam. Zeghal is currently the Prince Alaweed Bin Talal Professor in Contemporary Islamic Thought and Life at Harvard University's department of Near Eastern Languages and Civilisations and the Committee on the Study of Religion. Her book *Sacred Politics: The State and Islam in the Arab Middle East* (Princeton University Press) is forthcoming.

Mark Sedgwick

Mark Sedgwick is Associate Professor at Aarhus University, Denmark, where he is also coordinator of the Unit for Arab and Islamic Studies. After studying modern history at Oxford, he was awarded a PhD in Islamic history at the University of Bergen, Norway. His publications include *Muhammad Abduh* (Oxford: Oneworld, 2009), *Islam and Muslims* (Boston: Intercultural Press, 2006) and *Against the Modern World* (New York: Oxford University Press, 2004). His fields of research have included Sufism, sectarianism, esotericism and terrorism, and he is now researching Islam in Europe.

Omar Alí-de-Unzaga

Omar Alí-de-Unzaga is Academic Coordinator of Qur'anic Studies and Research Associate at the Institute of Ismaili Studies (IIS), London. He was a student of Mohammed Arkoun at the IIS, after which he obtained a PhD from the University of Cambridge. He is also the Series Editor of the Qur'anic Studies Series (for which Arkoun was part of the Editorial Board) published by OUP in association with the IIS. He has edited *Fortresses of the Intellect: Ismaili and Other Islamic Studies in Honour of Farhad Daftary* (London: I.B. Tauris, 2011). He is currently working on a monograph entitled *A Philosophical Reading of Scripture: Qur'anic Exegesis in the Epistles of the Pure Brethren* (Rasā'il Ikhwān al-Ṣafā') and is preparing a critical edition and translation of the *Epistle on Character Traits* of the Ikhwan al-Safa'.

R. Stephen Humphreys

Professor Humphreys is primarily a specialist in medieval Islamic history and culture. Many of his publications deal with this period, including *From Saladin to the Mongols* (State University of New York Press, 1977) and *Islamic History: A Framework for Inquiry* (Princeton University Press, 1991). In recent years his research has focused on the early Islamic period, as reflected in *Mu'awiya ibn Abi Sufyan: From Arabia to Empire* (Oneworld, 2006). He has an active interest and involvement in contemporary Muslim societies and has published a memoir based on his experience of the Middle East since the 1960s, *Between Memory and Desire: the Middle East in a Troubled Age* (University of California Press, 1999; reprinted 2005). Since 1990, he has taught at the University of California at Santa Barbara, where he holds the King Abdul Aziz Al Saud Chair in Islamic Studies. He has held visiting lectureships in Cairo, Leiden, Berlin and Paris, and was a visiting fellow at All Souls College, Oxford from 2006 to 2007. He was editor-in-chief of the *International Journal of Middle East Studies* from 1994 to 1999, and president of the Middle East Studies Association of North America in 2001.

Souleymane Bachir Diagne

Souleymane Bachir Diagne has taught philosophy at Cheikh Anta Diop University, Dakar, Senegal, for twenty years. From 1999 until 2007, he was Professor of Philosophy and Religion at Northwestern University and now teaches at Columbia University as a Professor in the Departments of French and Philosophy. Professor Diagne's fields of research include the history of algebraic logic, the history of philosophy, Islamic philosophy, and African philosophy. Among Diagne's publications in the history of logic and algebra are *Boole, l'oiseau de nuit en plein jour* (Paris, Belin, 1989), and a translation and presentation in French of Boole's *Laws of Thought* (Paris, Vrin, 1992). Diagne's most recent publications are *Comment philosopher en Islam?* (Paris, Panama, 2008), a study of the Indian poet and philosopher Muhammad Iqbal, *Islam and the Open Society. Fidelity and Movement in the Philosophy of Muhammad Iqbal* (Dakar, Codesria, 2010), *Bergson postcolonial. L'élan vital dans la pensée de Léopold Sédar Senghor et de Mohamed Iqbal* (Paris, Editions du CNRS, 2011) and *African Art as Philosophy : Senghor, Bergson, and the Idea of Negritude* (Seagull, 2011).

Stefan Wild

Stefan Wild was director of the German Oriental Institute in Beirut, Lebanon from 1968 to 1973; Professor at the University of Amsterdam from 1974 to 1977; Professor of Semitic Languages and Islamic Studies from 1977 to 2002; and is now Professor Emeritus at Bonn University. He has written a study of Lebanese place-names, has worked on Classical Arabic lexicography and Classical and Modern Arabic thought and literature, and edited two books on the Qur'an. He was editor and co-editor of *Die Welt des Islams. International Journal for the Study of Modern Islam* (Leiden) from 1981 to 2009. In 2003–04 he was a Fellow of the Wissenschaftskolleg in Berlin and was awarded the Prize of the Helga und Edzard Reuter Foundation in 2005.

Ursula Günther

Ursula Günther studied Arabic Islamic Studies and Romance Languages and Literature in Tübingen, Paris and Hamburg. She was awarded her PhD on the works of Mohammed Arkoun at the University of Hamburg, where she also conducted research on Islam and the transition process in South Africa. She is currently a research fellow at the University of Hamburg's Faculty of Education, researching religious education among "Muslim" adolescents in Germany. Her publications include *Mohammed Arkoun: ein moderner Kritiker der islamischen Vernunft* (Würzburg, 2004), chapters on Arkoun's approach to the Qur'an, chapters on aspects of Islam in South and sub-Saharan Africa and in Algeria, Muslim feminism (*Die Frau in der Revolte: Fatima Mernissis feministische Gesellschaftskritik*, Hamburg, 1993), and chapters on gender, interreligious and intercultural education.

Index